THE END OF ISLAM?

THE END OF ISLAM?

The Scourge of Islamism:
The Use and Abuse of the Quran

by

ABI T. AUDI

THE END OF ISLAM?

Copyright © 2017 by   Abi T. Audi

World Ahead Press is a division of WND Books. The views and opinions expressed in this book are those of the author and do not necessarily reflect the official policy or position or WND Books.

Paperback ISBN: 978-1-944212-88-9
eBook ISBN: 978-1-944212-89-6

Printed in the United States of America
16 17 18 19 20 21 LSI 9 8 7 6 5 4 3 2 1

To my Father
And all the victims of Islamic terrorism
To the Yazidis
To the Buddhas of Bamiyan
To Palmyra

"I have felt enough contempt at the false gods and their imaginary kingdoms of heaven which only bring hell on earth,"

"At the fake religions and their unholy wars waged in the name of God, against God."

- Abir Taha, *The Epic of Arya - In Search of the Sacred Light*

CONTENTS

THE END OF ISLAM?

FOREWORD

On September 11th, 2001, in a horrific act of human sacrifice on the altar of a faith gone mad in the name of a certain Allah, World War III was declared in the most brutal manner by Islamist lunatics against the "infidel" West, which terrorists saw as best represented by the Twin Towers, capitalist symbols of Western "arrogance" and "greed." The attacks of 9/11 signalled the beginning of a new era in the short-lived unipolar world led by the sole remaining American Superpower. It was all but official: barely over a decade after the fall of communism, the invisible green empire (green being the colour of Islam) had replaced the evil red empire as the West's enemy number one.

From this fateful day on, in the eyes of horrified Westerners, the "bad guys" were no longer the communists but rather the Islamic terrorists who viewed the West as decadent, immoral, unjust, godless and hence unworthy of existence (omit *godless* and you could argue that Islamists are the natural heirs of communism when it comes to how they view the West).

According to such Islamic radicals, Allah himself had decreed that the West, with its culture, history, and religion, be eradicated. Indeed, these extremists considered that the Free World was Ard al kuffar, the land of the infidels which should be purged from all decadence and, along with all other nations on the Earth, be ruled by the sharia, the law of Allah. Only then could the Ummah, the Islamic Universal Nation or Caliphate, be established, having as its ideal the Caliphate that prophet Muhammad had built (and which was later ruled, after his death, by Al Khulafaa Al rashidun, the "wise rulers"), and Judgment Day would be at hand, whereby the good Muslims will be rewarded and the godless rest will be punished.

Such perverted idealism, mixed with the worst cruelty, characterises the simple-minded but very dangerous Islamist ideology espoused by the likes of Osama bin Laden and members of al-Qaeda's numerous surrogate groups and branches, from Afghanistan's Taliban to Egypt's Islamic Brotherhood, from Syria's al-Nusra and Daesh (the Islamic State) to Nigeria's Boko Haram, and inspires until this day young Muslim radicals all around the world, whether they live in the suburbs of Paris or in the remotest village of China.

Immediately following the 9/11 attacks, Western bookshops witnessed a drastic surge in their book sales on Islam and Islamism, for Westerners were at a loss to understand why and how human beings could murder innocent civilians (men, women, children, elderly) simply because they worshipped God in a different manner (or - shock! Horror! - did not worship Him at all). In the name of what God and religion could such horrendous acts be perpetrated? What kind of God condones terrorism, cold-blooded murder?

Of course, terrorism is by no means a modern phenomenon, nor is it restricted to Islam. In fact, it has existed since the dawn of mankind. But one could easily argue that Islamic terrorism is by far the greatest threat in modern times, with its far-reaching, global dimension. Nowadays, Islamic terrorism has become a pivotal subject in international affairs; indeed, the Third World War, the war on terrorism, is a war against

Islamic terrorism. The beginning of the twenty-first century has been marred by that scourge, a bloody century which does not augur well for the rest of the new millennium.

For those who thought that 9/11 was a freakish, isolated terrorist act perpetrated by mad radicals, the Bali bombings in 2002, the Madrid train bombings in 2004, the London bombings in 2005, the Mumbai attacks in 2008, and, almost a decade after 9/11, the Moscow metro bombing in 2010 all served to remind them that Islamic terrorism is here to stay, if nothing is done to eradicate this modern plague. In January 2015, the Charlie Hebdo massacre that shook France, then the massacres in Denmark in February of that same year, and many other atrocities committed by Islamic terrorists (and the list is indeed very long) came to ascertain that this threat was rapidly turning into an international problem, since no country was immune from its mad hatred.

And, more recently, the horrendous Paris attacks of November 13th, 2015, the deadliest attacks against France since World War II, followed by the equally horrendous Brussels bombings of March 2016, Orlando's terrorist attack of June 12th, 2016, then the Nice massacre of July 14th, 2016, and many other atrocities committed by Islamic terrorists, including large-scale massacres that are happening almost on a daily basis in Syria and Iraq, were a very painful and violent wake up call to Westerners in particular and all lovers of culture and civilisation in general to fight that black plague. World War III had officially been declared by Daesh against the civilised world; indeed, against mankind at large. Or is it simply, as critics of Islam claim, the religion of Muhammad itself which is waging war against the whole world?

All these horrifying terrorist acts only added to a strong and increasing interest in Islam and Islamism and their relationship with terrorism. Questions such as the following were raised within intellectual circles by the media and the public at large: Why? Why do they hate us? What kind of a religion condones the most barbaric violence against innocent civilians? In the name of what God are defenceless men, women, children, elderly people murdered in cold blood? What is this ideology which quotes verses of violence "revealed" by Allah himself and exhorts its followers to slay all people from other faiths? Could such a mad and evil creed survive in the era of democracy and human rights? Thus, books about Islamic fundamentalism abound today, especially with the Islamic State now in vogue, for Westerners want to attempt to understand that hateful, barbaric, destructive phenomenon shaking world politics, wreaking havoc on the four corners of the planet and reaching inside their own homelands through the long tentacles of terrorism, the scourge of the twenty-first century, indeed the scourge of all times.

However, whereas most of these books treat the consequences of this Islamist plague, terrorism, and whereas other publications address its socio-political causes (poverty, illiteracy, crisis of identity and so forth) as well as the psychological instability of the perpetrators, very few actually treat and delve deeply into its *cause* and source, which is arguably the Quran itself, the fount of inspiration to the terrorists. Islam, in the mind of so many people, including Muslims, has become synonymous with terrorism. Therefore, in order to understand the Islamist phenomenon and terrorism, and in order to confirm or deny whether Islam equals terrorism, we must do the inconceivable, indeed the unacceptable (in the eyes of Muslims): we must objectively and courageously dissect the Quran itself, this controversial book which Muslims believe was revealed to Prophet Muhammad by Allah himself, and whose verses are used *à la lettre* by the terrorists to justify their crimes against humanity. Otherwise, we would only be treating the symptoms of Islamism - terrorism - through bombs, and not the causes, the intellectual (or rather anti-intellectual) causes behind this scourge.

Intellectual terrorism breeds actual terrorism. Islamism is behind most of terrorist acts today; ergo, is Islam itself the culprit? Are Islam, Islamism, and terrorism the same thing, or are they different? That is the brave and very necessary question that this book asks and attempts to answer in the most objective manner, seeking truth for its own sake, for only truth shall set Muslims free from what they perceive as God's word.

There are generally two kinds of opinions on Islam: non-Muslim critics who condemn it, focusing on the verses of violence which terrorists use and abuse to justify their atrocities; and there are the Muslim moderates who defend their religion from the accusation of violence or even terrorism, rejecting outright any criticism of it and simply saying it is a "religion of peace" and "this is not Islam," remaining silent when the many verses of violence are quoted as justification for murder, or merely repeating that these verses are "taken out of context," or worse, that "these verses have had their historical context in the past, and hence were justified at that time." And that means that dozens if not hundreds of Quranic verses lose their universality *as verses for all times*, which consequently leads to the need for the critical rereading of the so-called holy text.

Both aforementioned opinions, both opposite sides of the spectrum only see one side of the coin. Both are incomplete conceptions of Islam. Both deny its dual nature where darkness and light, violence and peace, cruelty and mercy are woven together in an Arab yin-yang, if you will.

This book is objective: it shows both sides of Islam, neither condemning nor defending it. In this sense, it is probably a rare, even unique book, since it is solely concerned with the truth about this religion and its "holy book," away from both undeserved praise and unjust condemnation.

This book neither attacks nor defends Islam. Its sole purpose is the truth about this faith espoused by over 1.5 billion people around the globe. It simply shows Islam as it is: darkness flirting with light, a free fall from the peak of cruelty to the depths of mercy, and then up again to the apex of violence and wrath.

The truth is, like any other religion, Islam and its legacy has its good and bad sides, and yet its warlike, violent nature always seems to overshadow its brighter, lesser-known, neglected side; neglected, it must be said, by both its foes and followers, let alone its fundamentalist followers.

As said above, this book is neutral towards Islam, neither praising nor attacking it. Freedom of belief (or unbelief) is a basic human right. What this book does, however, and with great strength, is attack the murderers who use and abuse, pervert and misrepresent the Quran's verses to justify the worst atrocities against fellow humans who happen to be of different faith (and sometimes even from the same faith as well), and thereby not just commit the greatest blasphemy against God himself but also destroy the sanctity and credibility of the very religion they pretend to preach with their bloody swords forever stained with the blood of innocents.

Every Muslim should read this book. It will be hard. Facing the crisis that is ripping his religion apart will be no easy task to even the most open-minded Muslim. Reading the verses of violence in his holy book will be painful, but less painful than the accusation of terrorism levelled against his religion and his god. And yet every Muslim has to face this reality. He has to face all sides of his holy book and decide, with everything that it entails, which is real Islam: the verses of violence that are present (in the context of the war during the time of Islam) and being used and abused by extremists to justify the worst atrocities against both Muslims and non-Muslims? Or espouse the verses of peace and mercy that are just as present - albeit to a lesser degree, it must be said - but largely unpublicised or unheeded? Or accept both as paradoxically forming one single book? It goes without saying that a critical reading of a "God-revealed" book requires courage, boldness of the spirit, and, above all, intellectual conscience.

Likewise, every non-Muslim should read this book. Terrorism has reached deep inside his own homeland; no one is immune from the imminent and global threat of Islamic terrorism, from East to West and North to South. Unfortunately, and perhaps unfairly, this must be said: wherever Muslims reside, terrorism is latent. All non-Muslims should read this book in order to understand that Islamic terrorists are basing themselves and justifying their atrocities based on existing verses that are used and abused, and in order to understand that terrorism starts in the mind, in the terrorist thought that is Islamist thought.

The only people who will truly be annoyed, or rather enraged, by this book and who will reject it outright as "blasphemous" and condemn its author as a "heretic," are the terrorists themselves, and the takfiri sheikhs behind them, their gurus. And it is good that they will, for they should. They are the enemies not just of real Islam, or at least the softer, brighter side of Islam, but of mankind, culture and civilisation. Islamism is a scourge, a curse against life, freedom, enlightenment, and against Islam itself; that is, if Islam is different from it, and that is what this book explores.

In any case, whatever "real Islam" is, it is high time, to save what can still be saved of that religion. It is high time moderate Muslims, if they truly are the silent majority, became more vocal and stood up and rebelled against this plague. Otherwise Islam, Islamism, and terrorism will forever be tangled together, mixed and mixed up, until all three collapse with the death of the last terrorist.

Abi T. Audi
October 15th, 2016

PREFACE

I n addition to my utter aversion to the darkness, violence, ignorance, and fanaticism of the Islamist scourge and its countless movements around the globe, it is a personal grudge that I mainly hold against this cultural black hole. Indeed, the tentacles of this dark beast reached and forever stained my personal life and the innocence of my childhood many years ago. I had just turned twelve when my father, a prominent secular, progressive, enlightened politician, was murdered in cold blood by Islamic fundamentalists, his body riddled with countless bullets of blind hatred and ignorance.

My father was staunchly opposed to the "Islamic Revolution" and the attempts to export this revolution to other secular Middle Eastern countries. This opposition was the cause behind his assassination: a fatwa, or religious edict, was issued and called for his death. It was a death sentence pronounced by an evil prominent cleric and executed by his ruthless henchmen. This cowardly, despicable crime outraged the whole nation. Indeed, my father was widely respected and admired by his fellow citizens of all faiths and political affiliations for his nobility, his honesty, his integrity, his moderation, his secularism, his patriotism, and his enlightened and progressive views.

My father's brutal murder left a gaping hole in my heart and an indelible wound in my soul. The deep wound, however, was not just emotional but also intellectual: my whole outlook on life was moulded by this traumatic loss, my father's violent death. Not only had I lost a loving father and role model, I had also lost faith in this unmerciful "God" and his religions, which hitherto had only sown death and destruction. I became an avowed atheist. Of course, Islamism was enemy number one; the plague that had to be destroyed lest the Middle East drown in the mud of ignorance, fanaticism, obscurantism, and backwardness. Sadly, my worst fears and expectations have all but materialised today, as the black plague of Islamism invades the whole Muslim world and even threatens the West and the rest of the world with its satanic tentacles that reach far and wide.

Later in my life, as I grew more discontented with materialistic and nihilistic atheism, I embraced spirituality in my late twenties, and I thereby came to realise that there might be a God after all, but that God is Life, He cannot be above or against Life. I espoused a pantheistic outlook on life, rejecting transcendentalist monotheism as life denial. The *real* God, not the God of religions, therefore could and should be redeemed from his unholy followers, fundamentalists of all religions, who commit the worst atrocities in his name. To kill in the name of God, I thought, was to commit the greatest blasphemy, for God is love, otherwise He doesn't exist.

My burgeoning spirituality only reinforced my resolve to fight the Islamist scourge in order to redeem the real God, not the "god" made in man's image, but rather the God who made man in His image; thus, I wrote:

"I am searching for the Light . . . not the light made by man, but the Light that made man."

When my father died, I lost faith in God. When I lived, I lost faith in men. I thought that goodness had died in man. But spirituality gave me hope; hope that there could be a God after all, the real God. In order to restore my faith in God and in life, the enemies of God and life had to be fought and destroyed. Destroying the scourge of Islamic terrorism thus became my sacred mission, and it must be the sacred mission of all enlightened minds. But it goes without saying that terrorism cannot be destroyed with weapons only. Its ideological foundations must be uprooted, discredited, disproved, if this plague is to be wiped off the earth, if the world is to be rid of this evil.

The terrorist "mind," for lack of a better word (or rather "no mind," since it is utter ignorance) must be destroyed by destroying the ideology that lies behind it and feeds it. The *real* war on terror is an intellectual war. The Age of the Enlightenment defeated the Inquisition with reason. So, too, must the enlightened Easterners defeat their own oriental version of the Inquisition: Islamism. When the light of the free spirit shines, the darkness of ignorance and fanaticism retreats like a shadow.

This book is my modest intellectual contribution to the global war on terrorism, which should be comprehensive: military, cultural, spiritual, and moral. The pen of enlightenment and the sword of justice will prevail. Truth shall prevail against the lies of millennia, and the light shall shine again from the midst of darkness. The sons of Light and Life should and shall defeat the sons of darkness, death, and ignorance.

Abi T. Audi
October 15th, 2016

INTRODUCTION

ISLAM IN CRISIS

'Sometimes people don't want to hear the truth because they don't want their illusions destroyed."

- FRIEDRICH NIETZSCHE

*"I*n *the name of Allah the compassionate and merciful."* Thus begins the Quran, the holy book of Islam believed by its followers, the Muslims or Muslimeen, *"those who have submitted"* (to the will of God), to have been revealed by Allah to the Prophet Muhammad through the angel Gabriel. The words *mercy, peace, compassion,* and *forgiveness* do indeed appear several times in the Quran, a fact which has prompted and encouraged moderate Muslims to claim, and even to insist, that Islam is a "religion of peace." To these moderate Muslims, Islam ("submission," "surrender") rhymes with salam ("peace").

Is Islam therefore a "religion of peace," as moderate Muslims affirm, quoting the verses on mercy and compassion in the Quran? Alas, the answer to that question turns into a resounding "no" when one reads on and, confused, finds very different (actually diametrically opposed) verses, verses of violence understandably described as "evil" by critics of Islam. Verses such as the following where the supposedly "merciful"

Allah exhorts his followers to *"slay the idolaters wherever you find them, and take them captives and besiege them and lie in wait for them in every ambush"* (Quran 9:5) . . . *"I will instil terror into the hearts of the unbelievers, smite ye above their necks and smite all their fingertips"* (Quran 8:12) . . . *"they should be murdered or crucified or their hands and their feet should be cut off on opposite sides"* (Quran 5:33) . . . *"And prepare against them whatever you are able of power and of steeds of war by which you may terrify the enemy of Allah and your enemy and others besides them whom you do not know [but] whom Allah knows. And whatever you spend in the cause of Allah will be fully repaid to you, and you will not be wronged . . . "* (Quran, 5:33).

One cannot but wonder as one reads such verses: where has the "merciful" Allah suddenly vanished? And there is no wonder that such verses make the "divinely-inspired" Quran prone to criticism, and even cynicism, by detractors of Islam who cite such verses of violence to denigrate those who advocate that Islam is a religion of peace, compassion and forgiveness.

The Quran reader, there and then, upon noticing these conflicting, even antithetical, verses, is directly faced with a dilemma and a paradox, as he asks himself, perplexed: how could a "merciful" and "compassionate" God exhort his followers to slaughter the "unbelievers" unless they *"repent and establish worship and pay the poor-due, for Lo! Allah is Forgiving, Merciful"* (Quran 9:5)? Indeed, mercy and cruelty make strange bedfellows in many Quranic verses . . . hence, questioning the peace-loving and non-violent nature of Islam becomes legitimate.

As one reads on and encounters many more conflicts between verses in Islam's holy book, one would undoubtedly wonder: how could the *same* book preach mercy and forgiveness on the one hand, and violence and intolerance on the other? In that inherent and structural contradiction lies, first, the root of the plague of Islamic terrorism, and, second, the crisis of Islam today; a crisis which threatens its very existence as a religion which is still trapped in the seventh century and which remains largely impervious to, and firmly resisting the modern world's humanist values and secular way of life, due to the prevalence of extremist religious scholars, and the constant silence or silencing of enlightened Muslims who find themselves under the continuous threat of being declared "apostates" and thus sentenced to death by the so-called fatwas.

We are confronted here with two opposing views of Islam: on the one hand, we have the moderate Muslims who paint such a rosy picture of Islam, describing it as "a religion of peace and mercy." Allah the Almighty, they claim, is first and foremost a merciful and compassionate *(rahmaan al raheem)* God. And, on the other hand, we have the critics of Islam who insist on their part that the religion of Muhammad is a "tyrannical," "fanatical" religion of war which oppresses women, stifles all freedoms, unabashedly preaches violence, and all but condones terrorism (though it solemnly names it jihad). The big dilemma is that both views come up with verses from the same Quran to support the veracity and legitimacy of their claims, the fact which nurtures rising doubts regarding Islam, or at least its dualistic, antithetical nature.

In fact, since the horrific 9/11 attacks on the World Trade Center, and with the continuous massacres perpetrated by Islamist mass murderers in the name of Islam, most Westerners—and, let's admit it, most non-Muslims on the four corners of the planet *too*—perceive Islam with utmost suspicion, even revulsion, considering it an intolerant, violence-prone religion totally incompatible with modernity's values of secularism and human rights— namely the right to freedom of expression, equality between the sexes, tolerance and openness, and, most importantly, pluralism and the inalienable right of individuals and communities to live according to their own beliefs (or lack thereof).

The black plague, the epitome of Satanism calling itself the Islamic State in Iraq and the Levant (ISIL, or simply IS), the notorious Daesh, along with its other al-Qaeda-affiliated allies like al-Nusra Front and Boko Haram, all these terrorist groups which are wreaking havoc in the Middle East and Africa, and now in the West, are disturbingly claiming that, by committing all their heinous and monstrous acts, they are merely applying the Quran and thereby they, and they alone, represent "real Islam." Thus, they justify their awful, barbaric atrocities by basing them on existing verses of the Quran which, according to Muslims, is God's word. Could Allah's word be considered sacred by both peaceful moderates and extremist murderers?

What kind of a "God," one feels compelled to ask, condones, and, even calls for, the shooting, throat-slitting, beheading, burning alive, stoning to death, torture, amputation, disfiguration, oppression, and humiliation of innocent civilians, whether they be men, women, children, or elderly? What kind of a "God" condones the desecration of tombs and profanation of shrines? The abduction, rape, and enslavement of women? The burning and destruction of places of worship? The pillaging, plundering, and destruction of priceless artefacts, statues and monuments, and entire ancient cities classified as World Cultural Heritage? And many other acts that defy and violate all religions and universal human values and go against human conscience, indeed humanity, culture and civilisation?

Let us say out loud what everyone dares only whisper: if *this* is Allah, if Daesh's Allah is the real God, who needs Satan? The truth of the matter is that, by all universal human standards and values, Daesh's Allah *is* Satan. No human being could argue otherwise. No Muslim can and should condone such monsters and subhuman, barbaric cavemen. There is no controversy over the fact that ISIL represents pure evil.

It is easy, therefore, to condemn Daesh. Its members are so flagrantly and grotesquely evil that no human being could do otherwise. However, the more sensitive and explosive question is the following: is *that* the true Allah? Is *that* true Islam? Does Daesh represent true Islam? Are these monsters *really* applying the Quran and its verses? Critics of Islam answer with a resounding "Yes!" whereas moderate Muslims reply with an equally firm "No!" So, who is right? Who should we believe?

If, however, the answer were that easy, if the answer to that crucial question posed above were a simple, clear-cut "yes" or "no," the reader would not be holding this book in his or her hands. Indeed, the answer is a complex one, especially when we draw a clear distinction between Islam and Islamism (and thence terrorism). And that cannot be done without examining and even dissecting the Quran itself, delving into its verses, particularly those verses that have been overused and abused. And that precisely is the aim of this book: to talk not *about* the Quran but rather to let the Quran itself do the talking and reveal to us the true nature of Islam. That is the most objective way to find and tell the truth about that religion.

If Christianity is the religion of love and forgiveness, Buddhism the religion of compassion and detachment, Hinduism the religion of truth and wisdom, what is Islam? How to define the religion of Muhammad? Is Islam the religion of war, fear, and wrath? Or is it the religion of peace, mercy, and tolerance? Why is Islam impossible to define save in contradictory terms? Even a moderate Muslim would be forced to admit that flagrant incitement to violence literally drips from the aforementioned verses.

Of course, the moderate Muslim would try to justify the verses of extreme violence mentioned above as being revealed "in the context of war"; yet the hard fact is that, firstly, Islam has *always* been at war with other faiths; and secondly, most of the verses of violence in the Quran are open-ended, meaning that the historical context is not mentioned in the surrounding text. In other words, they are part of the eternal, unalterable "word of Allah," and just as relevant or essential as anything else in the Quran. And therein lies the complexity of the task undertaken by this book: indeed, Islamic terrorists are precisely using the verses of violence which, it must be said and admitted, are sadly characteristic of this holy book, in order to justify their barbaric acts, killing, maiming, burning in the name of Allah.

Therefore, even if moderate Muslims insist for their part that these verses of violence were written in a historical context of war and conquests, the fundamental problem is, and remains, that they form an integral part of the Quran just like other verses, which makes the Quran and the Hadith (reports of Muhammad's words and actions outside of the

Quran), almost unique among all the sacred writings in the entire world because they alone urge the followers to make war on "unbelievers" or "infidels." Readers of the Quran will notice that one in every 55 verses in Islam's holy book consists of Allah exhorting Muslims to wage war on "unbelievers." In fact, the Quran contains at least 109 verses advocating the use of violence to spread Islam. More precisely, there are 123 verses in the Quran pertaining to killing and fighting.

Fortunately, there are verses of peace and tolerance in the Quran that counterbalance the verses of wrath and hate that preach jihad, or holy war, violence, and forced conversion or slaughter of "unbelievers" or "infidels." That being said, the warlike nature and inclination toward violence that characterise the Quran have led many Western scholars and historians to describe Islam as a religion of war which condones and even encourages terrorism. This unholy link to terrorism is the main symptom characterising the crisis of Islam today.

The year 2011 witnessed a turning point in modern Arab history, as the Tunisian and Egyptian revolutions heralded what came to be known as the "Arab Spring." However, these two originally democratically inspired, modernist and secular revolutions were later hijacked by Islamists in the subsequent legislative and presidential elections, and the other Arab countries followed suit, as the Libyan al-Qaeda-affiliated "rebels" turned to and espoused the sharia or Islamic Law as a model for the post-Qaddafi New Libya. The same Islamist extremists marred and discredited the so-called "Syrian Revolution," which questionably claimed to echo a legitimate popular call for more openness and freedoms, with their obscurantist ideology of darkness and ignorance and their horrific atrocities against Syrian civilians. ISIL's terrible crimes against humanity in Iraq and its expansion to Africa, Yemen, and even to Afghanistan underline the danger posed by Islamic extremism which has become synonymous with terrorism.

Thus, the Arab world has lately been witnessing, at a fast and alarming pace and on a wide scale, a resurgence of Islamic fundamentalism, whether in its most violent and extremist form (al-Qaeda and its many branches, such as al-Nusra, the Islamic State, and so forth) or in its "softer" version (the Salafists, the Muslim Brotherhood, the Jamaa Islamiyya). Nearly everywhere in the Arab world, in Egypt, Tunisia, Libya, Iraq, Syria, and so on, the Islamist scourge has tainted and hijacked the so-called (and now ineptly named) "Arab Spring," which was initially a genuine call and cry for freedom and justice aimed at toppling corrupt autocratic regimes and replacing them with democratic, liberal political systems that ensure basic freedoms and human rights to all citizens.

Consequently, instead of an Arab Spring, we are witnessing an Islamist Fall, indeed the dark winter of Arab thought. Instead of the dream of freedom, progress, and justice, we are witnessing the nightmare of medieval, obscurantist, tyrannical and fanatical theocracies replacing modern secular regimes. This is a total catastrophe for the region which threatens the whole world's security and stability (the *Charlie Hebdo* massacre, Paris, Brussels, Orlando, and Nice attacks, and terrorist acts in Australia and Denmark and elsewhere are but signs of worse things to come when "Western" Islamist rebels fighting under Daesh's Satanic banner in Syria and Iraq return "home" to their generous hosting communities.

Because of this spread of Islamic fundamentalist thought throughout the Arab world and among the Muslim communities of Europe, Islam and Islamism have become confused with each other, intermingled and inseparable in the eyes of most Westerners and non-Muslims around the world. Islamism has hijacked Islam and has become the standard-bearer of Muhammad's religion, taking centre stage in many Arab countries.

Consequently, it is becoming more and more difficult, or rather nearly impossible, for moderate Muslims to defend their religion from the Islamist onslaught, as Islamism has over the years become intimately linked to terrorism in the eyes of the world, especially since the 9/11 attacks. It has become nearly impossible to distinguish Islamism from terrorism. The more worrying thing, however, is that the same difficulty is nowadays experienced when one attempts to distinguish Islam from Islamism. Thus, Islam, Islamism and terrorism are today nearly totally mixed and mixed up in the minds of many.

Based on all of the preceding, it is clear that Islam today is facing a spiritual, ideological and existential crisis. It is more and more difficult nowadays for Islam to be separated and distinguished from the scourge of Islamism, the scourge of terrorism, fanaticism, dogmatism, misogyny, backwardness, violence, and barbaric cruelty. Muslims everywhere in the world are viewed with suspicion and suspected of being terrorists, all because of the stain of Islamism on every follower of Muhammad; a stain which has become almost impossible to remove, lest moderate Muslims rise up and take back their religion from the bloodied hands of the murderers who have hijacked their religion. Unfortunately, we have yet to witness a Muslim uprising against Islamism. Moderate Muslims prefer to bury their heads in the sand and deny this crisis altogether, while Islamic terrorism quickly spreads across and beyond the Muslim world like an epidemic.

Muslim moderates insist that their religion has been hijacked by a fringe minority of zealots and murderous fanatics who are distorting Islam, arguing that Islam cannot be confused with Islamism or terrorism. The problem, however, is that these terrorists are using the very Quran to justify their heinous acts, thus totally distorting and undermining the religion itself and its holy book. It is now, therefore, a crisis within Islam itself that the followers of Muhammad are facing.

Consequently, critics of Islam contend that, when a religion is so closely associated with terrorism because of a few extremist zealots, it is time to question how and why this association took place, what made this unholy union possible: is it only a wrongful, twisted and distorted interpretation and practice of Islam on the part of the Islamists? Or does the Quran itself contain the seeds of its own destruction, the seeds of extremism and violence that result in terrorism? The fact that there is such a controversy by itself confirms that there is indeed a crisis facing Islam in the modern era.

Now that we've (easily) established that Islam is in crisis, in deep crisis, the next question that naturally and logically follows is: why? Why has this religion, among all other religions, become intrinsically and intimately linked to Islamism and thence, to terrorism?

Three main reasons stand behind the current crisis facing Islam:

First, there are many contradictions in the Quran between what critics of Islam have termed *evil* (or, at the very least, negative) verses that promote violence and killing, superseding peaceful earlier verses (the Quran having been written in stages over a long period of time). Thus, verses of peace and war, of compassion and violence, of mercy and cruelty, are all mixed together, and mixed up, in the same book, just pages (indeed, paragraphs) away from each other. The crucial questions which come to the mind of the average reader, as well as to the serious researcher or scholar, are the following: were these inherent contradictions intended by those who have written the Quran? And, if so, to what end? Could the "word of Allah" be incoherent and contradictory? And, if Muslims believe that the Quran was truly revealed by God, one feels compelled to ask: is there an "original" Quran, and another, partly falsified, written after the death of the Prophet to serve political ends of dominion? Is there a Quran of Muhammad and another Quran, the actual one? Such questions are legitimate in the light of the contradictory, even antithetical, nature of the book; a contradiction that is leading to this bloody chaos wreaking havoc the world over at the hands of the Islamists in the name of Islam.

So, another likelihood which makes more sense but bears devastating consequences, is that the original text was edited, or rather perverted. That would be a much more plausible possibility, though rejected outright by all Muslims who consider and insist that the Quran is the unadulterated word of Allah. Nevertheless, this very doubt or possibility begs the (forbidden) question: was the Quran edited? If, as Muslims affirm, it was not, then how could the "Great Allah" contradict himself and be incoherent? And if it was edited, then Islam loses its validity as a genuine, divinely-inspired religion. Those are the hard facts that Muslims refuse to face, insisting that the actual Quran, the one we hold in our hands today, is "perfect" and hence untouchable, beyond criticism. The few bold Muslims who dare criticise their holy book or call for its revision and reform end up slaughtered, beheaded, hacked to death, or living in hiding. It is far too early to hope for a Muslim "Age of Enlightenment," although it is long overdue.

Second among the main reasons behind the crisis facing Islam today is that, whatever the causes of the inconsistencies and contradictions in the Quran, the fact (and the result) of such contradictions is that Islam, a religion which is followed by over 1.5 billion persons throughout the world, is also espoused by radical Islamists who use and abuse the Quran's verses of violence as holy justification for their acts of terror, as they kill, torture and maim countless innocent civilians worldwide in the name of Allah. The Quran is also used by these same Islamists, both so-called moderates and radicals) to oppress women and deny them their basic human rights and freedoms and, more importantly, their dignity and self-esteem as daughters of life.

Moderate Muslims continuously and stubbornly argue that, "Islam and Islamism are not the same thing," that Islamism "is not true Islam," and that "Islam and the Muslims" and "Muslims and terrorists" are not the same thing. But the problem is that the Islamists base their beliefs and justify their acts of terror based on *actual*, existing texts in the Quran. Hence the question that begs itself is are these Islamic terrorists acting as true Muslims when they slaughter non-Muslims? If the answer is yes, then Islam loses its legitimacy as a religion altogether, because almost all religions preach love and tolerance and none calls for exterminating "unbelievers." If, on the other hand, the answer is no, then what to make of Allah's own exhortations (and there are many scattered throughout "his" book) to slaughter non-Muslims or "unbelievers"?

Islam, Islamism, and terrorism have become so organically linked nowadays that the crisis undermining Islam as a religion threatens its very existence. The crisis started with the 9/11 attacks, which caused a backlash against Muslims living in the US, including the vast majority of peaceful, law-abiding Muslim citizens, and culminated in the unspeakable horrors perpetrated by Daesh today. Thus, ever since the attacks on the Twin Towers in 2001, Islamophobia has been on the rise in the West, coupled with a wider interest in the religion of Muhammad, as Westerners struggle to comprehend the motives behind terrorism and why Islam is so violence-prone.

Never has a religion been so associated with terrorism. So many crimes have been, and continue to be, committed in the name of Allah. The crisis is not just caused by the fact, disturbing as it is, that Muslims are killing in the name of God. The Crusaders didn't fare better when they waged their holy wars and killed in the name of Jesus who only preached love and remains innocent of the blood spilled in his name. But it must be said that the Crusaders, as well as the Inquisition, could never justify their crimes and atrocities by citing any verse from the New Testament, as the latter is totally devoid of any verse of violence. So, too, does the Old Testament devote entire chapters to war. The real crisis, rather, lies in the fact that Islamists are *still* using *their own* religion's written verses to justify their crimes. *That* is the danger posed by Islamism and against Islam: the actual scriptures, and more specifically the Quran, are being selectively used, taken out of context, and abused by Islamists to justify their atrocious crimes fuelled by blind hatred and mad ignorance.

Moderate Muslims dwell on the fact that fundamentalists take the verses of violence "out of context" and use them to conduct jihad and slaughter infidels. Yet, the problem is that even if they are taken out of context, these verses exist nonetheless; they are an integral part of the Quran, just like the rest of the verses, and thus have as much weight and value according to Islam. The second problem with the accusation of supposedly taking verses out of context is that Islamic history has *always* been in the context of war, invasions, and conquests! The context has always been one of violence, forced conversion.

The third reason why Islam is in crisis today is because it is incompatible with modernity, especially the sharia or Islamic law, which includes, at worst, the barbaric ancient acts of beheading, amputation, stoning, flogging, and so forth, and, at best, repression of free speech, freedom of belief, and all freedoms, including polygamy, gender inequality, and so forth. Therefore, it goes without saying that sharia goes against all of modernity's values: human rights, women's rights, basic freedoms, progress, tolerance, and secularism (separation of state and religion). Indeed, the sharia is totalitarian in nature, as it contains a vast body of regulations touching every aspect of life, without taking into account the basic principle of modernity which is the right of the individual to choose to live and think freely.

The Islamists call for the rigorous application of the sharia in the social, economic, and cultural fields in a way which is incompatible with our present day and age ruled by the universal values of human rights. For example, sharia calls for cutting off the hands of thieves, beheading criminals, and lashing offenders, practices which violate all human rights and hurt all modern sensitivities, as do its forced covering of women and the separation of the sexes. Moreover, Islamists want these laws to be imposed on both Muslims and non-Muslims living in a Muslim country, the fact which violates the rights of ethnic and religious minorities living in Muslim countries.

Another (deeply disturbing) way Islam is incompatible with modernity is the law of retaliation: Islam allows an injured plaintiff to exact legal revenge, literal punishment of "an eye for an eye" (as we shall see later). It is a literal law of retaliation which reminds us of the Old Testament.

Indeed, the Quran (5:45) says:

"And we ordained therein for them: Life for life, eye for eye, nose for nose, ear for ear, tooth for tooth and wounds equal for equal. But if anyone remits the retaliation by way of charity, it shall be for him an expiation" (*Hilali* and *Khan, The Noble Quran,* Riyadh: Darussalam, 1996).

This passage allows for a compensation or indemnity instead of imposing the literal punishment of eye for an eye. But the problem is the *literal* law of retaliation. The *Hadith* and later rulings show that this law was actually carried out, and in modern times continues to be carried out in traditional Islamic countries.

For all the aforementioned reasons, Islam is in deep crisis today. Can it overcome this crisis, or is this the end? Will Islam share the fate of Christianity in the West, which was, after the Inquisition, forcibly all but driven out of the public sphere through the Enlightenment's separation of Church and State, and relegated to a mainly private or ceremonial, even folkloric, rite?

Islam is in crisis. Muslim moderates can go on burying their heads in the sand and saying "there is no crisis, that is not real Islam," still, it is not by doing so that they'd be doing their religion a service but rather by facing the causes of that crisis. They, not the critics of Islam, stand to lose most from ignoring that crisis which can only be resolved by, first, being acknowledged, then faced; and at a later stage—that is, if we do get there—by finding solutions to save what could still be saved of that religion and reform it before Daesh becomes Islam's *only* face, the ugliest face of barbaric violence, fanaticism and ignorance.

Islam is nowadays demonised because of the Islamist demons themselves who commit unspeakable atrocities in the name of "Allah," thereby doing neither their God nor their religion a favour, but rather destroying Islam themselves. If Islam collapses one day, it would be not because of its enemies but because of its fiercest zealots, who in the final analysis turned out to be its fiercest enemies.

Islamic obscurantism definitely reminds us of the Old Testament's many verses preaching violence and the many atrocities committed by the Medieval Church during the Inquisition. The sharia's harsh punishments like burning alive, stoning to death, amputations, and beheadings were practiced by most societies in ancient times. Nonetheless, the crucial difference is that these practices were done many, many centuries ago and are no longer applied today! So, what is needed for Muslims is to "move with the times" and not stick to the verses of violence that might have been "normal" in those ancient days when human rights were inexistent, but that are absolutely incompatible with human rights today.

What is true Islam? Is there a difference between Islam and Islamism, true Islam and terrorism pure and simple? This book precisely aims to answer this question objectively, disinterestedly, for truth's own sake. As such, it neither condemns nor defends Islam. It does, however, condemn in the strongest possible manner obscurantist Islamism and its unholy offspring, Islamic terrorism, that scourge which distorts, misuses, and abuses the Quran in order to justify its unspeakable horrors in the name of Allah.

As said previously, this book neither defends nor attacks Islam. It shows the facts—namely how Islamists are appropriating and selecting Islamic verses to carry out acts in the name of God, against God! And against all universal human and religious values. The verses themselves speak. But in dissecting the verses of Islam's holy book, I show how the verses of violence are selectively used, overused, and abused by Islamists, whereas the positive verses of peace, tolerance, mercy, and compassion go largely unheeded and are almost never quoted or applied by these same Islamists who pretend to follow their religion to the letter.

So, Islam, religion of war or religion of mercy? That is the question which the present work endeavours to answer objectively, simply by basing itself on the Quran itself in its entirety, analysing all its verses, both the tolerant and intolerant ones, both the violent and peaceful ones. Let Allah's word speak for itself to reveal to us its true nature. But before we analyse the verses which are at the heart of the controversy and crisis gripping Islam today, let us first explain how Islam and Islamism came to be mixed and mixed up because of the use and abuse of the scriptures by extremists.

CHAPTER ONE

ISLAM AND ISLAMISM:
IS THERE *REALLY* A DIFFERENCE?

"There is no moderate or immoderate Islam.
Islam is Islam, and that's it."

RECEP TAYYIP ERDOGAN, PRESIDENT OF TURKEY

- "THIS IS NOT REAL ISLAM" - OR IS IT?

"This is not real Islam!" This is the mantra that moderate Muslims keep repeating after each terrorist act to defend their religion against the barbaric atrocities committed by Islamic terrorists. However, repeating this mantra over and over again will not change the fact that this sentence is becoming incomprehensible for non-Muslims, especially after the advent of the black plague calling itself the Islamic State or Daesh, the epitome of barbarism, cruelty, fanaticism and ignorance. With the chronic crisis that is jeopardising the very existence of Islam in the twenty-first century, one cannot but ask: Aren't moderate Muslims in denial, indeed in very deep denial, when they simply refuse to acknowledge this existential crisis? And it is precisely this denial which is preventing them from efficiently opposing the extremists who have hijacked their religion, and consequently from saving what still can be saved of their faith.

The so-called "Arab Spring," much acclaimed at first as a truly secular, modernist, and democratic upheaval, especially in Tunisia and Egypt, soon turned out to be an Islamist nightmare which unleashed the most barbaric movement of all time: the Islamic State. How can we believe this sentence, "this is not real Islam," when Islamic terrorists keep saying, and insisting, that they are applying the Quran to the letter, using *existing* verses to justify their inhuman, horrific acts? Moderate Muslims, and Muslim reformist scholars in particular, must have the courage and integrity to say it: the problem lies in (part of) the scriptures themselves, which contain highly controversial and very incriminating verses, and not just the lunatic zealots applying them.

Muslims must swallow this bitter pill, this reality pill, before they can even hope for a recovery; and that recovery is called *reform*. But for now, let us focus on explaining how Islam, Islamism, and terrorism came to be so inextricably intertwined in an infernal web of violence and fanaticism.

The 9/11 attacks climaxed almost two decades of terrorist acts committed by al-Qaeda (and the Taliban in Afghanistan) in the name of jihad or holy war, in the name of and for the sake of Allah. The attacks against the Twin Towers in 2001, followed by the attacks in Madrid, London, Bali, Mumbai, Sharm el-Sheikh, and elsewhere marked the emergence of al-Qaeda (whose members were ironically supported as "freedom fighters" by the USA against the Soviet occupation of Afghanistan in the 1970s and 1980s) as a global terrorist organisation and brought Islamism to the forefront, with a rising interest in, and suspicion of, Islam, as Westerners to this day still struggle to comprehend this warlike religion as well as the Islamist phenomenon, its extremist product, the dark side of Islam. And isn't fundamentalism the dark side of every religion? Ever since, Islam has been mixed, and more often than not, mixed up, with Islamism, which in its turn has become synonymous with terrorism. Of course, terrorism is not restricted to Islamism, but the latter is a prominent, indeed nearly exclusive, sponsor of terrorism, especially in the twenty-first century.

To make things worse, the much vaunted but quickly discredited Arab Spring, far from being the enlightened revolution that Arab secular and modern intellectuals were aspiring to, a revolution that would usher in a new era of freedom and self-determination for the peoples of the Middle East, has instead turned out to be an Islamist Fall; a cultural nightmare; the night of the Arab mind and soul; a cultural time warp throwing the region back into the Middle Ages as more and more Arab countries fell into the venomous tentacles of Islamism. Secular Arab regimes thus collapsed and were replaced with al-Qaeda-affiliated militias who claim to uphold "true Islam." Indeed, the satanic ISIL jihadis affirm that by spreading death, destruction, and terror, they are being, by their definition, "good Muslims."

How did Islam come to be associated with its most extreme zealots, who represent a minority among Muslims? The fact is that, because of the historical context and legacy of Islam and its bellicose nature glorifying jihad, some Islamic versions or interpretations of the Quran and other scriptures—namely, the Salafist version and its unholy offspring, takfirism, are more prone to terrorism than any other religious creeds or groups. Moreover, because of the inexplicable silence of moderate Muslims in the face of horrific deeds committed by Islamic terrorists, the Quran has become some sort of a manifesto for terror in the hands of these few extremists and mass murderers who are misusing and abusing the scriptures in their justification of the most despicable acts of terrorism.

Why, one feels compelled to ask, this deafening silence among Muslims in the face of such atrocities? The problem might be, in the eyes of many Muslims, that condemning these religious extremists would be tantamount to condemning the verses of the Quran themselves which they are continuously quoting, especially those calling for jihad or religious war or struggle, and consequently condemning the *Quran* itself, which would be considered blasphemy, or even apostasy, dangerous words which have lethal consequences in Islam.

Thus, strangely, but not surprisingly, many moderate Muslims have condemned the burning of the Islamic State flag (a symbolic act proposed by secular moderates of all faiths in Lebanon to condemn this terrorist group which had savagely murdered Lebanese soldiers in Northern Lebanon). The flag-burning proposal had sadly and unfortunately caused an uproar among Lebanese Muslims, extremists and moderates alike, simply because that flag contains the holy words; indeed, the holiest words of the Quran: "There is no god but God" and "Muhammad is the Messenger of God." Because of this uproar which threatened civil peace, the demonstrators finally decided to symbolically burn a black flag similar to Daesh's but instead containing the words "terrorism has no religion." Civil strife was thus averted, but this dangerous and telling incident showed how hard it is for Muslims to recognise the crisis facing their religion, let alone consider reforming their faith.

The result of this fear-based and fear-ridden inaction among Muslims to condemn these terrorists is that everywhere they go nowadays, all Muslims are more or less put in the same basket and suspected because of their religion. Their silence and inaction have done great damage to their religion; nearly as much as the damage caused by Islamic extremists. Consequently, and due to this inaction, Westerners (and many other non-Muslims around the globe) accuse Islam of being an intolerant religion and Muslims of being closet terrorists or members of terrorist sleeper cells ready to strike at any moment for the sake of the glory of Allah. Whether Muslims like it or not, Islam and Islamism have become closely entangled, locked in an unholy union.

That being said, religious extremism is, of course, not limited to Islam. Throughout history, men of all faiths have killed in the name of "God" (Jewish fundamentalists, the Crusades, the Inquisition, Hindu extremists). Today, however, Muslim reactionary fundamentalists, Salafists, are singled out as being terrorists, of turning supposedly divine commandments into a license to kill all "non-believers"; thus, the believers of other faiths, whether Jews, Christians, Hindus, Buddhists, Yazidis, and even other Islamic sects such as the Shias and Sufis (Islamic mystics), are all considered kuffars or kaffirs (infidels) by these extremists, and should consequently all be killed. Islamic terrorists have often said they are striking out against their enemies and oppressors in the name of Allah. They unabashedly and proudly admit that they are applying the Quran, leading, through their own bloody murders and crimes against humanity, the vast majority of mankind to link Islam with terrorism.

To be fair, many Islamic scholars and moderate Muslims *do* speak out against terrorism, as they affirm and insist that such terrorist acts not only violate the spirit of the Quran, but its letter as well. These moderates insist that Islam is a religion of peace and mercy and quote relevant verses to justify their theory. For their part, critics contend that the terrorists are using *actual* scriptures, verses of violence in the Quran, which means (and that is the disturbing part) that, in so doing, they are just being "true Muslims." Islamism has indeed been described by its opponents as nothing but a brand of totalitarianism rooted in a sacred text.

Islamism is thus an extremist and at times violent ideology, which is nowadays confused with Islam. Whether there is a real difference between Islam and Islamism is a legitimate question today that needs to be answered lest Islam remain in crisis, and the Muslims remain entrenched in their denial, which does more harm than good to their faith.

Those who feel no hostility toward Islam and Muslims insist that a distinction must be made between Islam and its fundamentalist, extremist version, lest we risk antagonising or alienating over 1.5 billion people around the globe. Yet, making this distinction is proving to be very difficult presently for the reasons we have mentioned above.

- COLONIALISM: THE ROOTS OF THE UNHOLY UNION

Islam was founded in AD 622 by Muhammad, a simple shepherd from Arabia who proclaimed himself a prophet, indeed the Messenger of God, after claiming to have received, although illiterate, a revelation from Allah: the Quran, a feat of literary style. Soon after founding his religion, Muhammad fled the city of Mecca after he and his followers were persecuted, only to return to it triumphantly as a ruler in 630. The Muslims began as an obscure group in the Arabian Peninsula, but after a century of wars and conquests, they erected an empire stretching from Spain to India. Islam was thus spread with the sword. No one can deny that fact. This religion will be linked to war throughout history.

Muslims believe their faith is "God's religion," and they consider it the "perfect religion," compared to what they describe as flawed and imperfect religions such as Judaism and Christianity, despite the fact that Islam recognises the latter as "celestial religions." As for other religions such as Hinduism and Buddhism, Muslims simplistically dismiss them altogether as being polytheistic heresies. This inflated self-image and feeling of superiority was understandably justified and bolstered by Islam's glorious early history, when Islamic civilisation was the world's most advanced in terms of medical, scientific, literary, and technical achievements. The vast Muslim empire gave the followers of Muhammad a natural sense of extreme pride and led them to conclude that theirs was Allah's only religion and the supreme, eternal truth, as their prophet proclaimed himself "the last prophet."

However, that pride would soon fade with the end of Islam's age of glory. Indeed, as early as the thirteenth century began Islam's irreversible decline and the irresistible rise of the Christian West. Nonetheless, for the next five centuries, Muslims remained generally isolated from the rest of the world, particularly the Christian world which they knew so little about. Napoleon's invasion of Egypt in 1798 signalled the beginning of centuries of European invasions, conquests, and domination of the Muslim world. The colonialism that ensued greatly increased the feeling of injustice and oppression in the hearts and minds of Muslims, already relegated to the status of occupied and oppressed peoples by the now culturally and technologically superior West.

As a reaction to colonialism, some Muslims embraced a radical ideology known as *Islamism*, which also later came to be known as fundamentalist, radical or political (militant) Islam, an avowedly anti-liberal, anti-capitalist and anti-Western ideology which sought to restore the lost pride of the now oppressed Muslims. Islamic radicals seek, as they claim, to get back the "golden past" by restoring the Caliphate on the same fundamental pillars, namely the sharia, the Islamic law, which is derived from the Quran and the Hadiths, or the life and sayings of the prophet Muhammad.

The attitude towards the system in place and methods used by Islamists to attain power or gain influence vary: some (like the Muslim Brotherhood) *claim* to be peaceful and moderate (but seldom are) and consequently respect, accept, and espouse the democratic process, while others (like al-Qaeda and its surrogates) are openly radical, violent and seek a violent overthrow of secular governments which are deemed "godless" and whose rulers are accused of being "puppets of the West."

However, whether moderate or radical, peaceful or violent, Islamism is an ideology that demands man's total and strict adherence to the sharia, the sacred law of Islam. It rejects other religions at worst as false and flawed or, at best, as imperfect, and considers their followers as heretics or infidels, and has a deep hostility towards the liberal democratic West and its "decadent" values. For Islamists, Islam is not only a religion but also a political system which covers all aspects of life; it is both Din wa Dunya (religion and life), the sacred and the temporal. Islamism is thus a religious form of totalitarianism with no separation between state and religion. When it gains power, it turns into a theocracy, as is the case in Saudi Arabia or Iran and other countries where the sharia is mostly and widely applied.

Those moderate Muslims and friends of Islam who try to distinguish between Islam and Islamism affirm that, whereas Islam is a faith, Islamism is a totalitarian ideology which seeks to pervade, control, and infringe on, people's personal lives, behaviour, and way of thinking. Nonetheless, critics of Islam who see no difference between these two doctrines affirm for their part that Islam itself is both a faith and an ideology which encompasses all aspects, public and private, of a person's life: religious, economic, social, cultural, political, even sexual life is dictated by the Quran which is some sort of a manual of life covering absolutely everything one could think of. Where, then, critics of Islam contend, is the freedom of belief, the thrill of intellectual and spiritual exploration, if everything is written for us in advance, and holds as supreme truth, forever and until the end of time?

To go back to colonialism which was the main trigger that ignited the fire of resentment towards the West and modernity in general, the Islamist ideology considers that Muslims can only recover their former glory, and stop being subservient to and oppressed by the West, by being "good Muslims" and returning to the old Islamic tradition, to the roots of their religion (hence the term *fundamentalist*) and that can only be made possible by totally applying the sharia, a medieval, cruel, and inhumane law which violates basic universal human rights, as we shall describe later in this book.

Islamism has been on the rise for more than a quarter of a century now, an inexorable rise which started *faute de mieux* after the demise of Communism (due to the absence of an alternative ideology opposing the West), and culminated after the so-called Arab Spring, which began as a secular revolution but was later hijacked by the more close-knit and organised Islamist parties and groups, through the ballot box (Egypt) or by force (Libya). However, in spite of its recent revival and expansion throughout the Arab world, Islamism still doesn't enjoy widespread support among Muslims, as less than 10 percent of Muhammad's faithful follow the Islamist approach.

That said, Islamism, a Third-Worldist, anti-Western ideology, is today a powerful force to reckon with, especially without an ideological alternative after the fall of the Communist utopia. Indeed, Islamists run or participate in governments in Iran, Iraq, Lebanon, Saudi Arabia, Turkey, Libya, Morocco, Pakistan, and Afghanistan, or are an important force of opposition in Tunisia, Palestine, and Egypt, among other Muslim countries. Some of these Islamist groups, like Lebanon's Hezbollah and the Justice and Development Party of Turkey, accept and work within the democratic process. Others like Pakistan's Jamaat-e-Islami, the Taliban, the F.I.S, al-Qaeda, Islamic State, al-Nusra, and Egypt's Islamic Jihad preach violent jihad and conduct attacks on a religious basis. Islamists are divided into traditionalists, "guardians of the tradition," like Salafism or the Wahhabi movement, or the more moderate "vanguard of change" like the Muslim Brotherhood in Egypt which, it must be said, is not peaceful at all despite its claims, especially after president al-Sisi took over power following a popular overthrow of al-Morsi's Islamist regime. The Syrian case, for its part, unveils the bloody and violent nature of the Muslim Brotherhood.

Another cause of religious radicalisation among Muslim communities in the West (and this phenomenon has proven to be as dangerous as in the rest of the world) is their feeling of marginalisation and their crisis of identity, as Muslims feel that they do not belong to their host communities, neither in the cultural nor in the religious sense. In this sense, radical Islam or Islamism is presenting itself in the West as the anti-imperialist "ideology of the poor" even among non-Muslim lower classes (and we have seen a number of native French and German citizens, among others, convert to Islam and join the jihad in Syria alongside the Islamic State). But while recognising that part of this is true, we must state the fact that the identity crisis among Muslims in Western countries is caused to a large extent by Muslims themselves, as they refuse to integrate and instead stick to their social and religious traditions that contradict the Western way of life, thus forming impenetrable cultural ghettoes where fundamentalist thought spreads like a disease and where no Westerner dares set foot, not even the police. That is the sad case with some districts in and around Brussels, Paris, and London, to name but a few European cities struggling with serious security issues caused by Muslim immigrants.

- TWO ISLAMS?

As noted, Muslims today face this pressing and crucial question which most people around the globe are asking themselves: is there a difference between Islam and Islamism?

Or are they two sides of the same coin, different shades of the same colour? Are radical Islamists acting as "true Muslims" by following the scriptures, or are they deviant Muslims, distorting an otherwise peaceful and tolerant religion? Could there be *another* Islam, a lesser-known, forgotten, peaceful Islam that is endangered by the beliefs and practices of radical Islamists, determined to impose their own agenda upon their co-religionists? This confusion and controversy surrounding the Quran's true message is perhaps the greatest challenge facing Islam today and one which is of inevitable concern to the rest of the world.

So, is there a difference between Islam and Islamism? In answering that question, Muslims and non-Muslims fall under two main categories:

First, there are those moderate Muslims and non-Muslims sympathetic to that religion who claim and insist that there is a distinction between Islam and Islamism. These moderate Muslims and their sympathisers argue that Islam is a religion of peace which has been distorted and misconstrued, even hijacked, by religious extremists' beliefs and violent acts committed on the basis of a flawed and twisted - or rather a lack of - understanding and misrepresentation of the scriptures, namely the Quran (which means "recitation" - because the Quran was first heard in sermons and public readings), and the Sunna (which in its written form, Hadith, is part of the Islamic canon). They say that Islamism is a radical version of Islam which distorts its true message, which is essentially that of peace and tolerance. They affirm that whereas Islam is a religion, Islamism is a political ideology wrapped in religious garb and rhetoric and its purpose, like any political ideology, is to attain power.

Moderate Muslim scholars and laymen distinguish between the ideology of *Islamism* which actively, and, more often than not, violently, seeks to impose Islamic laws on both Muslims and non-Muslims, and mainstream Islam, which is a faith. Others distinguish *Islamist* from *Islamic*, arguing that whereas the latter refers to a religion and culture in existence over a millennium, and is therefore innocent of the crimes committed by Islamist terrorists, the former is a modern political and religious phenomenon which is the main inspiration behind the scourge of terrorism dominating and shaking world politics for the last few decades. These moderates refer to the "positive" verses in the Quran to justify their claim, arguing that, even if these verses are lesser known and not mediatised, still they, too, form an integral part of their holy book which is essentially a "good" book preaching peace and tolerance like most other religions.

At the other end of the spectrum are both the critics of Islam and the Islamists themselves who affirm and insist for their part that there is no distinction whatsoever between Islam and Islamism, for two diametrically opposed reasons: whereas the Islamists claim that they are merely being "true Muslims" or "good Muslims" following the word of Allah, the critics of Islam condemn both the religion and the movement which they insist are essentially the same thing. Those who hold that there is no distinction base their argument on the fact that religion in Islam is not a private matter; indeed, their claim is justified as the Islamic faith does not separate state and religion, politics and society. Therefore, there can be no pluralism or secular society where Islam is the religion of the land.

Islamists who commit acts of terror affirm that they are not misinterpreting the Quran given that the actual verses they refer to in order to justify their acts of violence are very clear and beyond any misinterpretation. They claim that they are following the letter of the Islamic scriptures, namely the Quran, the Sunna and the Hadith. Indeed, they act on the basis of fatwas which quote verses of the Quran, and therefore, they justify their acts as totally in line with the word of Allah.

The problem, critics of Islam assert, therefore lies in the sacred scriptures themselves. The terrorists are using and abusing verses that are *actually* in the Quran. If, these critics believe, these "evil" verses are part of the Quran, then a true Muslim is an Islamist (and an Islamist is a true Muslim) and therefore a terrorist.

Usually, the distinction between Islam and Islamism is made especially by moderate Muslims, whereas Islamists proudly claim that they are but true Muslims. However, critics argue that the difference between Islam and Islamism is a difference of degree, not of nature, given that the Quran and the sharia themselves are used by Islamists to justify their acts of terror. The many verses of violence and exhortations to fight in the Quran are very clear and leave no room for controversy or interpretation. Therefore, critics assert, there is no such thing as a moderate Muslim; in fact, according to their logic (as well as that of the Islamists), a Muslim who is moderate is not being a true Muslim!

These critics conclude that it is absurd to suggest that Islamism is a distortion of Islam to show it as warlike and intolerant, as one need only look at the Quran and read what is right there in the text, multiple times. In fact, Muslim terrorists take these verses which preach violence and jihad as literally as anything else in the Quran, because, its critics affirm, it *is* literal. That is the problem and the crisis facing Islam today.

- IS THE PROBLEM WITH ISLAM, MUSLIMS, OR BOTH?

Could the problem not be with Islam itself but rather with (some) Muslims who misunderstand and thus use their religion in the wrong way? Could the distinction between Islam and Islamism be a false one, and could the quandary lie in Muslims themselves, who misinterpret the scriptures and take them out of context to justify unlawful or violent acts? Whereas moderate Muslims insist on that distinction, most Islamists speak out against it and oppose the use of the term *Islamist*, insisting that they are merely Muslims, or rather "good Muslims," and affirm that their beliefs and actions merely reflect Allah's only religion. The Quran 3:19 does state: "Truly, the religion with God is Islam."

For its part, the Muslim Brotherhood in Egypt uses the motto: "The Quran is our constitution." That says it all; Islamism in a nutshell. To these fundamentalists, Islam is an all-encompassing religion covering all areas of life; it is at once religion and life (Din wa Dunya), a religion and a state (Din wa Dawla), the "perfect," complete religion, the supreme truth, the unalterable word of Allah. Consequently, the Muslim brothers call for implementing the sharia and reject all non-Muslim "imperialist" influence and "puppets of the West" in the Muslim world.

The Islamist agenda aims to remove secular liberal regimes in the Muslim world and its higher aim and dream is to convert the whole world to the religion of Muhammad. Therefore, as we asked previously, could the problem lie with Muslims themselves? Is it possible that moderate Islam and moderate Muslims simply do not exist (the latter not being typical Muslims)? Is *real* Islam, Islamism?

Sayyid Qutb, the Muslim Brotherhood's "intellectual godfather," whose radical beliefs spurred some to call him "the founding father and leading theoretician" of modern jihadis such as Osama bin Laden, called for the elimination of what he termed "ignorance" (jahiliyya) —in other words, non-Muslim rule— through the forced conversion to Islam, in his eyes the only truth, and through the establishment of sharia, which he considered to be an all-encompassing and political and socio-economic system. By so doing, Muslims, he argued, should oppose all Western-style "corrupt and "godless" ideologies such as socialism or liberal democracy. Qutb thus preached jihad to eradicate secular modern Arab regimes and spread Islam to the four corners of the globe through the sword.

Shia fundamentalism differs little from its Sunni counterpart concerning the need to establish the rule of the sharia. Ayatollah Khomeini's beliefs were similar to Sunni Islamic thinkers like Qutb. He believed that only a return to early Islamic rule would restore this religion's glory and supremacy; he thus advocated the violent overthrow of modern secular Arab regimes, accusing their rulers of being mere "puppets" of colonialism. Where Shia fundamentalists differ from Sunni fundamentalists is their advocacy of the rule of what Iranians call *Velayat-e Faqih* ("the rule of the Jurisprudent," Khomeini in the case of the Islamic Republic of Iran), instead of the Muslim Caliphate that Sunni zealots of the Islamic State and *al-Nusra* Front struggle to establish.

Velayat e Faqih is also a type of theocracy where senior Islamic jurists exercise temporal power. A fundamentalist Plato's Republic, if you will. Shia fundamentalism also constitutes a relatively more moderate version of Islam which embraces the concept of *Ijtihaad,* a process by which the imams or scholars seek to reform and update Islamic laws and to make religious practices more flexible to fit the socio-political and cultural context; an Islam that moves with the times, one might say, at least theoretically. It is therefore a law-making process, an independent scholarly interpretation of the legal sources of Islam, the Quran and the Sunna. In this process, the "spirit" counts as much as the "letter" of the scriptures (or so it is supposed to, in principle).

A term which is much used nowadays by Islamic terrorists is *takfir* (the accusation of blasphemy). Justification for attacks on Muslims deemed "incorrect" or "impious" (these latter include atheists and agnostics) often comes as takfir, an implicit death threat, since under traditional sharia law the punishment for apostasy in Islam is death. As for the justification for attacks on non-Muslims, it is often the grave accusation that those "infidels" or "apostates" or "enemies of Allah." Jihadis are thus called takfiris, those who accuse all others of being kaffirs. Boko Haram is a typical takfiri group, just like the Islamic State.

Because of the stigma of violence which stains Muhammad's religion today, this unholy union which mixes (or mixes up, depending on one's views) Islam and Islamism, Geert Wilders, the controversial far-right Dutch politician, as well as other nationalist politicians in Europe, have suggested a ban on Islam itself by criminalising its holy book, the Quran. As with the case of Islamists, but for diametrically opposed reasons, Wilders refuses to distinguish between Islam and Islamism for, to him, the problem plaguing Western societies is Islam, full stop.

Wilders considers that terrorism, fanaticism, tyranny, the oppression of women, and so on, are not perversions of Islam, but rather its very essence. "The word 'Islamism' suggests that there is a moderate Islam and a non-moderate Islam," he told Jonathan Kay on May 8th, 2011 during an interview in Toronto. "And I believe that this is a distinction that doesn't exist. It's like Prime Minister of Turkey Recep Tayyip Erdogan, said, 'There is no moderate or immoderate Islam. Islam is Islam, and that's it.' This is the Islam of the Quran."

Declaring Islamism a threat, and even a plague, isn't controversial; even moderate Muslims condemn the radical views and untold atrocities committed by Islamists. However, declaring Islam a menace is considered "hate speech" in the West. Whereas the former is an ideology which seeks to impose an intolerant version of Islam on all Muslims and non-Muslims and forcibly spread the faith throughout the world, the latter is a religion espoused by one-quarter of the world's population, the fact which begs the following questions: is there a fundamentalist version of Islam? Are there two Islams or just one?

The problem, as we have seen, is that the scriptures are used and abused by Islamists to justify their violent acts. Wilders views Islam not at all as a religion but rather as "a backward political ideology" which he deems "violent, intolerant, and totalitarian," hiding behind religious garb and language. He considers its warmongering nature, its preaching of violence, its call to eliminate all non-Muslims, and its totalitarian nature as incompatible with modernity and human rights. He argues that whereas other religions separate between the temporal and the spiritual, Islam doesn't draw any distinction between the public and the private and demands submission (the very word *Islaam* indeed means "submission") in every aspect of life.

Pious Muslims, even moderates, agree with Islamists, and with Wilders, when it comes to Islam's non-separation between religion and state, arguing that Islam can never be secular or allow secularism. They thereby unintentionally give critics of Islam a further argument that Islam and Islamism are one. And this argument makes these critics stick to their verdict that there is no such thing as "moderate" and "extremist" Islam, there is only one Islam.

The non-separation between religion and state can only mean one thing: that the non-Muslims would be ruled by Islamic law, the sharia. Hence the question: is Islam a totalitarian religion? Not just Islamism, but Islam itself? The religion, the book, the practice, the actions, when it comes to the basic tenets of modernity: citizenship, pluralism, liberties, the right to difference? We shall see this incompatibility between Islam and modernity in the subsequent chapters. But for now we can say that two central concepts from traditional Islam, sharia and jihad (Islamic Holy Law and Islamic Holy War or struggle), have been revived and extended by modern Islamists in ways which are incompatible with the United Nations Universal Declaration of Human Rights, especially with regard to equality before the law and equality between men and women.

If Islam is incompatible with modernity, could and should the real distinction consequently be between Islam and Muslims? And between moderate and extremist Muslims? Wilders and other critics of Islam affirm that while there are moderate Muslims, there is no such thing as moderate Islam. Even though the religion of Muhammad has one book and one God, it is manifested very differently across the globe; thus Muslims could range from peace-loving citizens to fanatic terrorists.

Wilders says: "Now you can certainly make a distinction among the people. There are moderate Muslims, who are the majority in our Western societies, and non-moderate Muslims. But Islam itself has only one form. The totalitarian ideology contained in the Quran has no room for moderation. If you really look at what the Quran says, in fact, you could argue that 'moderate' Muslims are not Muslims at all. It tells us that if you do not act on even one verse, then you are an apostate."

Wilders goes on to conclude in an Interview with The Guardian newspaper in 2008, "I don't hate Muslims. I hate their book and their ideology."

This hostility towards Islam and (most) Muslims is shared by Samuel Huntington, famous author of *The Clash of Civilisations*. To Huntington, all Muslims are closet Islamists. Muslims, he claims, form a distinct anti-secular civilisation. Islam and secularism are not compatible.

To examine the veracity of the critics of Islam, as well as the claims by moderate Muslims and radical Muslims, an objective analysis should shed the light on the true nature of this religion embraced by over a billion and a half people across the globe. The fact of the matter is that Islam is a religion and, like all other religions, it has a wide array of followers, ranging from the moderates to the extremists, from the progressives to the conservatives, fighting amongst themselves over which interpretation of their faith best fits its true nature and current times. Islamism, on the other hand, is the desire to impose any one of these interpretations over everyone else through state law or terrorism.

We shall see in the coming chapters the truth about this religion and attempt to distinguish it from its extremist, fanatical, and violent version, namely Islamism. But a warning to moderate Muslims and to the West, indeed to all lovers of culture and civilisation: if this confusion between Islam and Islamism it not dealt with, we are headed down a dangerous path. Common people in the West will start to bundle all Muslims with Islamists, which would mean a war between Islam and the whole world. This clash of civilisations and religions is what al-Qaeda and its daughters Daesh and al-Nusra and others wanted to trigger with the attacks of September 11th, and still attempt to trigger to this day; a hostile response to Islamist terrorism could then quickly become hostility to all Muslims and thus undermine this religion and its relationship with the civilised world.

PART ONE

ISLAM: RELIGION OF WAR?
THE USED AND ABUSED VERSES

"We came to you with slaughter."
- Islamic State's motto

"I have come to you with slaughter."
(Prophet Muhammad quoted in *Saheeh, Hadith* narrated by
shaykh'abd as-salaam ash Shaami)

"Slay the idolaters wherever you find them . . .
I will instil terror into the hearts of the unbelievers,
smite ye above their necks . . . They should be
murdered or crucified . . . "
(Quran, 9:5; 8:12; 5:33)

CHAPTER TWO

ISLAMIC INTOLERANCE: NO MERCY FOR UNBELIEVERS AND "INFIDELS"

"The darkest night is ignorance."

- LORD BUDDHA

"*Truly, the religion with God is Islam*" (Quran, 3:19): thus proclaims the holy book of Islam. It follows from this "exclusivity" with God that, since Islam is God's only religion and hence the best religion, all other religions are deemed inferior and incomplete. This gives Muslims, or at least Islamists, the justification to consider all followers of other faiths as kaffirs, infidels or unbelievers unworthy of mercy or even of life.

Is Islam intolerant—indeed, the most intolerant religion in the world, as its critics claim? The first answer that comes to mind is, seeing the atrocities, mass murders, and crimes against humanity committed by its fervent followers, the Islamists, yes, it is, especially when we consider the fact that there are over 500 verses of violence and intolerance against "unbelievers" in the Quran (in other words, every twelfth verse of Islam's holy book). However, to be fair and objective, and to render justice where justice is due, we shall see in the second part of this book that these intolerant verses which are overused and abused by Islamists to justify their intolerance towards (and atrocities against) other religions, are counterbalanced by verses of peace and tolerance which are just as Islamic as these ones.

These verses of intolerance are very explicit, whether we situate them in their historical context or not. And herein lies the very root of Islamist terrorism, as these verses that incite hatred and killing, regardless of the legitimate point of view that they should not be there in the first place in a religion, are taken out of their historical context (which is a context of constant war) by Islamists, while the verses of tolerance are totally ignored, as though they never existed. Indeed, Islam's violent verses are much more known and mediatised than the rarely quoted verses of peace and tolerance. The result of this discrepancy is that Islam is demonised by its critics and the world at large is given an image of Muhammad's religion that is a distorted and incomplete version of the whole faith which, like any other faith, contains both good and bad aspects, since religions are influenced by their historical context and culture.

Actually, at the time Islam flourished and expanded, the whole world was intolerant; cruelty, barbarism, and fanaticism were part of the region's common culture. Christ himself was crucified simply for preaching a religion of peace and love. Nonetheless, we must mention and expose these verses of intolerance and violence which are over-exploited by terrorists, since they also form a part of the holy book of Islam.

To go back to the question, is Islam intolerant? And in an attempt to give this religion a second chance, let us be tolerant and indulgent and give a second answer and say: no doubt it *partly* is. Now, one would ask, ow could a religion be *partly* intolerant? It either is or isn't. Well, the truth of the matter is that there are verses of tolerance *and* verses of intolerance in the same book. Infer from that what you may, but that is the reality with which we must deal if we are to judge that religion fairly and objectively. The problem becomes worse because Islamists only focus on the verses of intolerance as divine justification for their odious crimes.

So, Islam, a tolerant *and* intolerant religion? Yes, and yes. As uncanny as this may sound, it is both. The reasons for this yin-yang (darkness versus light) nature of this faith will be discussed later, as we delve into the possibility of perversion or misrepresentation of the text, or the two very different stages characterising Muhammad's rule, the first of which being peaceful, the second violent. But for now, let us examine the intolerant version of this religion, the "yin," or dark part, so to speak.

In this context, it must be said that the word Islam derives from the root Arabic word *taslim,* which means "submission" or "surrender" to Allah, and specifically to Allah's will, desires, and commands written in *His* book, the Quran. Although the word *taslim* may imply free will/choice to submit out of veneration to The Almighty, a big part of these divine desires and commands happens to be filled with exhortations to slaughter non-Muslims "wherever they are" if they do not convert to the only and supreme "truth" which is Islam.

As we have noted in the previous chapters, critics of Islam accuse it of unquestionably being a totalitarian, even tyrannical religion, an all-encompassing religion which controls every aspect, public and private, of life (laws, ethics, society, economics, for example). This leaves little room, indeed, tiny room, for tolerance for other faiths. It is hard to argue with this accusation of totalitarianism, since the problem with Islam is that it is not only a religion but also a political and socio-economic system; and that is what Islamists, as well as moderate Muslims, say and repeat out loud. Unlike Christianity ("give unto Caesar"), the Quran deals with, and interferes in, every sphere of life, not just the religious. It does not believe in the separation between the sacred and the secular; hence there is little freedom of expression and belief for both Muslims and non-Muslims in the Umma or Islamic Nation or Caliphate.

In the eyes of Muslims, "there is no God but Allah." Allah is the one and only God; Islam is the one and only religion, the perfect religion. The Muslim conception of Allah is that of an absolute and almighty (albeit "merciful") Judge, and His is a religion based on intimidation and fear which allows no freedom of thought or belief, although it explicitly and paradoxically states that, "There is no compulsion in religion" (la ikraha fil din)! Add to this the fact that Muslims believe that the Quran was revealed by God Himself, God the Omnipresent, the Omniscient, and who knows better than God?! The Quran, therefore, acquires this absolute sanctity and leaves no choice but to totally abide by it, and totally submit and surrender, taslim, to its tenets. Everything that needs to be known is written in Allah's sacred book; therefore, there is no need to inquire elsewhere or have other ideas about life, death, heaven, hell, justice, truth, and so on. The Quran is the only source of universal, eternal truth, and Allah's unalterable and unadulterated word, therefore Muslims and non-Muslims should submit to its divine dictates:

"The only true faith in God's sight is Islam. Those to whom the book was given disagreed among themselves only after knowledge had been given to them, being insolent among themselves. He who disbelieves the verses of Allah indeed Allah is swift in reckoning" (Quran, 3:19).

"You are the best nation ever to be brought forth for people. You order honour and forbid dishonour, and you believe in Allah. Had the people of the book believed, it would have surely been better for them. Some of them are believers, but most of them are evildoers" (Quran, 3:110).

It is a Manichean view of the world whereby one could say "either you are with Allah or you are with the devil." This black-and-white perspective leaves little room for tolerance or dialogue, doesn't it?

According to Muslims, Islam is God's final message to humanity. All of God's prophets have come to this world (mind you, Islam doesn't recognise the pre-Abrahamic religions and their prophets; only the three "celestial religions," or "religions of the Book," namely Judaism, Christianity, and Islam, and all the scriptures have been delivered. Thus, Muhammad is the last messenger of God; he is, as he himself proclaimed, the "last of the prophets" (khatimat al anbiya'a). Muslims believe that the time has come to purify, complete, and accomplish all the messages delivered by God's prophets into one message, and to proclaim that henceforth, there is only one religion - Islam - acceptable to God and that all should submit to Allah's will (Quran 3:19, 85). All the other roads "lead to perdition," and people who follow them are "lost" and "deluded." Besides Muslims, who follow the "right path" (*as siraat al mustaqeem*) and who are thus redeemed, the other "people of the Book" (Jews, Christians) can and should convert to the new religion, since their prophets were but mere forerunners to the last prophet, Allah's messenger Muhammad. So, it must be said here that when Islam accepted and recognised the other two Abrahamic monotheistic religions, Judaism and Christianity, the intent was to incorporate the Jews and Christians in the new, *and last,* faith.

Despite the explicit Quranic statement "There is no compulsion in religion," most religious minorities suffer persecution, oppression, genocide, or at least discrimination under Islamic rule. Indeed, the Quran as well as the sharia stipulate that non-Muslims must either convert to Islam or submit to Islamic rule; and in the latter case accept to fall under the status of dhimmis or ahl al-dimma, a category of second-class citizens who pay a war tax (jizya) just to stay alive. In return, the dhimmis are exempted from participating in Muslim wars, since these wars are sacred and should be exclusive to Muslims; *a mere exemption and not a privilege.* The dhimmis also benefit from protection from the caliphate and are free to follow their religious rites in their places of worship which are also protected.

However, it must be said that the concept of dhimmi, as demeaning as it is in the first place, has in addition been largely abused by Muslim zealots throughout history, as it ceased to be a utilitarian taxed exemption from war, and started to have blasphemous (takfiri) connotations. Ahl al dimma, the non- Muslims, the Ahl al-kitab *(Jews and Christians),* thus started to face systematic persecution and extermination:

they were forced to flee or suffer constant, sometimes brutal, persecution, if they refused to convert or submit to Islamic rule. As for the other non-Abrahamic religious communities (Buddhists, Hindus, Zoroastrians, Yazidis), they were and still are considered kaffirs, a label which equals death. It must be said here that the Islamic State's horrendous genocide of Yazidis (and its odious sexual enslavement of Yazidi women) in Iraq unfortunately betrays an ancient and deep-seated mainstream Muslim contempt for these so-called heretics, the fact which perhaps explains the shameful, unacceptable, and inexplicable silence and indifference of Muslim Iraqis towards the holocaust of their Yazidi compatriots at the hands of Daesh terrorists.

This persecution of non-Muslims applied and still applies to countries where Islam dominates and where Muslims are the majority (as in the Middle East, Sudan, Pakistan, Afghanistan, and so on). As for countries where Muslims are the minority (as in some African states, Thailand, the Philippines, India) Islamic extremists, such as the notorious Boko Haram and al-Shebab, spread terror and commit genocide against Christians and other minorities. These non-Muslim countries with Muslim minorities are characterised by strife and unrest and the permanent threat of terror. The aim of the Islamic terrorists in these countries, including the group calling itself Islamic State, is the establishment of the Islamic State (caliphate) and the rule of the sharia.

Not only is Islam intolerant towards non-Muslims (which it brands "unbelievers" or "infidels)," the hard fact is that there is hardly any tolerance or freedom for Muslims themselves. Indeed, any person born into a Muslim family is and should remain a Muslim for life, with no option to choose another religion or to simply choose to be an atheist or even an agnostic. Atheism or conversion to another religion is absolutely forbidden and is a grave crime in the eyes of Islam. Thus, a Muslim is not allowed to leave Islam lest he be branded an "apostate" (murtadd), the gravest of accusations, since it entails death. In fact, the religion of Muhammad encourages its followers to kill such apostates since "spilling their blood" (safk dammihim) becomes "halal" (permitted) and even a duty for any devout Muslim...

Islam is thus a religion of total submission to the will of Allah. Submission to Allah and his dictates is the fundamental duty of every Muslim. Under sharia rule, there is no room for freedom of thought or belief, no tolerance for unbelievers or infidels. If you don't believe in the religion of Allah, you die, leave the country, go into hiding, or simply become a closet atheist.

Moreover, being Muslim means being subjected to a series of compulsory duties and obligations which must be fulfilled throughout one's life. The first duty of a Muslim is performing the "five pillars" of Islam:

- The Shahada, declaring that "there is no god but Allah, and Muhammad is the prophet of God."

- Praying five times a day (including very early in the morning). These prayers are mandatory if the Muslim doesn't want to end up in hell.

- Fasting during the holy month of Ramadan, when the Quran was supposedly revealed by Allah to Muhammad. The Muslim is even forbidden to drink water under the scorching desert sun. So much for Allah's mercy...

- Giving charity to the poor and needy.
- The pilgrimage to Mecca at least once in a lifetime.

Compulsion begins at home; there is no free will or free thinking under sharia rule and hardly any religious and intellectual freedom even for Muslims themselves, because most Muslims believe that religion (exclusively Islam, since it is the supposed "religion of God") should form the basis of the social and political order. Otherwise, the state and society would be "godless" or, secular, in the Islamist lexicon), which is totally unacceptable to Allah. As for the interpretation of the divine scriptures, it is the exclusivity of the scholars, ulama, and hence no critical or rational reading of the text is allowed due to its sanctity. Thus, a Muslim who criticizes any part of the Quran finds himself immediately sentenced to death through a "fatwa" (religious edict) issued by any Muslim cleric. The same sentence threatens those who leave Islam. Every "unbeliever" will be punished, according to the Quran, or Allah's word:

> "Surely those who disbelieve, it being alike to them whether you warn them, or do not warn them, will not believe. Allah has set a seal upon their hearts and upon their hearing and there is a covering over their eyes, and there is a great punishment for them." (Quran, 2:6–7).

Islam does not allow secularism either, because, it believes there is no separation between the state and religion in this religion, since it is both "din wa dawla" (religion and state).

Nevertheless, this nefarious and notorious intolerance of other religions and secularism was not always a characteristic feature of Islam, which began as a peaceful movement whereby Muhammad preached sermons of peace and tolerance. Indeed, in Sûrah al-Baqarah 256, Allah says: *"Let there be no compulsion in religion."* However, this peaceful period did not last long, as few people were voluntarily converting to the new faith and many were plotting against it. Consequently, after an initial peaceful beginning, prior to Muhammad's emigration from Mecca to Medina in 622 CE, Islam was later spread by the sword, and that is how history and mankind's collective memory unfortunately remember this religion, which perfectly suits Islamists and Islamic terrorists; and therefore, sadly, the peaceful verse quoted above and many other verses of peace were superseded by more violent ones, like Surahs 8:12, 9:5, 47:4 and many others.

From 624 CE, the early Muslims conducted local wars against the opponents of the new faith, as well as against defenceless tribal and religious communities, to subjugate them to Islam. These initial small wars inaugurated a period of large-scale Islamic wars (al- Futuhat) from Asia, to Africa, to Europe and the Far East, in order to spread Islam and establish the Muslim empire, the caliphate - a universal state ruled by the sharia. The only way for non-Muslims to avoid being slaughtered was to forcibly convert to Islam. In Ibn Ishaq 814, Muhammad preaches: *"Submit and testify that there is no God but Allah and that Muhammad is the apostle of Allah before you lose your head."* In Sahih Muslim 31:5917, *the prophet of Allah exhorts his followers to "fight with them until they bear testimony to the fact that there is no god but Allah and Muhammad is his Messenger."*

The people of Mecca - more specifically the *Quraish* tribe - who initially refused to convert to Islam were forcibly expelled following Muhammad's last sermon in 632 CE. The Christians and Jews in Arabia were also forced to either accept Islam as their faith, leave their land, or be killed:

"Garments of fire have been prepared for the unbelievers. Scalding water shall be poured upon their heads, melting their skins and that which is in their bellies" (Quran, 22:19–22:23).

"Slay the idolaters wherever you find them, and take them captives and besiege them and lie in wait for them in every ambush" (Quran, 9:5).

"Unbelievers" or "infidels"- that is to say, all non-Muslims - were branded "evil" and the "enemies of God." They would either be tortured or killed if they did not convert to Islam, as the following verses show:

"Take him [the infidel] and fetter him and expose him to hell fire. And then insert him in a chain whereof the length is seventy cubits" (Quran, 69:30–37).

"I will instil terror into the hearts of the unbelievers, smite ye above their necks and smite all their fingertips of them" (Quran, 8:12).

"They should be murdered or crucified or their hands and their feet should be cut off on opposite sides" (Quran, 5:33).

"Fight everyone in the way of Allah and kill those who disbelieve in Allah" (Ibn Ishaq: 992).

"The punishment for those who wage war against God and His Prophet, and perpetrate disorders in the land, is to kill or hang them, or have a hand on one side and a foot on the other cut off, or banish them from the land. Such is their disgrace in the world, and in the Hereafter their doom shall be dreadful" (Quran, 5:33).

"Disbelievers fight for the devil, so fight the minions of the devil" (Quran, 4:76).

"Those who deny Muhammad's revelation are evil" (Quran, 7:177).

"The worst beasts in Allah's sight are the disbelievers" (Quran, 8:55).

"They are your enemy and the enemy of Allah" (Quran, 8:59-60).

As the preceding verses show, the Quran justifies any attack against "unbelievers," since they are "evil," or "deluded" at best; thus Allah urges his prophet:

"Prophet, make war on the unbelievers and the hypocrites and deal rigorously with them. Hell shall be their Home: an evil fate" (Quran, 9:73).

In accordance with their prophet's instructions, Muslims were not allowed to befriend or ally themselves with unbelievers, let alone marry them. Nor did they tolerate non-believers among friends and family who were consequently shunned or persecuted. According to Islam's holy book, a Muslim can only be friends with another Muslim "brother." People of other faiths are undesirables:

"Believers, do not choose the unbelievers rather than the faithful as your friends. Would you give Allah a clear proof against yourselves?" (Quran, 4:144)

"The believers should not take the unbelievers as friends or helpers in preference to the believers. He who does this does not belong to Allah in anything, unless you have a fear of them" (Quran, 3:28).

Nonetheless, it is worth noting here that in some Muslim societies, a Muslim man is allowed to marry a Christian or a Jewish woman, as Christians and Jews are Ahl al-Kitab (People of the Book); the woman can even keep her original faith. Conversely, a Muslim woman is not allowed to marry a non-Muslim (be he a Christian, a Jew, or a person of another faith) unless he converts to Islam. Otherwise she will be considered a murtadda, an apostate; a flagrant discrimination between the sexes.

To go back to the Quran's instructions to Muslims regarding unbelievers, specific orders were given to the followers of Muhammad to slay non-Muslims or expel them out of the holy land of Islam, unless they repent and convert to the new faith:

"When you meet the unbelievers in the Jihad strike off their heads and, when you have laid them low, bind your captives firmly. Then grant them their freedom or take ransom from them, until War shall lay down her burdens" (Quran, 47:4).

"The only reward of those who make war upon Allah and His messenger and strive after corruption in the land will be that they will be killed or crucified, or have their hands and feet and alternate sides cut off, or will be expelled out of the land. Such will be their degradation in the world, and in the Hereafter theirs will be an awful doom; Save those who repent before ye overpower them. For know that Allah is Forgiving, merciful" (Quran, 5:33–34).

Most moderate Muslims say that the preceding verses were revealed to the Prophet during a specific period of war. The extremists who are implementing these "divine" orders and instructions against innocent civilians today in Syria, Egypt, Tunisia, Libya, Lebanon, Brussels, London, Paris, Nice, Orlando, Nigeria, and so on say for their part that these verses are God's word to our Prophet, and to all Muslims around the world, and God's word is eternal, and never temporal, limited to a specific time or task. Thus these terrorists carry out their murders which they deem are justified by the Quran itself.

As for Christians and Jews, the prophet Muhammad had specific instructions to Muslims about these infidels who were nonetheless one step above heathens as the People of the Book, and yet still considered "lost" and "blind" and hence second-class citizens and who, as previously mentioned, were therefore forced to pay a tax in order to stay alive and practice their faith (very discreetly, of course, seeing that they had to subject themselves to Islamic rule):

"Fight those who do not believe in Allah nor the Last day, nor hold the forbidden which hath been forbidden by Allah and his messenger, nor acknowledge the Religion of Truth [Islam], from among the People of the Book, until they pay the Jizya (tax) with willing submission, and feel themselves subdued" (Quran, 9:29).

Therefore, following their prophet's exhortation, Muslims did not always forcibly convert the dhimmis to Islam (the two other options for such infidels were beheading or expulsion) as they realized, as Muhammad implied, that it would be more lucrative to make money off of them. And all this was done, of course, in the name of religious "tolerance."

Thus the following verses:

"Let there be no compulsion in religion: Truth stands out clear from Error" (Quran, 2:256),

"If it had been thy Lord's Will, they would all have believed, all who are on earth! Wilt thou then compel mankind, against their will, to believe?" (Quran, 10:99).

were, one could say, financially motivated, as tolerance had a price... Indeed, when you read the verse about the "Jizya" mentioned earlier, these verses lose their pure religious sense and motivation.

However, merely paying the *Jizya* does not make Christians and Jews worthy of a Muslim's friendship, as the following verses quoting the prophet show:

"Believers, take neither Jews nor Christians for your friends. They are friends with one another. Whoever of you seeks their friendship shall become one of their number. Allah does not guide the wrong-doers" (Quran, 5:51).

"Believers, do not seek the friendship of the infidels and those who were given the Book before you, who have made your religion a jest and a past-time" (*Quran*, 5:57).

Based on all of the above, one cannot but acknowledge that Islam, despite its many verses of peace, tolerance and pluralism, is undoubtedly a largely intolerant religion, intolerant towards non-believers and believers alike, since the former are shunned and the latter have to abide by the strictest rules and obligations. The religion of Muhammad is not open to any kind of dialogue with other religions, unless this dialogue leads to these religions' dissolution and incorporation in the perfect and complete religion of Allah. Neither is Islam open to self-examination or reform, let alone criticism, since *the* Book, the Quran, is the unadulterated and the unalterable word of Allah, the Almighty himself, creator of heaven and earth. The concept of interpretation, ijtihad, does not go, even with the most daring scholars, beyond the mere modernisation or easing of some rituals, without going further into a rational critique of the main issues such as the revelation and the eternity of the scriptures.

When a religion deems itself "perfect" and "complete" and God's "final message to mankind," Muhammad being the last prophet, this religion and its followers are not likely to accept other points of views from "lost" souls, or even "good" ones, for that matter; for how could man's word - however enlightened that man may be - compare with the word of *Allah*? Islamists of course have no trouble at all using and abusing these verses of intolerance towards non-Muslims in their fanatical, hateful and twisted ideology, as a "divine" justification for their violent and heinous acts.

CHAPTER THREE

"JIHAD," OR TERRORISM?
THE CULT OF VIOLENCE

"Be kind to all creatures; this is the true religion."
"See yourself in others. Then whom can you hurt?"

"One should not kill a living being, nor cause it to be killed, nor
should one incite another to kill. Do not injure any being,
either strong or weak, in the world."

"Not to do any harm, to perfectly effect what is beneficial.
That is the teaching of Buddha."

- LORD BUDDHA

"**Y**ou love life and we love death, which gives an example of what the Prophet Muhammad said." In this al-Qaeda video claiming responsibility for the 3/11/2004 Madrid bombings, were these terrorists echoing and heeding Muhammad's exhortation *"I love that I should be killed in the way of Allah"*? Allah's Apostle did say, *"Know that Paradise is under the shades of swords."* (Sahih Bukhari, 4:52:73).

Jihad is one of Islam's holiest precepts. Indeed, it is a religious duty - *Farida*. And, unfortunately, it is also Islamism's and Islamic terrorism's *main* precept. Jihad is what the Quran and Islamic terrorists have in common, which makes it an explosive and highly controversial subject. The terrorists affirm that the Quran verses exhort the Muslim to "strive and fight in the way of Allah" (which is none other than jihad). Now, with countless innocent civilians who fell, and still fall, on a daily basis, victim to the terrorists' jihad in the name of Allah in New York, Boston, Orlando, London, Paris, Nice, Brussels, Munich, Madrid, Syria, Iraq, Yemen, Tunisia, Egypt, Libya, Algeria... one cannot but wonder: how could God condone violence and terrorism? How could he order *his* believers to commit crimes against the humanity he himself created? Against man whom he created "in his own image," as Islam confirms? Herein lies the deep moral crisis facing Islam today and threatening its very existence.

Jihad has its own set of rules (one might even say some sort of legal framework) pertaining to the code of conduct during war, and this set of rules specifies what is to be considered holy war according to the Islamic Canon, "Share3," and what is not. Self-defence, sparing innocent and unarmed civilians, especially women, children and the elderly, refraining from shedding the blood of other Muslims, and so on, are the "rules of war" which Muhammad instituted as an ethical code of conduct during war. However, this jihad rule book was and still is not rigorous enough to prevent the use and abuse of Quranic verses on jihad and war to serve political motivations of power and dominion. Thus, in the absence of a well-framed legal code of war or jihad, or what should, from the religious point of view, be considered as legal war practices, a large manoeuvring room has been conveniently created for Islamists to manipulate these verses and launch their politically, rather than religiously, motivated "sacred" wars. Moreover, contrary to the church, for example, the absence of a clergy and of a strict religious hierarchy in Islam, as well as the absence of one unified interpretation of the scriptures, have paved the way for many religious groupings and interpretations of the text to mushroom in the most chaotic manner ever.

Still, the main problem with jihad, whether it is considered within the framework of Islamic jurisprudence or not, is the presence of explicit verses in the Quran on "jihad for the sake of Allah," which makes Islam a religion of war to a great extent. Indeed, there are over 100 verses in Islam's holy book preaching war to defend "the House of Islam," Deir Al Islam, which includes all Muslim countries. This war is not restricted to the citizens of this or that country; rather, it is the duty of all the Muslims in the world to participate in this war, to support - nusra - and defend the Muslim umma - nation - against its enemies. And herein lies the root of international terrorism: Muslims worldwide are commanded by Allah to support and defend their fellow Muslims against what they consider acts of aggression or persecution against them, which leaves a very large margin for Islamic terrorists to make *their* "holy wars."

It goes without saying that these verses of violence, once manipulated and distorted by takfiris, become an extremely dangerous and lethal religious weapon and have catastrophic consequences, since they are supposed to be Allah's word and will, they are thus given a divine weight and authority, as they form an integral part of the Quran.

While Muslim terrorists take these verses of violence as literally and as seriously as anything else in the *Quran*, and thus consider that *Jihad* is an essential part of Islam, moderate Muslims for their part remain silent as regards these crystal-clear exhortations to kill or main "infidels" in their holy book... Indeed, what could they say?

All Muslims, whether they are moderates or fundamentalists, agree on the legitimacy of defending Islam (jihad) against its enemies. But they disagree on the extent of jihad: Moderates restrict it to self-defence and respect its ethical rules or code of war, while the fundamentalist jihadis, benefiting from the vagueness and elasticity of this jihad jurisprudence, extend it to wage war against non-believers. And while the moderates' jihad is for the sole religious purpose of defending Islam and Muslims against their persecutors, and never to force non-Muslims to convert to Islam, the fundamentalists' jihad has political as well as religious connotations against those they call the "infidels," "unbelievers," "crusaders." Their purpose is to spread Islam by the sword and to establish the Islamic state, the international caliphate, by war and violence.

And what do these extremists have in their hands? They have verses that, according to them, cannot be interpreted otherwise; they have a "clear" divine license to kill in the name of God. And what is more dangerous is that it is the fundamentalist jihadis who accuse moderate Muslims of distorting - and not the other way around! - the "clear" verses of the scriptures, Allah's words, to justify their "cowardice," "hypocrisy," and "submission" to the "corrupt" rulers, who are accused of being "puppets of the West." Thus they declare them "enemies" of God too; and we all know what that accusation means: it is a recipe to kill them, a death sentence.

Thus, Islamist takfiris or Jihadis consider themselves as the only true Muslims, while they perceive all others as kaffirs. Their jihad is ruled, not by any human jurisprudence, but by the Quran itself, God's word and command. And, as jihad is one of the holiest commandments of Islam, they consider their holy war against Islam's enemies - the "infidels," the "unbelievers," the "crusaders" ... as the supreme act or practice of religious devotion: they pray not only with their lips but with their blood, or rather, the blood of others, the blood of innocents. Therefore, to them, there is no distinction whatsoever between Islam and Islamism (a distinction they deem ridiculous), and herein lies the great danger and the disturbing reality; a reality whereby Islam has become associated with terrorism, since Islamic terrorists see themselves at the end of the day as merely following Allah's word when they heed the dozens of verses on jihad which they take quite literary and consider divine commandments, without any *human intervention or interpretation*. And alas! Facing this fundamentalist takeover of Islam at an alarming pace, the overwhelming majority of Muslims remain silent, except for a few brave voices scattered here and there, towards the violence done in the name of this unholy *jihad* stained with the blood of innocents.

Those who defend Islam would argue that the crusaders, too, committed crimes in the name of God, and they certainly did not represent true Christianity, so why do we consider that Islamists represent Islam? The crucial difference lies in the fact that crusaders were not basing themselves on the Scriptures or Christ's teachings; quite the contrary. Conversely, the Islamists base their actions on the Quran's verses to justify their acts of violence and crimes against unbelievers'. The problem with Islam, critics say, lies not just in Islamists but also in the scriptures themselves.

As noted previously, jihad is one of Islam's highest precepts. But what exactly is jihad? Literally, jihad means "struggle." In the second part of this book, we shall explore the two concepts of jihad, lesser and greater, the former meaning the jihad of the sword, the latter the jihad of the soul. Islamists completely disregard the latter, which is of spiritual and peaceful nature. But for now and in this chapter, we shall purely explore the first concept of jihad, the literal war to spread Islam with the sword.

For Islamists, the literal jihad or holy war is the best form of worship of Allah. Jihad, at least the way Islamic terrorists interpret and practice it, is the incitement to commit indiscriminate, barbaric, large-scale murder, torture, burning, and maiming of kaffirs or "infidels," plundering their wealth, destroying their property or places of worship, occupying their land, raping their women and turning them into sex slaves. They apply this barbaric jihad on both non-Muslims and Muslims alike whom they consider have deviated from the Right Path, al-Sirat ai-Mustaqim, or God's commandments; that is, according to Islam as *they* interpret it.

In this context, it is useful, in order to understand the ultimate goal and far-reaching, destructive consequences of this holy concept, to see what two prominent Muslim leaders have said about jihad:

- Ayatollah Khomeini, the leader of Islamic Revolution in Iran, declared at the height of the revolution,

"Jihad means the conquest of all non-Muslim territories. Such a war may well be declared after the formation of an Islamic government worthy of that name . . . It will then be the duty of every able-bodied adult male Muslim to volunteer for this war of conquest, the final aim of which is to put Quranic law in power from one end of the earth to

the other. . . . We have no recourse other than to overthrow all governments that do not rest on pure Islamic principles . . . That is not only our duty in Iran, but it is also the duty of all Muslims in the world, in all Muslim countries to carry the Islamic political revolution to its final victory."

- Another Muslim leader, Sheikh Ahmed Ismail Hassan Yassin, the founder of Hamas, the faction of the Muslim Brotherhood in Palestine, declared,

"Kill all the unbelievers just as they would kill you all! Does this mean that Muslims should sit back until they are devoured by [the unbelievers]? Islam says: Kill them [the non-Muslims], put them to the sword and scatter [their armies]. Does this mean sitting back until [non-Muslims] overcome us? Islam says, 'Kill in the service of Allah those who may want to kill you!' Does this mean that we should surrender [to the enemy]? Islam says: 'Whatever good there is exists thanks to the sword and in the shadow of the sword!' People cannot be made obedient except with the sword! The sword is the key to Paradise, which can be opened only for the Holy Warriors! Sons of Islam everywhere, the Jihad is a duty - to establish the rule of Allah on earth and to liberate your countries and yourselves from America's domination and its Zionist allies, it is your battle - either victory or martyrdom."

As we clearly see from the two statements above, jihad's ultimate goal is to establish the "rule of Allah" on Earth. In other words, sharia or Islamic law.

Following is a very long, but not exhaustive list of the Quran's most explicit verses on jihad which are used (and abused) by Islamic terrorists to justify their horrific acts. The verb jahada, "to struggle" or "to strive," which is commonly found in the Quran, is used against unbelievers as the sacred duty of each Muslim; otherwise, they are "hypocrites," i.e. those who call themselves Muslims but do not act as such. In other words, an unabashed "apology of our jihad," as the terrorists would say! According to them, these verses are crystal-clear; there is no need for comments or explanations, there is no room for any "allegorical" interpretation. In order to assess or understand how Islamic terrorists are *reasoning*, taking the verses as they are, considering themselves God's beloved faithful and martyrs, we shall now fall silent and let the verses of the Quran speak for themselves:

"Fight those who believe neither in Allah nor the Last Day, nor hold that forbidden which hath been forbidden by Allah and His Messenger, nor acknowledge the religion of Truth, [even if they are] *of the People of the Book, until they pay the Jizya* [tax] *with willing submission, and feel themselves subdued"* (Quran, 9:29).

"So when the sacred months have passed away, then slay the idolaters wherever you find them, and take them captives and besiege them and lie in wait for them in every ambush, then if they repent and keep up prayer and pay the poor-rate, leave their way free to them" (Quran, 9:5: the "Verse of the Sword").

"Therefore, when you meet the unbelievers, smite at their necks; at length, when ye have thoroughly subdued them,

bind a bond firmly [on them]: *thereafter* [is the time for]
*either generosity or ransom: until the war lays down its
burdens"* (Quran, 47:4).

*"Then fight in the cause of Allah, and know that Allah
heareth and knoweth all things"* (Quran, 2:244).

*"Fighting is prescribed for you, and ye dislike it. But it
is possible that ye dislike a thing which is good for you,
and that ye love a thing which is bad for you. But Allah
knoweth, and ye know not"* (Quran, 2:216).

*"As to those who reject faith, I will punish them with
terrible agony in this world and in the Hereafter, nor will
they have anyone to help"* (Quran, 3:56).

*"Soon shall we cast terror into the hearts of the unbelievers,
for that they joined companions with Allah, for which he
had sent no authority"* (Quran, 3:151).

*"Let those fight in the way of Allah who sell the life of this
world for the other. Whoso fighteth in the way of Allah, be
he slain or be he victorious, on him we shall bestow a vast
reward"* (Quran, 4:74).

"Those who believe fight in the cause of Allah."
(Quran, 4:76).

*"They but wish that ye should reject faith, as they do,
and thus be on the same footing* [as they]; *But take not
friends from their ranks until they flee in the way of Allah*
[From what is forbidden]. *But if they turn renegades,
seize them and slay them wherever ye find them; and* [in

any case] *take no friends or helpers from their ranks"* (Quran, 4:89).

"And be not weak-hearted in pursuit of the enemy; if you suffer pain, then surely they [too] suffer pain as you suffer pain..." (Quran, 4:104).

"The punishment of those who wage war against Allah and his messenger and strive to make mischief in the land is only this, that they should be murdered or crucified or their hands and their feet should be cut off on opposite sides or they should be imprisoned; this shall be as a disgrace for them in this world, and in the hereafter they shall have a grievous chastisement" (Quran, 5:33).

"I will cast terror into the hearts of those who disbelieve. Therefore strike off their heads and strike off every fingertip of them" (Quran, 8:12).

"O ye who believe! When ye meet those who disbelieve in battle, turn not your backs to them. Whoso on that day turneth his back to them, unless manoeuvring for battle or intent to join a company, he truly hath incurred wrath from Allah, and his habitation will be hell, a hapless journey's end" (Quran, 8:15).

"If thou comest on them in the war, deal with them so as to strike fear in those who are behind them, that haply they may remember" (Quran, 8:57).

"And let not those who disbelieve suppose that they can outstrip [Allah's purpose]. Lo! they cannot escape. Make

ready for them all thou canst of [armed] *force and of horses tethered, that thereby ye may dismay the enemy of Allah and your enemy"* (Quran, 8:59-60).

"O Prophet, exhort the believers to fight." (Quran, 8:65).

"Fight them, Allah will punish them by your hands and bring them to disgrace." (Quran, 9:14).

"Those who believe, and have left their homes and striven with their wealth and their lives in Allah's way [jihad] *are of much greater worth in Allah's sight. These are they who are triumphant"* (Quran, 9:20).

"And the Jews say: Ezra is the son of Allah; and the Christians say: The Messiah is the son of Allah; these are the words of their mouths; they imitate the saying of those who disbelieved before; may Allah destroy them; how they are turned away!" (Quran, 9:30).

"O ye who believe! What is the matter with you, that, when ye are asked to go forth in the cause of Allah, ye cling heavily to the earth? Do ye prefer the life of this world to the Hereafter? But little is the comfort of this life, as compared with the hereafter. Unless ye go forth, he will punish you with a grievous penalty, and put others in your place" (Quran, 9:38–39).

"Go forth, light-armed and heavy-armed, and strive with your wealth and your lives in the way of Allah! That is best for you if ye but knew" (Quran, 9:41).

"But the Messenger, and those who believe with him, strive and fight with their wealth and their persons: for them are [all] good things: and it is they who will prosper" (Quran, 9:88).

"Allah hath purchased of the believers their persons and their goods; for theirs [in return] is the garden [of Paradise]: they fight in his cause, and slay and are slain: a promise binding on him in truth, through the Law, the Gospel, and the Quran: and who is more faithful to his covenant than Allah? Then rejoice in the bargain which ye have concluded: that is the achievement supreme" (*Quran*, 9:111).

"Therefore listen not to the unbelievers, but strive against them [Jihad] with the utmost strenuousness..." (Quran, 25:52).

"If the hypocrites, and those in whose hearts is a disease, and the alarmists in the city do not cease, We verily shall urge thee on against them, then they will be your neighbours in it but a little while. Accursed, they will be seized wherever found and slain with a [fierce] slaughter" (Quran, 33:60–62).

"Those who reject Allah follow vanities, while those who believe follow the truth from their lord. Thus does Allah set forth form men their lessons by similitudes. Therefore when you meet in battle those who disbelieve, then smite the necks until when you have overcome them, then make (them) prisoners" (Quran, 47:3–4).

"Be not weary and faint-hearted, crying for peace, when ye should be uppermost, for Allah is with you" (Quran, 47:35).

"There is no blame for the blind, nor is there blame for the lame, nor is there blame for the sick [that they go not forth to war]. *And whoso obeyeth Allah and His messenger, He will make him enter Gardens underneath which rivers flow; and whoso turneth back, him will He punish with a painful doom"* (Quran, 48:17).

"Muhammad is the messenger of Allah. And those with him are hard (ruthless) against the disbelievers and merciful among themselves" (Quran, 48:29).

"Surely Allah loves those who fight in his way" (Quran, 61:4).

"He it is who has sent his Messenger (Muhammad) *with guidance and the religion of truth* (Islam) *to make it victorious over all religions even though the infidels may resist"* (Quran, 61:9).

"O ye who believe! Shall I lead you to a bargain that will save you from a grievous Penalty? - That ye believe in Allah and His Messenger, and that ye strive (your utmost) in the cause of Allah, with your property and your persons: That will be best for you, if ye but knew! He will forgive you your sins, and admit you to gardens beneath which rivers flow, and to beautiful mansions in gardens of eternity" (Quran, 61:10–12).

"O Prophet! Strive against the disbelievers and the hypocrites, and be stern with them. Hell will be their home, a hapless journey's end" (Quran, 66:9).

"O Prophet! Strive hard against the unbelievers and the hypocrites and be unyielding to them; and their abode is hell, and evil is the destination" (Quran, 9:73).

"Therefore, the curse of Allah is upon the unbelievers!" (Quran, 2:89).

"Whoever is an enemy to Allah and His angels and messengers, to Gabriel and Michael, lo! Allah is an enemy of the unbelievers" (Quran, 2:97).

"Slay them [unbelievers] wherever you find them. Drive them out of the places from which they drove you, for persecution is worse than slaughter. . . Such is the reward of those who reject faith" (Quran, 2:191).

"Fight against them [unbelievers] until there is no dissension, and the religion is for Allah" (Quran, 2:193).

"But those who believe and those who migrate and struggle in the way of Allah, those, have hope of the mercy of Allah" (Quran, 2:218).

"Those who disbelieve, neither their riches nor their children shall save them from Allah. They shall become the fuel of the fire" (Quran, 3:10).

"And those who believe fight in the way of Allah, but those who disbelieve fight in cause of evil. Therefore, fight against

those guided by Satan" (Quran, 4:76).

"For the unbelievers are to you open enemies" (Quran, 4:101).

"How many a village have we laid in ruin! In the night our might fell upon it, or at midday when they were drowsy" (Quran, 7:4).

"Fight them [the unbelievers] *until persecution is no more and the religion of Allah reigns supreme"* (Quran, 8:39).

"Those who believe and migrated from their homes and fought for the Way of Allah, and those who have sheltered them and helped them they are truly the believers" (Quran, 8:74). *"For four months you shall journey freely in the land. But know that you shall not render Allah incapable, and that Allah will humiliate the unbelievers . . . .And give glad tidings to the unbelievers of a painful punishment . . . .When the sacred months are over, slay the idolaters wherever you find them. Take them and confine them, then lie in ambush everywhere for them"* (Quran, 9:1, 3, 5).

"Fight them [the unbelievers], *Allah will punish them with your hands and degrade them. He will grant you victory over them and heal the chests of a believing nation"* (Quran, 9:14).

"Do you consider giving drink to the pilgrims and inhabiting the sacred mosque is the same as one who believes in Allah and the last day, and struggles in the

Way of Allah? These are not held equal by Allah. Allah does not guide the harm-doers. Those who believe, and migrated, and struggle in the Way of Allah with their wealth and their persons are greater in rank with Allah" (Quran, 9:19).

"Then, Allah caused his tranquillity [sechina] *to descend upon his messenger and the believers; he sent legions you did not see and sternly punished the unbelievers. Such is the recompense of the unbelievers"* (Quran, 9:26).

"It is he who has sent forth his messenger with guidance and the religion of truth to uplift it above every religion, no matter how much the idolaters hate it" (Quran, 9:33).

"Those who believe in Allah and the last day will not ask your permission so that they may struggle with their wealth and their selves" (Quran, 9:44).

"Hell shall encompass the unbelievers" (Quran, 9:49).

"Believers, fight the unbelievers who are near you. Let them find firmness in you. Know that Allah is with those who are cautious" (Quran, 9:123)

"But the unbelievers shall be the destroyed losers. He will bring their deeds to nothing" (Quran, 47:8).

"It was he who expelled the unbelievers among the people of the book from their homes into the first exile. You did not think that they would go out, and they thought their fortresses would protect them from Allah. But Allah came upon them from where they did not expect, casting

terror into their hearts that their homes were destroyed by their own hands as well as by the hands of the believers. Therefore, take heed you that have eyes. Had it been that Allah had not decreed that they should be dispersed, he would have surely punished them in this world. And in the everlasting life the punishment of the fire awaits them" (Quran, 59:2-3).

"He has sent His messenger with the guidance and the true religion, and will make it dominate all religions, in spite of the idol worshippers" (Quran, 61:9).

"The unbelievers among the People of the Book and the idolaters shall be forever in the fire of Jahannam [hell]. *They are the worst of all creatures"* (Quran, 98:6).

"Fighting is enjoined on you, and it is an object of dislike to you; and it may be that you dislike a thing while it is good for you, and it may be that you love a thing while it is evil for you, and Allah knows, while you do not know" (Quran, 2:216–218).

"And fight in the way of Allah, and know that Allah is Hearing, Knowing" (Quran, 2:244).

"How many of the prophets fought (in Allah's way) [jihad], *and with them (fought) large bands of godly men? But they never lost heart if they met with disaster in Allah's way* [lost a battle], *nor did they weaken (in will) nor give in. And Allah loves those who are firm and steadfast* [in jihad]" (Quran, 3:146).

"Come, fight in Allah's way, or defend yourselves" (*Quran*, 3:165-67).

"And reckon not those who are killed in Allah's way as dead; nay, they are alive (and) are provided sustenance from their Lord" (Quran, 3:169).

"Therefore let those fight in the way of Allah, who sell this world's life for the hereafter; and whoever fights in the way of Allah, then be he slain or be he victorious, We shall grant him a mighty reward" (Quran, 4:74).

"And what reason have you that you should not fight in the way of Allah and of the weak among the men and the women and the children, (of) those who say: Our Lord! Cause us to go forth from this town, whose people are oppressors, and give us from Thee a guardian and give us from Thee a helper" (Quran, 4:75).

"Those who believe fight in the way of Allah, and those who disbelieve fight in the way of the Satan. Fight therefore against the friends of the Satan; surely the strategy of the Satan is weak" (Quran, 4:76).

"Have you not seen those to whom it was said: Withhold your hands, and keep up prayer and pay the poor-rate; but when fighting is prescribed for them, lo! A party of them fear men as they ought to have feared Allah, or (even) with a greater fear, and say: Our Lord! Why hast Thou ordained fighting for us? Wherefore didst Thou not grant us a delay to a near end? Say: the provision of this world is short, and

the hereafter is better for him who guards (against evil); and you shall not be wronged the husk of a date stone" (Quran, 4:77).

"O you who believe! When you go to war in Allah's way, make investigation, and do not say to anyone who offers you peace: You are not a believer. Do you seek goods of this world's life! But with Allah there are abundant gains; you too were such before, then Allah conferred a benefit on you; therefore make investigation; surely Allah is aware of what you do. The holders back from among the believers, not having any injury, and those who strive hard [jihad] in Allah's way with their property and their persons are not equal; Allah has made the strivers with their property and their persons to excel the holders back a (high) degree, and to each (class) Allah has promised good; and Allah shall grant to the strivers [jihadis] above the holders back a mighty reward" (Quran, 4:94–5).

"The punishment of those who wage war against Allah and His apostle and strive to make mischief in the land is only this, that they should be murdered or crucified or their hands and their feet should be cut off on opposite sides or they should be imprisoned; this shall be as a disgrace for them in this world, and in the hereafter they shall have a grievous chastisement" (Quran, 5:033).

"O you who believe! Be careful of (your duty to) Allah and seek means of nearness to Him and strive hard [at jihad] in His way that you may be successful" (Quran, 5:035).

"They ask thee (O Muhammad) of the spoils of war. Say: The spoils of war belong to Allah and the messenger, so keep your duty to Allah, and adjust the matter of your difference, and obey Allah and His messenger, if ye are (true) believers" (Quran, 8:001).

"When you sought aid from your Lord [at the Battle of Badr], *so He answered you: I will assist you* [in jihad] *with a thousand of the angels following one another"* (Quran, 8:9-10).

"And if they break their oaths after their agreement and (openly) revile your religion, then fight the leaders of unbelief - surely their oaths are nothing - so that they may desist. [9.13] *What! will you not fight a people who broke their oaths and aimed at the expulsion of the Apostle"* (Quran, 9:12–14).

"What! do you think that you will be left alone while Allah has not yet known those of you who have struggled hard [jihad] *and have not taken any one as an adherent besides Allah and His Apostle and the believers; and Allah is aware of what you do"* (Quran, 9:016).

"Surely the number of months with Allah is twelve months in Allah's ordinance since the day when He created the heavens and the earth, of these four being sacred; that is the right reckoning; therefore be not unjust to yourselves regarding them, and fight the polytheists all together as they fight you all together; and know that Allah is with those who guard (against evil)" (Quran, 9:036).

"Therefore if Allah brings you back to a party of them and then they ask your permission to go forth, say: By no means shall you ever go forth with me and by no means shall you fight an enemy with me [in jihad]; *surely you chose to sit the first time, therefore sit (now) with those who remain behind"* (Quran, 9:83).

"And whenever a chapter is revealed, saying: Believe in Allah and strive hard [in *Jihad*] *along with His Apostle, those having ampleness of means ask permission of you and say: Leave us* (behind), *that we may be with those who sit"* (Quran, 9:86).

"Surely Allah has bought of the believers their persons and their property for this, that they shall have the garden; they fight in Allah's way, so they slay and are slain; a promise which is binding on Him in the Taurat [Old Testament] *and the Injeel* [New Testament] *and the Quran; and who is more faithful to his covenant than Allah? Rejoice therefore in the pledge which you have made; and that is the mighty achievement"* (Quran, 9:111).

"O you who believe! Fight those of the unbelievers who are near to you and let them find in you hardness; and know that Allah is with those who guard (against evil)*"* (Quran, 9:123).

"But verily thy Lord - to those who leave their homes after trials and persecutions - and who thereafter strive and fight for the faith and patiently persevere - Thy Lord, after all this is oft-forgiving, Most Merciful" (Quran, 16:110).

"And those who leave their homes for the cause of Allah, and are then slain or die, Allah will, surely, provide for them a goodly provision. And, surely, Allah is the Best of providers" (Quran, 22:58).

"And strive hard [in *Jihad*] *in* (the way of) *Allah, (such) a striving is due to Him; He has chosen you and has not laid upon you a hardship in religion; the faith of your father Ibrahim"* (Quran, 22:78).

"And they swear by Allah with the most energetic of their oaths that if you command them they would certainly go forth [to jihad]. *Say: Swear not; reasonable obedience* (is desired); *surely Allah is aware of what you do"* (Quran, 24:53).

"So obey not the unbelievers and fight strenuously with them in many a strenuous fight" (Quran, 25:52).

"And whoever strives hard [in jihad], *he strives only for his own soul; most surely Allah is Self-sufficient, above* (need of) *the worlds"* (Quran, 29:6).

"And (as for) *those who strive hard* [in jihad] *for Us* [Allah], *We will most certainly guide them in Our ways; and Allah is most surely with the doers of good"* (Quran, 29:69).

"And verily they had already sworn unto Allah that they would not turn their backs (to the foe) [in *Jihad* battle]. *An oath to Allah must be answered for"* (Quran, 33:15).

"Of the believers are men who are true to that which they covenanted with Allah. Some of them have paid their vow by death (in battle), *and some of them still are waiting; and they have not altered in the least"* (Quran, 33:23).

"And Allah turned back the unbelievers in their rage; they did not obtain any advantage, and Allah sufficed the believers in fighting; and Allah is Strong, Mighty" (Quran, 33:25–27).

"And those who believe say: Why has not a chapter been revealed? But when a decisive chapter is revealed, and fighting [jihad] *is mentioned therein you see those in whose hearts is a disease look to you with the look of one fainting because of death. Woe to them then!"* (Quran, 47:20).

"Those who were left behind will say, when ye set forth to capture booty: Let us go with you. They fain would change the verdict of Allah. Say (unto them, O Muhammad): Ye shall not go with us. Thus hath Allah said beforehand. Then they will say: Ye are envious of us. Nay, but they understand not, save a little... Say to those of the dwellers of the desert who were left behind: You shall soon be invited (to fight) *against a people possessing mighty prowess; you will fight against them until they submit; then if you obey, Allah will grant you a good reward* [booty]; *and if you turn back as you turned back before, He will punish you with a painful punishment... There is no blame for the blind, nor is there blame for the lame, nor is there blame for the sick* (that they go not forth to war). *And whoso*

JIHAD," OR TERRORISM? THE CULT OF VIOLENCE

obeyeth Allah and His messenger [by going on *Jihad*], *He will make him enter Gardens underneath which rivers flow; and whoso turneth back* [from *Jihad*], *him will He punish with a painful doom... Certainly Allah was well pleased with the believers when they swore allegiance to you under the tree, and He knew what was in their hearts, so He sent down tranquillity on them and rewarded them with a near victory,* [48.19] *And much booty that they will capture. Allah is ever Mighty, Wise"* (Quran, 48:15–24).

"And yet another (blessing) *that you love: help from Allah and a victory* [in *Jihad*] *near at hand; and give good news to the believers* (Quran, 61:13).

The many verses above not only exhort the Muslims to wage jihad, but they also urge them to use the most barbaric violence: beheading the kaffirs or "infidels." Two verses are crystal-clear in their advocacy of beheading:

"I will instil terror into the hearts of the unbelievers: smite ye above their necks" (Quran, 8:12).

"Therefore, when ye meet the Unbelievers, strike off their heads" (Quran, 47:4).

Based on the aforementioned verses, Islamic militants consider their case closed against their opponents or critics, whether Muslims or not. In their eyes, the authoritative *Quran*, a purely revealed and untainted Book - which is thus impossible to distort - gives them the necessary "religious", "ethical", and "moral" tools for their "holy" war against al-kuffar. Indeed, they are following, as they claim, the cult of the rightful ancestors, al-Salaf al-Saleh, , meaning the Prophet and his first comrades, al-Sahaba.

A theory presents itself among those who seek to give an explanation to the dual, even antithetical, nature of Islam; a religion of mercy on the one hand, a religion of war on the other. This theory states that the earlier "Meccan" verses were peaceful; they coincided with a newly emerging faith which had yet to consolidate itself, and which was too weak to declare war against its potential or actual enemies who had their own religions, and definitely had their interests and socio-political status to defend; indeed, the caste system which was in place at that time viewed the new religion with utmost suspicion since it could challenge or jeopardise the solidly established status quo and thus threaten its authority. And then came the later verses, the Medina warlike verses, which coincided with Islam's expansion, after the religion of Muhammad took roots, and consolidated itself against its opponents; that is when Muslims became more confident, aggressive, and expansionist; and ruled by the sword.

So, verses *à la carte*, one might say! The Islamists definitely reject this theory as being blasphemous against The Almighty, as it views the divine scriptures as manipulative and temporal to fit temporary circumstances, the fact which dismisses their eternal and divine nature and authority.

Those who defend Islam warn of the "risks" of trying to interpret the Quran without the "assistance" of Muslim clerics, lest it is misconstrued. Critics reiterate: but how could verses that openly and explicitly exhort violence (and specifically instruct "believers" to "chop off the heads" of "infidels") be interpreted in a "different" way? It would be preposterous to try to find an "allegorical" dimension to verses which preach the spilling of blood in the name of Allah, these critics argue.

Violence has always characterised Islamic history, a turbulent history of wars and conquests. The Quran's verses on jihad, which today are used and abused by Islamic terrorists to justify the slaughter of "unbelievers," were also exploited much earlier in history by Muslim zealots to justify the genocide of tens of millions of Hindus during five centuries (beginning around AD 1000). Followers of Muhammad also slaughtered scores of Buddhists, nearly wiping this religion off the Indian subcontinent, as well as Jews and Christians in the Middle East, North Africa and parts of Europe. Zoroastrians were also despised as "heretics" or "pagans" and consequently persecuted and killed, exactly the same way the Islamic State terrorists slaughter the Yazidis today. Nowadays Zoroastrians live very discreetly in the Islamic Republic of Iran, practicing their religion in the shadows, whereas they had total religious freedom under the late Shah (who was believed to be Zoroastrian himself).

The critics' argument thus goes on: the fact of the matter, an undeniable fact which says a lot about Islam as a religion of war, is that Muhammad was not just a prophet but also - and more significantly - a military leader who, after a peaceful but unsuccessful period trying to win the hearts and minds of the people of Mecca, waged wars to forcibly convert "infidels" and "unbelievers" to the new faith.

According to Islamist literature, the warriors or jihadis' reward, should they be martyred, is 72 virgins waiting to mate with them in paradise. Otherwise, if they remain alive after battle, they would reap the spoils of war and fruits of their conquests on Earth by having countless women as sex slaves, and booty. As for those Muslims who do not participate in jihad, or those fighters who renege or hesitate to kill in the name of Allah, they are called "hypocrites," "cowards," and "weaklings" and thus threatened with hell if they do not behave as good Muslims, i.e. warriors.

An important point to be made is that the armies of Muhammad, who waged military campaigns under their prophet's leadership, made the most significant military conquests in the decades following his death, forcibly subjecting the people they conquered to the new faith. Muslim apologists would contend that the armies of Muhammad only attacked in self-defence, but this is clearly contradicted by history itself.

However, that being said, and to be objective in our analysis of Islam, in the second part of this book, we will show the "other," allegorical, spiritual side of jihad, and make a contrast between "greater" and "lesser" jihad and show how Islamists are only focusing on the latter and completely disregarding the former.

CHAPTER FOUR

WOMEN IN ISLAM:
ALLAH'S FORGOTTEN DAUGHTERS

"In all things, there is neither male nor female."
- LORD BUDDHA

"I look upon all creatures equally; none are less dear to me and none more dear."
- LORD KRISHNA

An issue of no lesser importance than any other when studying Islamic terrorism is the status of women, for the treatment of women shows the moral worth of any given society. And we have all seen with shock and horror on media channels how Daesh terrorists treated Yazidi women and girls in Iraq as sex slaves, beating and raping them, and even selling them like cattle. The mistreatment and abuse of women might be, to a certain extent, a common war practice, even among the most professional armies, including Western armies, but such practices are not ideologically motivated, i.e. stemming from a certain doctrine, as is the case with Islamic terrorists who again refer to the scriptures (the Quran and the Hadith) to justify, and even to praise the physical and sexual abuse and mistreatment of women, especially those of other faiths (or even from certain sects within Islam itself). Indeed, these women are considered infidels, and must either convert to Islam and mate with their new Muslim masters, or face their dismal fate as sex slaves to be bought and sold.

Islam saw the light in the Arabian Peninsula, a tribal community where burying newborn girls alive was a common habit or norm. And the new faith must be given credit for forbidding this ancient barbaric and criminal social custom, for lifting the status of women, and giving them *some* rights that were progressive *at that time.* Indeed, Muslims proudly proclaim that Islam gave women their rights "long before most of the rest of the world did, including the West," arguing that, before Islam, Arabs (and many other cultures) used to bury their unwanted baby girls alive. Furthermore, they claim that, at that time, other cultures and religions also treated women as second-class citizens (and to this day, a lot of cultures still do!); so, this, they say, must be taken into consideration before criticising the Quran's unequal treatment and consideration of women. While this claim is far from being totally correct (many other ancient cultures and religions treated women with respect and as equals, such as ancient Greece and Rome in the West and Buddhism in the East, to name but three examples among many), still, it is fair to say that Islam did uplift women's status in Arabia, and was thus progressive to a certain degree in this regard.

- LOVE, RESPECT, AND PROTECTION:

Islam, in its Book, teaches that women must be loved, respected, and protected. Consider the two verses below (love between a man and a woman):

> *"And of His Signs is that He created mates for you from yourselves that you might find peace of mind in*

them, and He put between you love and compassion" (Quran, 30:21).

"It is He Who created from a single person, and made his mate of like nature in order that he might dwell with her - in love" (Quran, 7:189).

- MATERIAL RIGHTS:

Not only did Islam forbid the horrifying and barbaric practice of burying baby girls alive, and taught Muslim men to love and protect them, it also went further to ensure their rights in inheritance, and this according to Allah's own will:

"Allah directs you with regard to your Children's (inheritance): to the male, a portion equal to that of two females . . . These are settled portions ordained by Allah" *(Quran, 4:11).*

Despite the fact that a daughter is entitled to inherit only half the portion of her father's property than that allotted to the son, still, that was a leap, a very progressive leap, in women's status and rights (but again, it must be said, *at that time*): women thus went from being buried alive to inheriting from the dead.

-1- FUNDAMENTAL INEQUALITY BETWEEN MEN AND WOMEN:

Nevertheless, and unfortunately, this is where the positive aspect of Islam regarding women ends. Indeed, for reasons related to the fundamental convictions of Islam and its cultural background, the religion of Muhammad does not recognise equality between men and women; it considers the female mentally and intellectually "inferior" to her male counterpart, and it views her with suspicion as to her intellectual, as well as to her religious, capacities. Indeed, the Quran, the main "divine source" of Islam, says on women's inferiority to men:

"Men are superior to women because Allah has made it so." (Quran, 4:34).

"Wives have the same rights as the husbands have on them in accordance with the generally known principles. Of course, men are a degree above them in status" (Quran, 2:228).

The Hadith, another main source of Islam, since it is the collection of the Prophet's teachings and instructions, helps clarify the status of woman in Islam with regard to her "intellectual deficiencies":

"The Prophet said, 'isn't the witness of a woman equal to half of that of a man?' the woman said, 'Yes,' he said, 'this is because of the deficiency of a woman's mind.'" (Bukhari: Vol. 3, Book 48, No. 826).

"Narrated Abu Said Al-Khudri: Once Allah's Apostle went out to the Musalla (to offer the prayer) *of 'Id-al-Adha or Al-Fitr prayer. Then he passed by the women and said, 'O women! Give alms, as I have seen that the majority of the dwellers of Hell-fire were you* (women).' *They asked, 'Why is it so, O Allah's Apostle?' He replied, 'You curse frequently and are ungrateful to your husbands. I have not seen anyone more deficient in intelligence and religion than you. A cautious sensible man could be led astray by some of you.'*

The women asked, 'O Allah's Apostle! What is deficient in our intelligence and religion?' He said, 'Is not the evidence of two women equal to the witness of one man?' They replied in the affirmative. **He said, "This is the deficiency in her intelligence.** *Isn't it true that a woman can neither pray nor fast during her menses?' The women replied in the affirmative. He said, 'This is the deficiency in her religion.'"* (Bukhari vol. 1, book 6, no. 301).

Based on the preceding verses and statements, and many others, critics of Islam would argue that the claim that *Islam gave Arab women their rights couldn't be further from the truth, and they would instead reply that, granted that* Islam gave Arab women a few rights in the (very) distant past, when newborn girls were buried alive, and when women were enslaved(and alas! they continue to be mistreated even in this day and age in certain backward parts of the world), still, the rest of the world, particularly the West, has come very far when it comes to women's rights. And, in the age of universal sacrosanct human rights, an age where women in civilised and advanced societies are now ministers, M.P.s, presidents, astronauts, soldiers, paratroopers, rocket scientists, should women in traditional Muslim societies (Saudi Arabia, Iran, Afghanistan, as well as in parts of Syria and Iraq that have fallen under Islamist rule) who are obliged to wear the burqa, niqab, or tchador, symbols of women's submission and oppression, and are forbidden to drive or walk in public or travel without the company of a male relative, let alone vote or run for public office, should these women who were unfortunate to be born in such backward, misogynistic societies be contented (even grateful) with the fact that they are no longer buried alive? Is *this* what Muslims consider "women's rights" and "respect for women"? Allowing women to simply *live*, whilst denying them their basic political, social, and cultural rights?

As they usually do when justifying their atrocities and crimes, Islamists (and unfortunately many moderate Muslims) base their misogynistic, discriminatory, and cruel treatment of women on the above (and many other) verses of the Quran, as well as on the prophet's sayings in Hadith, disregarding and totally ignoring the (very few, it must be said) other verses that give woman few of her unalienable rights to life and property, and, most importantly her right to be loved and respected.

Playing on the unexplainable duality and contradictions in the scriptures regarding many issues, including women, Islamists and many Muslims consider that women are inferior to men in every way, as Allah himself says in his book. Indeed, they use the verses of the Quran and the Hadith, and other literature of Islamic theology, including Muslim scholars such as Tabari, to enslave women and liken them to beasts - and treat them accordingly.

Their unethical and shocking stance towards women sees its justification in the *Ulama's* (theologians) teachings and interpretations of the Scriptures and *Hadith:*

> *"Treat women well, for they are (like) domestic animals with you and do not possess anything for themselves"* (Tabari, vol. 9, no. 1754).

So, Muslims, according to these extremists, should treat their women well, not because they too are worthy of love and respect as daughters of life and children of God, but because they are like . . . animals!? So much for giving women their "rights"...

Considering themselves as the "true Muslims" abiding by the *Quran*, the word of *Allah*, and following the Prophet's example and teachings in *Hadith*, the Islamists confirm that these two main sources show the true status of woman in Islam: an inferior creature.

Nothing could be clearer to Islamists to truly encapsulate the "slavish" status of women than the following two *Hadiths* (conversations with the Prophet):

> *"Narrated Abdullah ibn Amr ibn al-'As: the Prophet (peace be upon him) said: if one of you marries a woman or buys a slave, he should say: 'O Allah, I ask Thee for the good in her, and in the disposition Thou has given her; I take refuge in Thee from the evil in her, and in the disposition Thou hast given her.' When he buys a camel, he should take hold of the top of its hump and say the same kind of thing' "* (Hadith, Book 11, no. 2155).

> *"Anyone who incites a woman against her husband or a slave against his master is not one of us"* (*Hadith,* Book 12, no. 2170).

Whatever Muslim apologists claim, the truth of the matter is that Islam is a patriarchal religion which considers that women are born unequal to men not only in physical strength but also in mental capacities and judgment.

And, because women are unequal to men, men should be in charge of them, as they are inferior:

> *"Men are in charge of women, because Allah hath made one of them to excel the other, and because they spend of their property for the support of women"* (Quran, 4:34).

According to the same logic as well, a Muslim woman's testimony counts half of a man's testimony:

"And let two men from among you bear witness to all such documents [contracts of loans without interest]. *But if two men be not available, there should be one man and two women to bear witness so that if one of the women forgets (anything), the other may remind her."* (*Quran*, 2:282), (Maududi, vol. 1, p. 205).

Thus, the merit of the witness of a woman, in the court of law, is simply half of that of a man.

The preceding statements are very shocking in our day and age of universal suffrage and equal human rights. It is quite incredible to see that some people on this earth *still* consider that women are inferior to men, and, more so, *intellectually*; a claim that is widely contradicted by women's stellar success in academic institutions and in professions that are usually reserved for men.

According to Islamic theology, not only are women deficient in intelligence but also in religion, the fact which makes them unworthy of Allah's love and respect. So why should common mortals love and respect women?

Furthermore, a woman is expendable; she could easily be replaced by other, better wives, so she'd better behave lest she lose her husband:

"Maybe, his Lord, if he divorce you, will give him in your place wives better than you, submissive, faithful, obedient, penitent, adorers, fasters, widows and virgins" (*Quran*, 66:5).

According to the Hadith, which has nearly just as much authority as the Quran (for it contains the prophet's discourses on many matters), women are not to be trusted:

"Tell the men with you who have wives: never trust a woman" (Ishaq, 584).

"In hell I saw women hanging by their breasts. They had fathered bastards" (Ishaq, 185).

Since she is "deficient," a woman's judgment cannot be trusted. It follows from this that a man could easily accuse one of his (many) wives of any offence without any witnesses:

"As for those who accuse their wives but have no witnesses except themselves, let the testimony of one of them be four testimonies" (Quran, 24:6–7).

The problem is that Islamists in the twenty-first century are building their arguments against women based on religious teachings that go back 1,500 years, without taking into account the social, intellectual, and scientific progress that has been made since in the rest of the world; their argument is the same: Allah's word is eternal; thus, women should suffer inequality and oppression till the end of times. Based on the Scriptures, they do not recognise women as being equal to men. Since she is considered deficient, a woman's judgment cannot be trusted. -

Furthermore, women, in the eyes of Islamists, are second-grade creatures which should be viewed with utmost suspicion and disdain and treated as such, that is, repressed and oppressed. The undeniable fact, even for mainstream Muslim scholars, is that the Quran considers that women are unequal to men. But more undeniable is the way Islamists are abusing this "fundamental" inequality: whereas men are to enjoy life's many joys and benefits, women are only supposed to serve the males as slaves, and more precisely their sex slaves, and beget future jihadis: the warriors of Islam. Islamic State terrorists thus speak of "sex jihad" or jihad al-Nikaah, whereby fundamentalists Muslim women are sent to them, voluntarily, and as part of the war effort, to quench their sexual appetites...

In the Islamists' state ruled by sharia, the promised born-again Caliphate, the status of Muslim women should be the same as it used to be in the traditional societies in the 7th century. Thus, in an Islamic republic, women must be covered from head to toe by wearing either the tchador, the niqab or the burqa, because they trigger the lust of the flesh in men's minds. So, if men are lustful or sexually aroused, women are to blame! For in their view, woman instils vice and so her temptation is one of the most dangerous trials that confront Muslims. This is shown in the Hadith narrated by Usamah ibn Zaid, who said that the messenger of Allah said *"after me I have not left any affliction more harmful to men than women"* (Bukhari).

Women should also remain indoors and not get an education after the age of eight, or, better still, no education at all (the only exception as an Islamic republic is Iran, and Saudi Arabia to a much lesser extent, where women are allowed to study and work, and even hold political positions and play sports, of course, so long as they wear the Islamic garb.). The main reason behind the mandatory lack of education is that if women were to get an education, knowledge is power, they would demand their rights and their freedom and would want to emulate women in Western societies and thus be respected, equal, and emancipated. Therefore, they should be kept in total darkness so that they may not revolt against the male-dominated society and demand their rights.

-2 - WOMEN: SEX SLAVES?!

Because according to Allah's will and judgment, women are considered inferior to men in every respect, it follows that Islamists, his faithful servants, as they see themselves, despise these "inferior creatures" and treat them with disdain. And so, the only purpose of women on this earth is to provide pleasure for their male masters, and satisfy all their sexual urges.

Islamists find full justification for sexually abusing their women, as they please and when they please, in the following Quranic verse:

"Your women are your fields, so go into your fields as ye will" (Quran, 2:223).

Thus, a Muslim husband has sex with his wife, as a plow goes into a field . . . Indeed, the full verse goes as follows:

"Your women are a tilth for you (to cultivate) so go to your tilth as ye will, and send (good deeds) before you for your souls, and fear Allah, and know that ye will (one day) meet Him. Give glad tidings to believers, (O Muhammad)" (Quran, 2: 223).

Unfortunately, here again, as with the verses of violence, Islamists justify their mistreatment of women in the *actual*, existing scriptures . . .

Thus, in the Hadith, Malik 362:1221, Ibn Fahd said: "*'I have some slave girls who are better than my wives, but I do not desire that they should all become pregnant. Shall I do azl (withdrawal) with them?" Hajjaj said 'They are your fields of cultivation. If you wish to irrigate them do so, if not keep them dry'.*"

In Islam, the husband's sexual desires must immediately be met by the wife, anytime, anywhere. The wife is thus never allowed to withhold sex from her husband, as the few Hadiths below show:

> *"If a man is in a mood to have sexual intercourse the woman must come immediately even if she is baking bread at a communal oven"* (Tr. P 428, Hadith Tirmzi and others).

> *"Narrated by Abu Huraira: The Prophet said, 'If a man invites his wife to sleep with him and she refuses to come to him, then the angels send their curses on her till morning'* "(Bukhari: Vol 7, book 62, no. 121).

> *"If a woman refuses to come to bed when invited by her husband, she becomes the target of the curses of angels. Exactly the same happens if she deserts her husband's bed"* (*Bukhari*, p. 93).

> *"Abu Huraira (Allah be pleased with him) reported that Allah's Apostle (may peace be upon him) said: When a woman spends the night away from the bed of her husband, the angels curse her until morning."* (Muslim: book 8, no. 3366).

"The Prophet said: when a man calls his wife to bed and she does not come, the husband spends the night being angry with her, and the angels curse her until morning. The one who is in heaven is displeased with her until the husband is pleased with her" (Sahih Muslim Hadith, chapter 558).

As we've seen above with many Quranic verses and hadiths, a woman in Islam is forced to provide sex to her husband, regardless of her will, consent, or mood. So one would ask, isn't this a kind of "institutionalised" rape and/or sex slavery inflicted upon women by a faith which was, and is, supposed to protect and give them their rights as human beings?! This is very unsettling, to say the least.

Furthermore, Muslim men are entitled by law to have up to four wives, if they have enough money to sustain them and treat them equally. Well-off men exceed this number by far and have dozens of wives. The truth is that women in traditional Muslim societies have no freedom or independence, and they are not treated as human beings having emotions, sensitivities, dreams, ambitions. They are totally crushed, enslaved, and sexually abused in the name of the "God-given" inequality between them and their male masters.

So, the sad but hidden reality is that a woman in traditional Muslim societies must silently endure her horrible status as the (sexual) "property" of her husband.

- ON ADULTERY:

The Quran cautioned against any arbitrary accusation of adultery (zina); thus it requires four witnesses to prove such a crime:

"And those who accuse chaste women, and produce not four witnesses, flog them with eighty stripes, and reject their testimony forever, they indeed are the Fâsiqûn (liars, rebellious, disobedient to Allâh)" (Quran, An-Nur, 24:4).

The aforementioned verse clearly indicates that four witnesses are needed to prove that adultery has taken place. Nevertheless, if the husband himself is an eye witness to his wife's betrayal, and the unity of the family is jeopardised, then this condition of four witnesses is waived:

"And for those who accuse their wives, but have no witnesses except themselves, let the testimony of one of them be four testimonies (i.e. testifies four times) by Allâh that he is one of those who speak the truth. And the fifth (testimony) (should be) the invoking of the Curse of Allâh on him if he be of those who tell a lie (against her)" (Quran, An-Nur, 24:6–7).

- ON RAPE:

From the perspective of modernity and its values, Islam is viewed as a reactionary (although progressive 1,500 years ago!) male patriarchal religion that discriminates against woman in general, giving her very few of her rights as a human being. Here we can see the sharp contrast between a man's status and rights and a woman's non-status and non-rights (seeing that she is a non-entity) according to the Muslim faith or heritage. Indeed, in any part of the Muslim world, a married woman who is raped is called an adulterer and a single woman is a fornicator, whereas a man gets away with rape since he cannot be held responsible for his carnal desires (and anyway, the mentality goes, it is always the woman's fault since *she* provoked him with her "satanic wiles," as religious zealots would say!!). Therefore, in the case of rape, the burden of proof lies totally on the shoulders of the woman, not the opposite.

The Quran approves extremely harsh punishments for any sexual impropriety on the part of the woman, who in that case could be starved to death (Quran, 4:15), hanged, burned, shot, or stoned to death, and all this in accordance with religious tribal customs, more particularly the notorious act of "honour killing," which is nothing but killing without honour.

As for the act of raping a woman other than one's wife, it is practically impossible for the victim to prove it, since in order to do so, sharia demands that the woman must have four male witnesses to establish her allegation (which means that, in most cases, this is absolutely impossible); otherwise, they are called "liars":

> *"And those who accuse free women then do not bring four witnesses (to adultery), flog them" (Quran, 24:4).*

> *"Why did they not bring four witnesses of it? But as they have not brought witnesses they are liars before Allah" (Quran, 24:13).*

Thus, if the victim fails to prove rape, her predicament does not stop here, as she runs the risk of being convicted of committing adultery, a grave crime that calls for a punishment like stoning to death. Moreover, even in relatively modern Muslim societies (Jordan, for example), after a woman has been raped, her own family, instead of consoling her and seeking justice, has the right to execute her (again, the infamous "honour killing") in order to restore the so-called honour of the family!! In Iran, if a woman is raped, *she* is condemned to death (after being subjected to hundreds of lashes)!! There are simply no words to describe such an injustice wrought on women in traditional Muslim societies.

There have been many instances where Muslim women were killed because they have been raped (!!), a "crime" which many Islamic scholars and clerics often consider to be the fault of the woman, not the rapist (!!). Two very horrific examples that were cited by the United Nations Population Fund in 2000 involved an 18-year old woman in Bangladesh who was flogged to death for "immoral" behaviour, and an Egyptian case in which a father actually paraded his daughter's severed head through the streets while shouting, "I have avenged my honour"... Many such crimes also occur within Muslim communities in the West, where the sharia is applied; places that are "no-go zones" to the police and that escape the laws of the Western hosting nation. These *sharia* zones can be found in London and Stockholm, to cite but two of the most civilised cities on Earth.

Moreover, according to Islamists, women are considered part of the spoils of war. Consequently, conquering Muslim armies are allowed to take women as *sabaya*- which means (sex) slaves or prisoners of war. They base their enslavement of women "prisoners" on the following verse, among others:

"O Prophet! We have made lawful to thee thy wives to whom thou hast paid their dowers; and those whom thy right hand possesses out of the prisoners of war whom Allah

has assigned to thee; and daughters of thy paternal uncles and aunts, and daughters of thy maternal uncles and aunts, who migrated (from Mecca) *with thee; and any believing woman who dedicates her soul to the Prophet if the Prophet wishes to wed her;- this only for thee, and not for the Believers* (at large); *We know what We have appointed for them as to their wives and the captives whom their right hands possess; in order that there should be no difficulty for thee. And Allah is Oft-Forgiving, Most Merciful"* (Quran, 33:50).

Thus, Daesh murderers and warmongers saw it as completely legitimate to take the Yazidi women, after they conquered their lands in Iraq (Mount Sinjar), as sex slaves; beating and raping them, and proudly exhibiting them for trade, with a price tag on each according to *her value*; virgin girls got the highest price! These terrorists justified their horrific, monstrous crimes by verses in the Scriptures, saying that Allah himself allowed his prophet and followers to commit such practices.

- POLYGAMY:

Polygamy, an ancient, uncivilised custom which has all but disappeared a long time ago and is nearly inexistent and banned in our modern day and age and in most parts of the world, is nonetheless still widely practiced in many Muslim societies who consider it a normal thing. why? Because Allah approves it in his "Holy Book," the Quran, and the Prophet himself condoned it and practiced it, having taken several wives during his long life.

There are two clear passages in the Quran which mention and allow the practice of polygamy: 4:2–6 and 4:127–129. Indeed, according to Islam's holy book, a Muslim man can marry up to four wives:

> *"If ye fear that ye shall not be able to deal justly with the orphans, marry of the women, who seem good to you, two or three or four; but if ye fear that ye shall not be able to deal justly* (with them), *then marry only one wife, or those* (captives) *who have fallen in your possession. Thus it is more likely that ye will not do injustice"* (Quran, 4:3).

Although a big controversy surrounds this verse, particularly with regard to the condition of fair or equal treatment when it comes for a man to marry more than one woman (the husband *must* treat his numerous wives equally, otherwise he should marry only one), still, the principle of polygamy, which is forbidden by the civil marriage law because it transgresses the human dignity of women, stays valid and widely applied in Islam. Moreover, this inhumane practice is also being largely abused. Men in many Muslim societies are marrying more than four women; the fair or equal treatment being restricted or understood as being "financially fair" with the many wives without any other ethical, emotional, or psychological considerations. In other words, marry as many women that money can buy!!

Here again, Muslims show a stiff resistance to progress and fail to move with the times; hence, they stand nearly alone in our modern era with this morally and socially unacceptable practice based on scriptures that go back to the seventh century BC, when polygamy was a common practice...

To be fair, and as mentioned earlier, it must be said that, even though the Quran allows polygamy, still, it warns Muslims that *"ye will not be able to deal equally between (your) wives, however much ye wish (to do so)* (Quran, 4:129). Some moderate Muslim clerics have used this supplement to the verse permitting polygamy to argue that the verse preceding that supplement has been misrepresented and abused by most Muslims who rush to consider it an apology for polygamy, disregarding the warning attached to it. These moderate clerics have used the above verse to argue that monogamy is preferable to polygamy in Islam. But the bottom line is that, whether a Muslim man will or will not do justice to all four wives is his own choice, and marrying many wives is totally acceptable.

Furthermore, not only is the husband permitted to have up to four wives, but in Shia Islam, he can also have a "temporary wife" for a few hours or days at his discretion. This "temporary marriage" is referred to as "Zawaj al Mut'aa" (temporary "marriage of pleasure").

Although this kind of "sexual marriage" is regulated by a religious contract, and with the consent of the two parties, the man and the woman, still it leads to further and further degradation of women.

In the verse below, polygamy is considered to be a normal act since the term "wives" is used without any controversy:

"It is made lawful for you to go in unto your wives on the night of the fast" (Quran, 2:187).

In addition, the Arabic word *nikah,* which is the official or conventional term for *marriage* in Islam, bears sexual connotations: it literally means sexual intercourse, which empties marriage of its sacred nature, as is the case with Christianity for example.

Generally speaking, the status of women in Muslim societies is archaic, to say the least, and it touches their very human dignity: man can through nikah legally and officially marry up to four wives (referred to as marriage, though the term literally means intercourse), while at the same time conveniently having an unlimited number of "concubines" through mut'aa. Both kinds of marriages are perfectly legal according to the Quran.

Add to the "legal" wives those captives *"who have fallen in your hands* [as prisoners of war]" (Quran, 4:24) and *"the* (slaves) *that their right hands possesses"* (Quran, 23:1-6).

Also add to this the fact that women are simply exchangeable, as Islam allows divorce:

"And if ye wish to exchange one wife for another." (Quran, 4:20).

Thus, polygamy, accompanied by mistreatment and sexual and physical abuse of women, is still largely practiced in traditional Muslim societies. What allows this backward practice, which is so demeaning to women in the age of human rights and female emancipation, is that Prophet Muhammad himself, between the age of 49 and 63, married at least 12 times, with some Muslim scholars saying he had 23 wives, 28 women all in all in his life; women with no rights, and to this day their status has hardly changed in the Muslim world.

One might argue that it is also the woman's mistake when she accepts to marry a married man; however, this argument does not stand, since women in many Muslim communities are forced to get married and have no free will to marry a man whom they truly love.

- FORCED MARRIAGE AND DIVORCE:

Forced marriage is a well-known and widespread practice in Muslim societies throughout the ages and even to this day, particularly among the lower strata of society. Islamists, basing their beliefs and actions on the Scriptures, view women as the property of their fathers, and these latter are the only ones who might "transfer" that property to another man, the husband, who thus becomes the sole "guardian" of the woman since she is, according to them, and always based on the Quran and the Hadith, deficient in intelligence and inferior. Thus, the woman in the "perfect" Muslim society, the Islamist society, is never free; she only changes masters from the paternal to the marital home. According to the Muslim fundamentalist patriarchal view, she must be submitted to the male in the family, whoever he may be; her father, or her brother if the father is dead, then to the husband, then to the son if the husband passes away!

As regards divorce, the status of women is even worse. Islam, Sunni Islam in particular, allows a man to divorce his "undesirable" wife/wives by simply uttering the word *talaq* ("divorce") thrice. Actually, this has been a traditional custom to formalise divorce throughout the ages in Islamic societies. The actual verse says:

"Ye may divorce your wives twice; and then either retain them with humanity or dismiss them with kindness" (Quran, 2:229).

Worse still, if the father of the husband orders his son to divorce his wife, he must do so (*Hadith Tirmzi,* p. 440, and others). Thus, the marriage of a woman to her man is not substantive. It is precarious.

Whereas the husband can divorce his wife at will, a woman who seeks *khula,* divorce, from her man, without a just cause, shall not enter paradise (*Hadith Tirmzi,* p. 440, and others).

Islam speaks of Al Osma, which means that the divorce decision or initiation is kept to the husband. In sharp contrast, a Muslim woman cannot divorce her husband; it is nearly impossible; she has no such right. Indeed, Islam makes it difficult for women to divorce:

"Narrated Thawban: The Prophet (peace be upon him) said: if any woman asks her husband for divorce without some strong reason, the odour of Paradise will be forbidden to her" (Hadith, Book 12, no. 2218).

However, it must be said that in Shia Islam, divorce is made a little more complicated as there is a waiting period during which attempts are made (by both families and clerics) to reconcile the couple; some sort of marriage counselling, one might say. But the bottom line is that the husband has the sole right to divorce, unless he consents to his wife's wish to do so.

The verse in question (2:230), shown below, goes on to say a more perilous and terrifying consequence for a woman's dignity and respect:

"But if the husband divorces his wife (for the third time), *she shall not remain his lawful wife after this* (absolute) *divorce, unless she marries another husband and the second*

husband divorces her. [In that case] *there is no harm if they* [the first couple] *remarry"* (Quran, 2:230).

Thus, in addition to the arbitrary Islamic divorce law that gives men the sole authority to divorce or otherwise, there exists a remarriage law that is even more demeaning to women. It says that if the husband divorces his wife and wants to get her back, in order to make her lawful, she has to be given in marriage to another man and if her new husband divorces her, after consummation of the marriage, then and only then will she be made lawful to her original husband! The customary practice in such a case is to hire somebody called *mostahel,* and engage him as a husband to the divorced woman (at least for a night). He is supposed to divorce her in the morning as the only way for the original husband to take his divorcee back. Such a temporary marriage is called a *hilla* marriage.

Therefore, a wife may remarry her ex-husband if and only if she marries another man and then this second man divorces her.

In Islam, forced marriage and forced divorce are a common practice:

"Narrated Abdullah ibn Abbas: A woman embraced Islam during the time of the Apostle of Allah (peace be upon him); she then married. Her (former) husband then came to the Prophet (peace be upon him) and said: Apostle of Allah, I have already embrace Islam, and she had the knowledge about my Islam. The Apostle of Allah (peace be upon him) took her away from her latter husband and restored her to her former husband" (Hadith, Book 12, no. 2231).

- PAEDOPHILIA:

Paedophilia might be an odious, outrageous crime in our modern day and age, but centuries ago, it was more or less a common practice in traditional societies such as the pre-Islamic society in the Arab peninsula. Islam, being the natural product of that society, kept this tradition which lingers on in our day and age. It thus allows a man to marry a girl who hasn't reached puberty. Indeed, the following highly controversial Quranic verse prescribes the waiting period of a female who has not yet reached puberty:

> *"Such of your women as have passed the age of monthly courses, for them the prescribed period, if ye have any doubts, is three months, and for those who have not menstruated yet: for those who carry* (life within their wombs), *their period is until they deliver their burdens: and for those who fear Allah, He will make their path easy"* (Quran, 65:4).

In fact, as previously stated in this book, the Quran allows a Muslim man to marry a child as young as six years old, consummating the marriage by age nine. The dowry is given to the family in exchange for the girl.

Here again, it is common for Muslims to marry a prepubescent girl, following the model of the prophet Muhammad himself, whom they view as untainted by sin. ma'assum. It is well-known that the prophet married Aisha, his third wife, when she was only nine years old:

> *"The Prophet said to her (Aisha), 'You have been shown to me twice in my dream. I saw you pictured on a piece of silk and someone said (to me). 'This is your*

wife.' When I uncovered the picture, I saw that it was yours. I said, 'If this is from Allah, it will be done' " (Hadith, Sahih Bukhari 5:58:235).

-3- VIOLENCE: WIFE-BEATING IS CONDONED BY ISLAM:

Can a husband beat his wife? Islam condones "contained" (!) violence against women, both in the Quran and the Hadith. Thus, husbands can beat their wives as a punishment for misbehaviour, but not break their bones, whilst avoiding the face:

"If a woman's conduct is mischievous or immodest, the husband has the right to beat her up but must not break her bones" (Hadith Tirmzi, p. 439, and others).

"Narrated Abu Hurayrah: The Prophet (peace be upon him) said: when one of you inflicts a beating, he should avoid the face" (Abu Dawud, Book 38, no. 4478).

"Narrated Salim Umar Said: The Prophet forbade beating the face" (translation of Sahih Bukhari, vol. 7, Book 67, no. 449).

And, what's worse, a man does not have to say why he has beaten her:

"Narrated Umar ibn al-Khattab: 'the Prophet (peace be upon him) said: a man will not be asked as to why he beat his wife' " (Hadith, Book 11, no. 2142).

This absence of the need for justification gives a Muslim man a license to beat his wife at will and anytime for no reason at all . . . and Islamists of course rejoice in applying these instructions to the letter on their defenceless wives...

The Hadith below shows Muhammad hitting this girl-bride, *Aisha*, daughter of *Abu Bakr*:

"He (Muhammad) struck me [Aisha] on the chest which caused me pain" (Muslim, 2127). Furthermore, the following verse from Islam's holiest book advises men to beat their wives if they don't obey them:

> *"Men are the maintainers of women because Allah has made some of them to excel others and because they spend out of their property; the good women are therefore obedient, guarding the unseen as Allah has guarded; and* (as to) *those on whose part you fear desertion, admonish them, and leave them alone in the sleeping-places and* **beat them***; then if they obey you, do not seek a way against them; surely Allah is High, Great"* (Quran, 4:34).

This domestic violence sometimes acquires bizarre proportions, and this in our modern day and age which don't seem to have any impact on many Muslims regarding the prohibition of any kind of violence against women. They simply justify their horrific and demeaning mistreatment of their wives with the Holy Book's and Hadith's sayings. Indeed, a Mufti not long ago issued a grotesquely gruesome fatwa, in which he allowed a Muslim man to "eat his wife" if he were starving. No comment!

What's more, violence against women can take on particularly cruel forms, especially when it is *still* applied in the universal age of human rights, such as the barbaric stoning to death which is firmly applied in sharia, as we shall see in the chapter dedicated to Islamic law. In fact, women are specifically targeted in this brutal punishment, as far more women than men are stoned to death for adultery. For now, however, we can quote this deeply disturbing and grisly verse:

> *Imran b.Husain reported that a woman from Huhaina came to Allah's Apostle (may peace be upon him) and she had become pregnant because of adultery. She said; Allah's Apostle, I have done something for which* (prescribed punishment) *must be imposed upon me, so impose that. Allah's Apostle (may peace be upon him) called her master and said: Treat her well, and when she delivers bring her to me. He did accordingly. Then Allah's Apostle (may peace be upon him) pronounced judgment about her and her clothes were tied around her and then he commanded and she was stoned to death. He then prayed over her* (dead body). *Thereupon Umar said to him: Allah's Apostle, you offer prayer for her, whereas she had committed adultery! Thereupon he said: she has made such repentance that if it were to be divided among seventy men of Medina, it would be enough. Have you found any repentance better than this that she sacrificed her life for Allah, the Majestic?"* (Hadith, Book 17, no. 4207).

And last, but not least, a Muslim husband is *"legally"* allowed to lock his wife at home until death if he suspects that she is immoral:

"As for those of your women who are guilty of lewdness, call to witness four of you against them. And if they testify (to the truth of the allegation) then confine them to the houses until death take them or (until) Allah appoint for them a way (through new legislation)" (Quran, 4: 15).

-4- REPRESSED, OPPRESSED: THE VEIL OF IGNORANCE:

According to various interpretations of Islam, including mainstream ones, and it goes without saying that these include the Salafist interpretation, woman instils vice and so her temptation is one of the most dangerous trials that confront Muslims. A Hadith narrated by Usamah ibn Zaid mentions that the messenger of Allah, Muhammad, said *"after me I have not left any affliction more harmful to men than women"* (Bukhari).

Thus, because woman invokes temptation and sexual desire among men, *the lusts of the flesh*, she must be veiled from head to toe, paying the price of men's libido! She must also be hidden and forbidden to go outdoors, and forbidden as well in many backward Islamic societies (such as Afghanistan) and communities (Taliban, Daesh or Islamic State) to get an education after the age of eight, if any education at all. The question of her having dreams or ambitions is not even an issue in such backward societies.

Indeed, in many Muslim countries, women are subjected to the laws of *purdah,* or seclusion, which refers not only to the practice of facial veiling and body coverings, but also to the seclusion of women from all social and public life:

"It is forbidden for a woman to be seen by any man except her husband when she is made up or well-dressed" (Hadith Tirmzi, p 430, and others).

And men should admonish them if they are not obedient and submissive (as the aforementioned Quranic verse 4:34 states).

That submission and forced seclusion is why most women in the Muslim world are forced to wear the veil or hijab, or, worse, the burqa or niqab (in Saudi Arabia and many Gulf countries), or the tchador (in post-shah Iran and post-Saddam Iraq). And they are not permitted to go outdoors without the company of their male "guardians," be they their fathers, husbands, or brothers. And, when they do go outdoors, they should be covered from head to toe in order not to "tempt" men by showing their feminine wiles.

The following is what the Quran says about the veil or hijab:

"O Prophet, tell your wives and your daughters and the women of the believers to draw their cloaks close round them (when they go abroad). *That will be better, so that they may be recognised and not annoyed. Allah is ever Forgiving, Merciful"* (Quran 33:59).

"And say to the believing women that they cast down their looks and guard their private parts and do not display their ornaments except what appears thereof, and let them wear their head-coverings over their bosoms, and not display their ornaments except to their husbands or their fathers, or the fathers of their husbands, or their sons, or the sons

of their husbands, or their brothers, or their brothers'
sons, or their sisters' sons, or their women, or those whom
their right hands possess, or the male servants not having
need (of women), or the children who have not attained
knowledge of what is hidden of women; and let them not
strike their feet so that what they hide of their ornaments
may be known" (Quran, 24:31).

Islamists say that these verses are crystal clear: Muslim women must wear the veil, if not the full black garment niqab/ tchador, to prevent any sex appeal or temptation of men! And this instead of the latter controlling their animal instincts.

The truth is that these verses are affecting the lives of millions of women worldwide to this very day. And whereas the religious see in the veil a symbol of purity, the liberal world views it as a symbol of woman's oppression and servitude: logic says that one must tame or master his instincts, and not enslave the victims of his instincts! The debate about this issue is heating up in the West, in secular France in particular, on whether the government must ban the burqa (and lately the burqini, the Muslim swimming suit) in public places in order to preserve the secular image and character of the state and society, or whether to allow it in order to protect the so-called "freedom of faith." But how could the oppression of women be a part of any culture's faith?

However, the veil or burqa has become, not only a symbol of "faith" and "purity," in the eyes of Islamists, but more importantly a symbol of religious radicalisation and communitarianism, a symbol of identity for the Muslims in the West, unveiling their crisis of belonging, as well as their difficulty to integrate in Western societies and to embrace the values of modernity. Most Western countries have not banned the veil (and not even the grotesque burqa) because they fear it would constitute an infringement on "freedom of faith." But one must not forget woman's freedom, liberation, and equality with man; this is a battle that (Muslim) liberal women are fighting. They rely on this verse in the Quran that clearly says that righteousness is the best *cover*:

"O you Children of Adam! We have bestowed on you raiment to cover your shame as well as to be an adornment to you. But the raiment of righteousness, that is the best. Such are among the Signs of Allah, that they may receive admonition" (Quran 7:26).

The problem is that the Quran provides both sides with arguments, though the misogynistic Islamists, alas, clearly find more justification in the Scriptures for demeaning women than moderate Muslims who respect women and treat them as their partners instead of their servants.

Thus, those who insist that woman must wear the veil, present more arguments from hadith, the fatwas of the Prophet himself:

"A woman must veil herself even in the presence of her husband's father, brother and other male relations" (Hadith Tirmzi, p 432, and others).

Fundamentalist Muslim clergymen are using what they consider Allah's word - the Quran, and the Hadith of the prophet whom they consider untainted by sin - to debase the status of woman to the level of animals, and to enslave her, instead of preserving her purity, as they pretend. In October 2006, the Grand Mufti of Australia, Sheikh Taj El-Din Hilaly, shamefully compared, in a sense, a woman's uncovered body to raw meat, when he delivered a Ramadan sermon in Arabic in which he made shocking and demeaning statements about female clothing:

> *"If you take out uncovered meat and place it outside on the street, or in the garden or in the park, or in the backyard without a cover, and the cats come and eat it . . . whose fault is it, the cats' or the uncovered meat? The uncovered meat is the problem. If she was in her room, in her home, in her Hijab, no problem would have occurred."*

So, to this cleric, the problem is not with lustful, beastly men, but with women's *"uncovered meat"!* Women are likened to meat. That is their value to Islamists. And rape, to the latter, is the natural consequence and punishment for a woman who refuses to cover herself; rape is no longer a crime, it is sickly justified as: *"the meat was exposed!"* So, rape is the *woman's* fault. Anyone who does not find the above statement offensive, demeaning, and outrageous is a soulless savage.

It is notable that one of the hundreds of German women who were sexually assaulted in Cologne during the New Year festivities in 2016 by Muslim migrants records feeling (when she was grabbed by countless Muslim men who touched her sensitive areas) "like a piece of meat at a meat market." In Sweden, some signs were recently hung by Muslims on the streets which shocked public opinion. The signs warned: "If a woman does not cover herself, she only has herself to blame if she is raped."

Following are some other oppressive verses in Muslim scriptures as regards women:

A woman is not a believer if she undertakes a journey which may last three days or longer, unless she is accompanied by her husband, son, or father (Hadith Tirmzi, p. 431, and others).

A woman is forbidden to spend any money without the permission of her husband, and it includes giving food to the needy or feast to friends (Hadith Tirmzi, p. 265, and others).

A wife is forbidden to perform extra prayers or observe fasting (other than Ramadan) without the permission of her husband (Hadith Tirmzi, p. 300, and others).

"If prostration were a legitimate act other than to God, woman should have prostrated to her husband" (Hadith Tirmzi, p. 428, and others).

"Women who are ungrateful to their men are the denizens of hell; it is an act of ingratitude for a woman to say: 'I have never seen any good from you'" (Hadith Bukhari, p. 96).

A woman in many ways is deprived of the possession of her own body. Even her milk belongs to her husband. (Bukhari, p. 27). She is not allowed to practise birth control either.

-5- WOMEN IN ISLAM ARE CURSED, EVIL, CROOKED, UNCLEAN, IMPURE:

- a - *Women are cursed, evil creatures:*

In the eyes of many Muslims, women are simply bad luck, bad omen. They refer to sayings of the prophet Muhammad himself:

"Umar b.Muhammad b. Zaid reported that he heard his father narrating from Ibn Umar that Allah's Messenger

(may peace be upon him) had said. If bad luck is a fact, then it is in the horse, the woman and the house" (Hadith, Book 26, no. 5526).

"Narrated Sa'd ibn Malik: the Prophet (may peace be upon him) said: there is no hamah, no infection and no evil omen; if there is anything an evil omen, if is a house, a horse, and a woman" (Hadith, Book 29, no. 3911).

Most women are "evil" in nature and will end up in hell... That is how Islamic theology describes half of mankind. The "evil" character of women is emphasised by the following hadiths:

The majority of women *"will go to hell"* (Muslim, p. 1431).

"The majority of those who entered the fire of Hell were women" (Sahih Muslim Hadith, Chapter 1140).

"The Prophet said: 'I was shown the Hell Fire and the majority of its dwellers were women who are disbelievers or ungrateful.' When asked what they were ungrateful for, the Prophet answered, 'All the favours done for them by their husbands.'" (Bukhari Hadith, Vol. 1, Book 22, No 28).

Similarly, another hadith says,

"O womenfolk, you should ask for forgiveness for I saw you in bulk amongst the dwellers of Hell.' A wise lady said: Why is it, Allah's Apostle, that women comprise the bulk of the inhabitants of Hell? The Prophet observed: 'You curse too much and are ungrateful to your spouses. You lack common sense, fail in religion and rob the wisdom of the wise.' Upon this the woman remarked: What is wrong

with our common sense? The Prophet replied, 'Your lack
of common sense can be determined from the fact that the
evidence of two women is equal to one man. That is a
proof." (Muslim Hadith: Book 1, no.142).

Another hadith expresses woman's position bluntly when
it quotes Prophet Muhammad:

"I have not left any calamity more harmful to man than
women" (Sahih Bukhari, vol. 7, Book 62, no. 33).

Al-Ghazali, the renowned Islamic thinker, summed up
the 18 pains that had been inflicted on Muslim women as a
"punishment" for Eve's transgression in paradise.

The 18 punishments are:

- Menstruation.
- Childbirth.
- Separation from father and mother and marriage to a
  stranger.
- Pregnancy.
- Not having control over her own person.
- A lesser share in inheritance.
- Her liability to be divorced and inability to divorce.
- It being lawful for man to have 4 wives but for a woman to
  have only 1 husband.
- The fact that she must stay secluded in the house.
- The fact that she must keep her head covered inside the
  house.

- The fact that two women's testimonies have to be set against the testimony of one man.

- The fact that she must not go out of the house unless accompanied by a near relative.

- The fact that men take part in Friday and feast day funerals while women do not.

- Disqualification for rulership and judgeship.

- The fact that merit has 100 components, only one of which is attributable to women while 999 are attributed to men.

- The fact that if women are profligate they will be given only half as much torment as the rest of the community at the resurrection day.

- The fact that if their husbands die, they must observe a waiting period of 4 months and 10 days before they remarry.

- The fact that if their husbands divorce them, they must observe a waiting period of 3 months or 3 menstrual periods before remarrying.

- b - *Women are basically crooked:*

Anwar Shaikh, author of the book *Islam: An Arab National Movement*, unabashedly and shamelessly trumpets that Islam views woman as *"basically crooked"* and considers that man *"has the right to keep her under his constant vigil; she must never be left alone,"* for she is not to be trusted, neither intellectually nor morally, as the prophet considered *her "intellectually deficient"*... Woman, in the eyes of Islam, is thus an inferior, distrustful, contemptuous creature which should be kept under a man's strict control and guidance.

The Prophet said:

"Woman has been created from a rib, and will in no way be straightened for you" (Sahih Muslim Hadith, chapter 576). Not only is woman inferior to man, but she is also crooked... Another hadith reports these words from the messenger of Allah: *"Abu Hurayra (Allah be pleased with him) reported Allah's Messenger (may peace be upon him) as saying: 'woman is like a rib. When you attempt to straighten it, you would break it. And if you leave her alone you would benefit by her, and crookedness will remain in her'"* (Muslim, Book 08, no. 3466).

- c - *Women are unclean and impure:*

Islam, as we have seen above, allows men to have up to four wives and as many female war slaves (jawaris) as he likes. Nevertheless, and in a striking contradiction to this, women in Islam, a male and patriarchal religion par excellence, are deemed unclean, impure! In fact, in the eyes of Allah, women are so unclean and impure that if a man who intends to join a prayer and touches a woman after taking a bath, he must purify himself again before joining the prayer:

> *"Believers, approach not prayers with a mind befogged or intoxicated until you understand what you utter, nor when you are polluted, until after you have bathed. If you are ill, or on a journey, or come from answering the call of nature, or you have touched a woman, and you find no water, then take for yourselves clean dirt, and rub your faces and hands. Lo! Allah is Benign, Forgiving."* (Quran, 4:43).

"And if ye are unclean, purify yourselves. And if ye are sick or on a journey, or one of you cometh from the closet, or ye have had contact with women, and ye find not water, then go to clean, high ground and rub your faces and your hands with some of it" (Quran, 5:6).

Thus, women are deemed even inferior to dirt, since *dirt is supposed to purify the polluted hands and face of Muslims who have touched a woman.*

In fact, a Muslim clergyman, or even an ordinary religious Muslim, is not allowed to shake a woman's hand. And although a veiled woman cannot shake a man's hand either, this does not have the same dirt-like aspect or connotation, and no verse to our knowledge requests woman to clean herself after she touches a male. To designate by specific verses and hadiths the necessity for men to wash and clean themselves "from woman" (!!) before they pray carries this degrading view of women as *morally and spiritually impure creatures,* especially when we add to these verses the aforementioned ones that consider that the majority of women are going to *"nar jahanam"* – i.e. they will all end up consumed by the flames of hell! All these verses essentially mean that women are basically *dirty,* morally speaking; thus, the "faithful" must clean himself after he touches a woman's hand.

With this demeaning view of woman, asserted by clear verses and *Hadiths*, progressive and open-minded Muslim scholars find it very difficult to defend Islam, against their fundamentalist fellow scholars, as a religion that gives woman the basic rights of freedom and liberty as a human being, and that guarantees her socio-political and legal equality with man as a citizen; those basic and inalienable rights that are so characteristic of modernity and embraced by the civilised West. Indeed, taking the Scriptures (Allah's word) and hadith (the Prophet's word) as reference (and what greater references could there be, the Islamists argue?!), the battle for woman's equality and rights in Muslim societies is lost *in advance*; unfortunately and until further notice, it continues to be won by the fundamentalists.

A Bukhari hadith, putting women side by side with animals, says:

> "*Narrated 'Aisha: 'The things which annual prayers were mentioned before me (and those were): a dog, a donkey and a woman. I said, 'You have compared us (women) to donkeys and dogs. By Allah! I saw the Prophet praying while I used to lie in (my) bed between him and the Qibla [the direction of Mecca]. Whenever I was in need of something, I disliked to sit and trouble the Prophet. So, I would slip away by the side of his feet*" (Vol 1, Book 9 No.493).

And the demeaning view goes on, and this time through Allah's word. Eve's daughters are impure beings, and stupid, and they must *bleed* (menstruation) for it as their eternal punishment. *Allah, the merciful and the forgiving - Al rahman al rahim,* said:

> "*It is My obligation to make Eve bleed once every month as she made this tree bleed. I must also make Eve stupid, although I created her intelligent.' Because Allah afflicted Eve, all of the women of this world menstruate and are stupid*" (Tabari I: 280).

And who can contest Allah's judgment, would say the misogynistic, fundamentalist takfiris? For when God *speaks*, humans must utter no word. And thus spoke Allah. *Not only are women unclean but they are also stupid, of course.*

That is why, during menstruation, men should keep away from women, for the latter are filthy. The Quran says:

> *"If menstruation is a discomfort: therefore keep aloof from the women during the menstrual discharge and do not go near them until they have become clean; then when they have cleansed themselves, go in to them as Allah has commanded you: surely Allah loves those who turn much (to Him), and He loves those who purify themselves"* (Quran, 2:222).

To conclude, the truth is that Islamists, and, alas, the majority of Muslims, remain stuck in the seventh century and stick to the Quran's verses, which discriminate against women and call for their total submission to men; verses which are now outdated in the era of human rights and women's liberation. Muslims would argue that the Quran's word is eternal and unalterable and thus should apply for all eternity, regardless of any "progress" (which is viewed as "decadent"). Its dictates, therefore, however discriminatory or misogynistic, must still apply today just as they did at that time when women were not considered Allah's daughters but simply wombs for future jihadis.

Even if Islam did save women from being buried alive and did give them some rights, namely the right to live and own property, still these rights were quite basic and over 1,400 years have passed since then and there has been no progress whatsoever to this day in strict Muslim societies (which partly or totally apply sharia or Islamic Law). Thus Muslim women lack most of their rights, and all this according to Allah's will, Allah who is supposed to be All-compassionate, All-Merciful, All-Just, Unbiased, All-knowing and Most Wise. Muslim women seem to be the forgotten daughters of Allah. Why else would the Almighty call on his most "loyal followers," the Islamist jihadis, to treat women as their sex slaves?

Let us point out that what was acceptable 1,400 years ago is today considered barbaric and uncivilised, including stoning, beheading, lashing, burning alive, crucifying, and such, and so, too, the rights of Muslim women are long overdue but never granted because Islam (or Islamism) remains stuck in the seventh century since Muslims refuse to reform their religion which they claim is "perfect" as it represents Allah's unadulterated and eternal word. "How could you improve perfection," the Muslims reply to those critics who call on them to reform their religion in order to move with the times, completely oblivious to the fact that many of their holy book's verses can hardly be considered worthy of a loving, compassionate and merciful God, especially when it comes to the treatment of women whom he created too!

CHAPTER FIVE

THE JIHADI'S JANNAH:
PARADISE OF LUST AND LUXURY

"The way is not in the sky.
The way is in the heart."

— LORD BUDDHA

- THE HIGH VALUE OF "MARTYRDOM" IN ISLAM:

Istishhad (martyrdom). This is perhaps the most powerful word in the Islamic faith; certainly the most used and revered word in the Islamic lexicon. It bears a crucial significance since it means to die for the sake of *Allah,* to sacrifice one's life for the sake of jihad, or holy war. However, what might seem like the noblest deed - to sacrifice one's life for a higher cause, and what cause is higher than God? - has in fact been transformed, at the hands of the "Salafist jihadis," the Islamic fundamentalists, into an abhorrent act of cold-blooded murder and the most immoral act under the sun because it is done in the name of God and religion which are supposed to uplift and glorify life, rather than sow death and destruction.

Muslim apologists, and Islamists in particular, would argue here that all cultures highly value martyrdom for the sake of truth, and that martyrdom is not an exclusive Muslim value. The problem, whoever, and the significant difference with other cultures and religions, is that it is not when you *die* defending your kin, clan or country or even religious beliefs, but when you *kill* for their sake... or rather when you commit suicide but take dozens of other people with you in your death, and, what's more, innocent civilians, women, children (half of the horrendous Nice massacre's victims were children). Indeed, it is not so much that the jihadi - who considers himself the most loyal fighter of Allah and his messenger Muhammad - is killed, but that when he does so, he kills others, sacrifices others, most of the time innocent civilians, with him... so it is not such a selfless, noble act made in self-defence, but rather a despicable, immoral, and criminal act. In other words, it is a terrorist act so characteristic of Islamic fundamentalist violence these days.

Where is the "sacrifice" when the suicide bomber (most "martyrs" are nowadays suicide bombers killing innocent civilians and certainly not "hero martyrs") is taking the lives of countless innocent civilians along with his own worthless and wretched life? If one wants to commit suicide (which is a reprehensible thing in most religions), let him do so, but when you *force* suicide on others, it is sheer terrorism, especially when the victims are elderly people, women and children, and especially when the crime is committed in the name of God and religion, which are supposed to preach love and compassion, not hatred and murder.

When jihad and martyrdom go together, they make a lethal combination which spells doom on mankind and civilisation. When "martyrdom" is used to justify murder, it loses all its nobility. When "martyrs" are mad fanatics and suicide bombers, they are mass murderers. This word is today totally exploited by Islamists (due to its significance in Islam) in order to attract would-be suicide bombers who kill in the name of "God," who kill the *real* God each time they kill in his name.

To go back to the high value of martyrdom in the Muslim faith, this elevation of jihad to the highest of virtues makes this act of sacrifice (which is almost always accompanied, with Islamic terrorists, by murder) something particularly holy and the highest honour for all Muslims, for, according to the Quran and the hadiths, martyrs go straight to heaven to meet their reward: 72 *houris,* or beautiful virgins (as we shall see in the verse below) "whom no man or *Jinn* [genie] before them has touched." Thus, the "tradition of the virgins" has been and continues to be effectively exploited by terrorist Islamic organisations as an inducement to the so-called "martyrdom." In fact, most suicide bombers literally die with a smile on their face, imagining what awaits them in their "pornographic" heaven.

There are countless verses in the *Quran* and hadiths quoting Prophet Muhammad praising and encouraging martyrdom; those verses which are used and abused by the terrorist jihadis to wage war against their "enemies," indeed against civilisation and mankind at large. We will cite a few below as characteristic examples of the highest regard and honour reserved for martyred jihadis in Muslim sacred scriptures:

> *"It has been narrated on the authority of Masruq who said: 'we asked Abdullah about the Quranic verse:*
>
> *'Think not of those who are slain in Allah's way as dead. Nay, they are alive, finding their sustenance in the presence of their Lord'* (Quran, 3:169).

"*He said: We asked the meaning of the verse* (from the Prophet) *who said: 'The souls of the martyrs live in the bodies of green birds who have their nests in chandeliers hung from the throne of the Almighty. They eat the fruits of Paradise from wherever they like and then nestle in these chandeliers'* " (Sahih Muslim, 20:4651).

"*Let those fight in the cause of Allah who sell the life of this world for the hereafter. To him who fighteth in the cause of Allah, - whether he is slain or gets victory - Soon shall We give him a reward of great* (value)" (Quran, 4:74).

"*Verily for the Righteous there will be a fulfilment of* (the heart's) *desires; Gardens enclosed, and grapevines; And voluptuous women of equal age; And a cup full* (to the brim)" (Quran, 78:31–34).

"*The Prophet Muhammad was heard saying: 'The smallest reward for the people of Paradise is an abode where there are 80,000 servants and 72 wives, over which stands a dome decorated with pearls, aquamarine, and ruby, as wide as the distance from Al-Jabiyyah* [a Damascus suburb] *to Sana'a* [Yemen]' " (Sunan At-Tirmidhi, 4:21:2687).

[Note: It is therefore no sheer coincidence that the Terrorist jihadis are committing their horrific crimes against civilians in that geography stretching from Syria to Yemen, passing through Lebanon and Iraq, as they are promised an equal land and more in the heavens!]

"Nobody who dies and finds good from Allah (in the Hereafter) *would wish to come back to this world even if he were given the whole world and whatever is in it, except the martyr who, on seeing the superiority of martyrdom, would like to come back to the world and get killed again* (in Allah's Cause)" (Sahih Bukhari, 4:52:53).

"By Him in Whose Hands my life is! Were it not for some men amongst the believers who dislike to be left behind me and whom I cannot provide with means of conveyance, I would certainly never remain behind any Sariya' [army-unit] *setting out in Allah's Cause. By Him in whose hands my life is! I would love to be martyred in Allah's Cause and then get resurrected and then get martyred, and then get resurrected again and then get martyred and then get resurrected again and then get martyred"* (Sahih Bukhari, 4:52:54).

"Nobody who enters Paradise likes to go back to the world even if he got everything on the earth, except a Mujahid [Jihadi] *who wishes to return to the world so that he may be martyred ten times because of the dignity he receives* (from *Allah). Our Prophet told us about the message of our Lord that 'Whoever amongst us is killed will go to Paradise.' Umar asked the Prophet, 'Is it not true that our men who are killed will go to Paradise and theirs* [i.e. the Pagans] *will go to the* (Hell) *fire?' The Prophet said, 'Yes.'* " (Narrated Al-Mughira bin Shu'ba, Sahih Bukhari, 4:52:72 [see also Sahih Muslim, 20:4635]).

"If anyone fights in Allah's path as long as the time between two milkings of a she-camel, Paradise will be assured for him. If anyone sincerely asks Allah for being killed and then dies or is killed, there will be a reward of a martyr for him" (Sunan Abu Dawud, 14:2535).

"It has been narrated on the authority of Abu Huraira who said: I heard the Messenger of Allah (peace be upon him) say: 'By the Being in Whose Hand is my life, I love that I should be killed in the way of Allah; then I should be brought back to life and be killed again in His way'" (Sahih Muslim, 20:4631 [see also 20:4626]).

"I love that I should be killed in the way of Allah": the Prophet's wish for death, or rather his exhortation to kill and die in the name of Allah, has become a battle cry among his staunchest followers today: Islamic terrorists. Indeed, jihad and sexual reward have been inextricably intertwined in the Islamic terrorists' mind (if there is any mind at all), as they are promised by their gurus, the fundamentalist sheikhs, unbridled sex in the hereafter as a reward for dying as "martyrs." And that is the main reason, among others, why so many Muslim young men become suicide bombers. It is not, as Westerners tend to think, an act of desperation, it is rather a promise of a hedonistic heaven filled with beautiful virgins.

The urge to become a martyr through sacrificing one's life to a higher cause is not a unique urge; however, the difference with Islamists is that this urge is intimately related to the promise of mating with the houris (beautiful virgins) in the afterlife. That is how "martyrdom" has become so attractive to Allah's "beloved fighters," and that is why this desire for martyrdom has become a rallying cry for terrorists all over the world.

Indeed, not to desire death in battle against the "infidels" or "unbelievers" is considered shameful:

> *"It has been narrated on the authority of Abu Huraira that the Messenger of Allah (may peace be upon him) said: One who died but did not fight in the way of Allah nor did he express any desire* (or determination) *for Jihad died the death of a hypocrite"* (Sahih Muslim, 20:4696).

It is praiseworthy, for any Muslim to seek and love death as a martyr (which involves, we always remind, the death of countless others, alas, innocent, unarmed civilians, along with the jihadi terrorists who carry out the suicide attacks). Islamism, indeed, Islam itself in the minds of many, has thus become a death cult. The way to Jannah is through martyrdom. It is paved with corpses.

- JANNAH: THE JIHADI'S HEDONISTIC REWARD:

All religions promise paradise (except perhaps Buddhism, which affirms that nirvana could be achieved here on Earth). Islam is certainly no exception. The problem, however, is when this promised paradise becomes, as with the case of Islamism, an incentive to kill in order to reap the reward for jihad in the next life.

Now it is true that these rewards in heaven are promised by the Quran and hadiths to those who are martyred for the sake of Allah, nevertheless, the scriptures also state that true jihad and martyrdom must (mostly, not solely, it must be said) be in self-defence: therefore, whereas the Quran incites Muslims *to defend* the "Land of Islam" whilst sparing the lives of civilians and vulnerable persons (women, children, and the elderly), and for that the martyrs would be rewarded, Islamism, for its part, incites Muslims *to kill*; an act of aggression that spares no souls; indeed, these are merely cowardly, murderous acts directed against innocent civilians in their homes and public spaces, and not against soldiers on the battlefield. Thus Islamist jihad has become a licence to kill for the sake of the houris, and not for the sake of Allah!

The Islamist doctrine indeed promises its warriors the virgins in paradise along with other delights, as an incentive to go to war and "spread the word of Allah" with the sword. Jannah (heaven) thus becomes the main reason why Islamic terrorists slaughter Yazidis and Christians in Syria and Iraq: to get the promised virgins. Islamism, or the so-called jihadi Salafism, has become a mere call for murder in the twisted minds of these mad killers. So it is not so much a question of courage but rather of sick perversion and sex mania that pushes jihadis to commit all kinds of atrocities, in order to get the fair virgins.

Paradise, for these "martyrs," is naught but a brothel filled with lust and luxury and materialistic delights; quite an incentive for Bedouins living in the hellish desert centuries ago. In fact, Jannah, as described in Islamic literature, seems to be the characteristic product of a Bedouin's imagination: lush, green vegetation with all kinds of flowers, water, women. In fact, this paradise promises its seekers, the jihadis, beautiful virgins or houris, along with young boys(!!), water, wine, fruits and wealth. As one can notice, all these things are rare in the desert of Arabia. Nothing to do with the chaste, ethereal heaven of higher spheres of other religions like Hinduism or Christianity.

The following are the lusts of the flesh that await the Jihadi "martyr" upon his death:

-1- FAIR VIRGINS (HOURIS):

Houris are the most prized bounty that awaits Muslims who fall as martyrs in jihad:

"As to the Righteous (they will be) *in a position of Security, among Gardens and Springs; dressed in fine silk and in rich brocade, they will face each other; So; and We shall join them to Companions with beautiful, big, and lustrous eyes* (Quran, 44:51–54).

"As to the Righteous, they will be in Gardens, and in Happiness, - Enjoying the (Bliss) *which their Lord hath bestowed on them, and their Lord shall deliver them from the Penalty of the Fire.* (To them will be said:) *'Eat and drink ye, with profit and health, because of your* (good) *deeds.' They will recline* (with ease) *on Thrones (of dignity) arranged in ranks; and We shall join them to Companions, with beautiful, big, and lustrous eyes"* (Quran, 52:17–20).

"Therein are bashful virgins, chaste and fair... dark-eyed virgins sheltered in their tents whom neither man nor Jinn have touched before whom neither man nor jinnee will have touched before" (Quran, 55:70–77) ... *"virgins as fair as corals and rubies... virgins chaste and fair... they shall recline on green cushions and fine carpets"* (Quran, 55:58).

"And on Thrones (of Dignity), *raised high. We have created* (their Companions) *of special creation. And made them virgin - pure* (and undefiled) *- Beloved* (by nature), *equal in age - For the Companions of the Right Hand"* (Quran, 56:34–38).

For the "martyr" who dies for the sake of Allah, there await him 72 virgins:

"It was mentioned by Daraj Ibn Abi Hatim that Abu-al-Haytham Abdullah Ibn Wahb narrated from Abu Sa'id Al-Khudri, who heard the Prophet Muhammad saying: 'The smallest reward for the people of Paradise is an abode where there are 80,000 servants and 72 wives, over which stands a dome decorated with pearls, aquamarine, and ruby, as wide as the distance from Al-Jabiyyah [a Damascus suburb] to Sana'a' " (the Book of Sunan, volume IV, chapters on "The Features of Paradise as described by the Messenger of Allah," Chapter 21: "About the Smallest Reward for the People of Paradise," Hadith 2687).

These houris are real virgins, undefiled, offering themselves to the "faithful":

"The chastity of the black-eyed was not violated by man nor jinn" (Quran, 55: 74, *Surah Al-Rahman*).

"We created the houris and the virgins, loving companions for those on the right hand" (Quran, 56:7–40).

And, as a bonus, each follower will be able to perform wonderfully with his 72 sex *Houris*, since his sexual force will increase drastically for that matter:

"A man in paradise shall be given virility equal to that of one hundred men" (Tirmzi, vol. 2, p. 138).

The other relevant verses from the Quran are:

"As for the righteous, they shall surely triumph. Theirs shall be gardens and vineyards, and high-bosomed virgins for companions: a truly overflowing cup" (Quran, 78:31).

"They will sit with bashful, dark-eyed virgins, as chaste as the sheltered eggs of ostriches" (Quran, 37:40–48).

"Yes and We shall wed them to dark-eyed Houris" (*Quran*, 44:51-55).

"They shall recline on couches ranged in rows. To dark-eyed Houris (virgins) *we shall wed them"* (Quran, 52:17–20).

"Virgins as fair as corals and rubies. Then which of the favours of your Lord will you deny?" (Quran, 55:57–58).

"There is in Paradise a market wherein there will be no buying or selling, but will consist of men and women. When a man desires a beauty, he will have intercourse with her" (Fazlul Maulana, Tirmizi, Al Hadis, Book 4, Chapter 42, no. 34).

-2- YOUNG BOYS TOO!

Promised to the jihadis, young handsome boys too:

"Round about them will serve, to them, boys (handsome) *as pearls well-guarded"* (Quran, 52:24).

"Round about them will serve boys of perpetual freshness" (Quran, 56:17).

"And round about them will serve boys of perpetual freshness: if thou seest them, thou wouldst think them scattered pearls" (Quran, 76:19).

It is worth noting in this context that, in contradiction with the above, there are other verses in Islam that actually condemn homosexuality as a crime and an abomination; yet another contradiction in the "book of God," say critics of Islam. For example:

"We also sent Lut: He said to his people: 'Do ye commit lewdness such as no people in creation (ever) committed before you? For ye practice your lusts on men in preference to women: ye are indeed a people transgressing beyond bounds' " (Quran, 7:80–81).

According to the hadiths, notably Al Dawud, Tirmizi:

"May Allah curse him who does what Lut's people did."

"When a man mounts another man, the throne of God shakes."

"Kill the one who sodomises and the one who lets be done to him" (in reference to the active and passive partners in gay sexual intercourse).

There is at least one mention of lesbian behaviour mentioned in the *Hadith*:

"Sihaq (lesbian sexual activity) *of women is zina* (illegitimate sexual intercourse) *among them."*

-3- WATER: THE FOUNTAIN OF DELIGHT

One of the major problems in the desert of Arabia was shortage of pure water, one might even say that it was an item of luxury rarely found in Arabia and highly coveted by the Bedouins who named the Levant "the fertile crescent" because of its abundance of water and greenery. Based on that, one might not be surprised that the Muslim promise of paradise is filled with water, rivers, fountains and springs.

The relevant verses from the *Quran* are:

"This is the paradise which the righteous have been promised: it is watered by running streams" (Quran, 13:35).

"As for those that fear their Lord, theirs shall be gardens watered by running streams in which they will abide forever, and a goodly welcome from God" (*Quran,* 3:198).

"These shall be rewarded with forgiveness from their Lord and with gardens watered by running streams, where they shall dwell forever. Blessed is the reward of those who do good works" (Quran, 3:136).

The righteous (will be) amid gardens and fountains (of clear flowing water) *"* (Quran, 15:45).

"As for those who have faith and who do good work, God will admit them to gardens watered by running streams" (Quran, 22:23).

"Here is a Parable of the Garden which the righteous are promised: In it are rivers of water incorruptible" (Quran, 47:15).

"In them each will be two springs flowing free; Then which of the favours of your Lord will you deny? (Quran, 55:50–51).

"In them will be Two Springs pouring forth water in continuous abundance: Then which of the favours of your Lord will you deny?" (Quran, 55:66–67).

"As for the righteous, they shall be lodged in peace together amidst gardens and fountains" (Quran, 44:51–55).

"They shall recline on couches raised on high in the shade of thornless Lote trees and talhs; amidst gushing water" (*Quran*, 56:7–40).

For people living near the Mississippi, the above verses do not describe a distant heaven but reality.

-4- WINE:

In Islam, wine is allowed, indeed, promised, in heaven, though strictly forbidden on earth!! As with virgins and water, wine was yet another pleasure promised to the righteous Muslims, the jihadis.

Consequently, rivers of wine would flow alongside the pristine rivers of water, delighting the jihadis in Jannah:

"Here is a Parable of the Garden which the righteous are promised. In it are... rivers of wine" (Quran, 47:15).

"But the true servants of God shall be well provided for . . . they shall be served with goblet filled at a gushing fountain, white and delicious to those who drink it. It will neither dull their senses nor befuddle them" (Quran, 37:40–48).

"They shall recline on jewelled couches face to face, and there shalt wait on them immortal youths with bowls and ewers and a cup of purest wine" (Quran, 56:7-40).

"The righteous will surely dwell in bliss. Reclining upon soft couches they will gaze around them: and in their faces you shall mark the glow of joy. They shall be given a pure wine to drink, securely sealed, whose very dregs are musk" (Quran, 83:23–26).

-5- FRUITS:

To the spiritual person longing for elevation and a post-mortem journey into higher, subtler spheres in the ethereal world, climaxing in a total union with the Whole or Source, the jihadis' heaven will turn out to be a big materialistic and hedonistic disappointment. For this *Jannah* which is fuelling the imagination of the terrorists is purely made of human, all-too human delights and sensual pleasures, much like earth. In fact, it is but a mirror of their earthly desires and basic instincts: sex, food, and luxury . . . the fact of which suggests that this heaven is "pure" (rather, impure) utopia created to recruit jihadis for Allah's wars.

And so, here come the fruits to complete the picture for the Jihadis yearning for their fair virgins. Wine and fruits make a perfect combination and a delight to the senses and basic instincts and cravings of *Allah's* warriors.

Indeed, as with water and wine, fruits were also a rare treat in the desert of Arabia, where only dates and dry pomegranates were available. Consequently, the promised *Jannah* will be blessed with an endless supply of every variety of fruits:

> *"This is the paradise which the righteous have been promised... eternal are its fruits, and eternal are its shades"* (Quran, 13:35).

> *"But the true servants of God shall be well provided for, feasting on fruit and honoured in the gardens of delight"* (Quran, 37:40–48).

> *"Such will be the garden of which ye are made heirs for your deeds. Ye shall have therein abundance of fruit, from which ye shall have satisfaction"* (Quran, 43:68–73).

> *"Here is a Parable of the Garden which the righteous are promised: In it are rivers of milk of which the taste never changes; rivers of wine, a joy to those who drink; and rivers of honey pure and clear. In it there are for them all kinds of fruits; and grace from their Lord"* (Quran, 47:15).

> *"Containing all kinds of trees and delights. Then which of the favours of your Lord will you deny?"* (Quran, 55:47–49).

> *"In them there will be fruits of every kind, two and two. Then which of the favours of your Lord will you deny?"* (Quran, 55:52–53).

"The fruit of the gardens will be near and easy to reach. Then which of the favours of your Lord will you deny?" (Quran, 55:54–55).

"In them will be Fruits, and dates and pomegranates: then which of the favours of your Lord will you deny?" (Quran, 55:68–69).

"Secure against all ills, they shall call for every kind of fruit" (Quran, 44:51–55).

"They shall recline on jewelled couches face to face, and there shalt wait on them immortal youths with . . . fruits of their own choices and flesh of fowls that they relish" (Quran, 56:7–40).

"Reclining there upon soft couches, they shall feel neither the scorching heat nor the biting cold. Trees will spread their shade around them, and fruits will hang in clusters over them" (Quran, 76:13–21).

Here also, for people living in tropical islands, where water and fruit abound, this heaven is déjà vu.

-6- WEALTH:

As we have seen, the heaven promised by Islamists, and selectively and arbitrarily based on *Quranic* verses, is a materialistic and hedonistic place. And what better than money could be bestowed on the faithful to crown the basest human cravings like sex and food? Wealth thus comes as the final, crowning reward for jihadis who have served Allah well in jihad. Yet another contradiction in Islamic literature, since the Prophet made sure his followers would not be obsessed with worldly delights down under, only to get plenty of those up in heaven! Silk, gold, pearls, jewels, fine cushions and carpets . . . everything one could ever dream of on Earth will be provided in *Jannah*:

> *"As for those who have faith and who do good work, God will admit them to gardens watered by running streams. They shall be decked with pearls and bracelets of gold, and arrayed in garments of silk"* (Quran, 22–23).

> *"Enter Ye the Garden, Ye and your wives, in beauty and rejoicing. To them will be passed round, dishes and goblets of gold: there will be there all that soul could desire, all that the eyes could delight in: and ye shall abide there in"* (Quran, 43:68–73).

> *"They shall recline on green cushions and fine carpets. Then which of the favours of your Lord will you deny?"* (Quran, 55:70–77).

> *"As for the righteous, they shall be lodged in peace together amidst gardens and fountains, arrayed in rich silks and fine brocade"* (Quran, 44:51–55).

> *"They will recline on carpets, whose inner linings will be of rich brocade"* (Quran, 55:54–55).

> *"They shall recline on jewelled couches"* (Quran, 56:7–40).

> *"They shall be arrayed in garments of fine green silk and rich brocade, and adorned with bracelets of silver"* (Quran, 76:13–21).

Based on the words of the Quran, the Islamic Paradise of the jihadis is like the lure of the siren: follow Allah's instructions and will, and you shall receive all the earthly delights and sensual pleasures in heaven.

CHAPTER SIX

ALLAH'S HELL:
ETERNAL SUFFERING FOR UNBELIEVERS

"Hell is empty and all the devils are here."

- WILLIAM SHAKESPEARE

- AND THEY (THE UNBELIEVERS) LIVED MISERABLY EVER AFTER

Every religion, with the exception of Buddhism, restricts heaven to its followers, and excludes the followers of other religions for the simple reason that they are not embracing the "true faith." Indeed, each religion proclaims that its own will go to heaven and live happily ever after, while the sons of other creeds will go to hell and will burn in its flames for all eternity. Religions negate each other, and are mutually exclusive. All religions, with no exception, have been in constant war, hot and cold, against each other throughout history; hence the necessity of an honest and serious interfaith dialogue in order to have a better life in the here and now.

Islam is no exception. Like all other religion, it promises Muslims *Jannah*, heaven, and threatens all non-Muslims (and, it goes without saying, the atheists or agnostics) with eternal punishment in *Jahannam*, hell: Hindus, Buddhists, Zoroastrians... are considered pagans, polytheists, and hence infidels or unbelievers (kaffirs or kuffar); they will inevitably go to hell and will burn there forever. The same goes for the atheists or apostates. As for the Jews and the Christians, although theirs are monotheistic (Abrahamic) religions and they are called the People of the Book *(Ahl Al Kitab)*, still, they are considered respectively *Al Maghdoob 'Alayhim* (the ones upon whom is anger) and *Al Daalleen* (the deviants, or the ones who have gone astray); they would endure hardships and suffering in hell, if they do not come back to the "right path," that is, Islam.

This is Islam's teleological order, *grosso modo.*

Definitely, the zealots of Islam, the fundamentalists or Salafists, embrace this Jannah-Jahannam scenario and push it to the extreme: they are *Takfiris*, they accuse the followers of all other creeds of blasphemy, and, instead of waiting for the Day of Judgment - Yawm Al Hissab or Qiyama - to come, when "Allah will keep his own with Him in heaven, and send the rest to hell," they themselves take God's place, judge the kuffar and daalleen, and *send them to hell:* they burn and kill them here on Earth! They thus consider themselves as fulfilling Allah's *will*, referring to the verses in the Quran itself to face or challenge their critics, including the moderate Muslim critics. They use the "legitimate" weapon of the Scriptures to justify their crimes; to draw their swords and guns against the "unbelievers."

The most famous verse these zealots use (and misuse, and abuse) is the one about Al Tahrim ("prohibition") which encapsulates the way Islam views "unbelievers." In this verse, Allah exhorts his messenger to kill them:

> *"O prophet, strive hard against the unbelievers and the hypocrites, and be unyielding to them. Hell will be their home, a hapless journey's end"* (Quran, 8:15).

What's more, unbelievers will suffer excruciating and continuous pain in hell for all eternity:

"They will dwell therein for all the time that the heavens and the earth endure" (Quran, 11:107).

Allah's wrath will fall on those who did not heed his messenger's call to bow before his will. Of course, according to the takfiris, all non-Muslims fall under the "unbelievers" or "infidels" category, as well as those Muslims who were not true to their religion or who have transgressed some of its (many) instructions and warnings. However, since the Almighty Allah is wise and merciful, he could choose to make the punishment of hell temporary; that is a bonus that non-Muslims do not have, since they are doomed for all eternity, they have no hope of being redeemed (unless they repent and convert to Islam, of course):

"Those who reject Faith, and die rejecting, on them is Allah's curse, and the curse of angels, and of all mankind. They will abide therein: Their penalty will not be lightened, nor will they receive respite" (Quran, 2:161–162). *"They are* (men) *whom Allah hath cursed: And those whom Allah Hath cursed, thou wilt find, have no one to help"* (Quran, 4:52).

The punishments of Jahannam have been outlined extensively in numerous verses in the Quran, as we shall see below. The unbelievers will endure the worst kind of suffering in hell: the Quran states that these cursed souls will be punished forever and that each time they endure the most excruciating physical pain, that of being burned, it will feel new, since inhabitants of Jahannam are given new skin so as to suffer from the start again:

"Lo! Those who disbelieve Our revelations shall be cast into hell, We shall expose them to the Fire. As often as their skins are consumed We shall exchange them for fresh skins that they may taste the agony of punishment" (Quran, 4:56).

The punishment of inhabitants of hell having their skin burned and then renewed only to be burned again for all eternity is mentioned again in verse 22:20. Verse 18:28 says these unbelievers will be drinking *"water like melted brass, that will scald their faces,"* and is also detailed in verse 22:19, which also mentions the "garment of fire" that the dwellers will wear in Jahannam while verse 22:21 reveals the punishment of *"maces of iron* (to punish) *them."*

"Islamic" Hell has a two-fold aim: first, to torture all the kaffirs for all eternity and, second, according to Islam's critics, to terrorise people into accepting Islam. They say that, as one reads with horror the verses detailing the kind of torture unbelievers endure down under, one cannot but understand that these verses were written with the main purpose of sowing extreme fear in the hearts and minds of those who do not embrace Islam or those Muslims who steer away from its precepts.

Muslim clerics do not all agree on whether Jahannam is exclusively reserved for infidels, as some also believe that it is also reserved for bad Muslims. But for Islamist takfiris, the purpose of hell is *not* to punish the Muslim wrong-doers, provided they don't renounce their religion (murtaddeen); no wonder then, when we see the terrorist thugs of Daesh, al-Nusra, Ahrar al-Sham, al-Qaeda, Taliban, Boko Haram, al-Shebab, and the like, kill, steal, and rape without the slightest remorse; so long as they remain Muslims, they can be forgiven or, worse, rewarded, because they are murdering the "unbelievers," stealing their money, confiscating their properties and assets, and raping their women. In stark contrast to this divine mercy, a flaming hell is reserved only for all non-Muslims, no matter how pious and God-fearing they may have been. In that sense, "Islamic" hell is exclusively for non-Muslims, be they good or bad persons, sinner or saints. What about the millions of people born before Islam? Were they all doomed to go to hell? That is a question which also embarrasses many moderate Muslims, for they have no answer to that great injustice on the part of the merciful *Allah*.

- GUARDIANS AND INMATES OF JAHANNAM

In Islam, hell, in Arabic *Jahannam* or *Nar* (which also means "fire") - is known to be a huge fiery blaze which consumes the skin of those cursed by Allah for not having followed the "right path" (al Siraat al mustaqeem) set forth by Muhammad. Jahannam is described in the Quran as having seven gates, each for a specific group of sinners according to their degrees based on their deeds. The Quran designated the occupants of Jahannam in several verses. The inhabitants of Jahannam thus fall into two broad categories: what we may call the inmates (the "sinners") and the guardians (the "angels").

Among the first category of inhabitants (the "sinners") is the sub-category of what the Quran calls "the hypocrites, " those who have not followed the true precepts of Islam. Muslims who have gone astray or who are deluded, one might say. They are the worst class of sinners and consequently occupy the lowest degree of hell: *"The Hypocrites will be in the lowest depths of the Fire"* (Quran, 4:145).

Hypocrites, however, are not the only inhabitants of Islamic hell. Indeed, the *Quran* states that both hypocrites and disbelievers will all be in hell in verse 4:140: *"Surely Allah will gather together the hypocrites and the unbelievers all in hell."* The second sub-category of sinners is thus the polytheists or disbelievers (commonly referred to as kaffirs or "infidels"). These include both the disbelievers among the "People of the Book" (Christians and Jews) as well as pagans:

> *"Surely those who disbelieve from among the followers of the Book and the polytheists shall be in the fire of hell, abiding therein; they are the worst of men"* (Quran, 98:6).

In short, Islamic hell, this huge flaring prison, this nightmarish inferno, comprises all non-Muslims (or all non-"real" Muslims, given that "bad" Muslims are not real Muslims). Some verses of the Quran also include various other groups of people described as inhabitants of Jahannam such as sinners and criminals, tyrants, the unjust, transgressors, and people who commit suicide and murder. The hadiths add to this long list of the damned the arrogant, the proud and the haughty.

As for the other category of inhabitants of *Jahannam,* namely those who are guarding it, there are nineteen "angels" who are responsible for punishing sinners . . . a most unlikely role for an angel, to say the least! The leader of these "angels," according to the Quran, is Maalik, who in the words of Prophet Muhammad, is *"very severe and harsh."* This "angel" is so cruel that he will listen to the condemned person's pleas of clemency and absolution for their punishments after 1,000 years to finally deny these pleas!

According to Muslim scriptures, all the people mentioned above will experience the fiery blaze and boiling water burning their skin over and over again, and they shall be engulfed in shades of black smoke that will choke them. This nightmare will last for all eternity in an endless cycle of physical pain, anguish and despair. That is the punishment that fits the crime of unbelief.

What's more, Prophet Muhammad gave his followers a grim vision of their own future as he told them that, out of every one thousand people entering the afterlife, nine hundred and ninety-nine of them will end up in hell.

- THE DAY OF JUDGMENT AND THE WEIGHING PROCESS

The Day of Judgment (Yaym al Qiyama) is a harrowing experience for all Muslims, given the fact that Prophet Muhammad predicted that most of them will go to hell; one of Muhammad's most quoted statements is: *"My Ummah* [nation, meaning Muslims] *will be fragmented into 72 sects, all of them will go to hell, except one which shall be redeemed."* This statement has caused, and continues to cause, countless inter-sectarian wars among Muslims, as each sect considers itself the redeemed one designated by the Prophet.

The Day of Judgment is also a terrifying experience since Muslims are all too aware of what awaits them in hell. In any case, the purpose of this day of reckoning is for Allah to judge each man's soul according to its earthly deeds or misdeeds. It is up to God to determine whether this soul, after its brief passage on Earth, deserves to go heaven or to hell, for all eternity. According to Islam, on this crucial day, which occurs at the end of times, all the dead are awakened in their tombs to face (the day of Hashr) their fate in the afterlife.

That is when the weighing process takes place. The anxiety reaches its peak as the uncertainty each soul faces is absolutely terrifying until the final sentence or verdict is pronounced by the Almighty through his angels Mounkar and Nakir, whose primary task is to test the faith of the dead in their grave. Good and bad deeds acquired in each soul's lifetime are then weighed on a scale, and consequently the soul is held accountable for these very deeds, according to the intention behind each deed. Good deeds weigh more than bad ones.

When the good deeds outweigh the bad deeds, the righteous Muslim enters Jannah (heaven), and when the bad deeds outweigh the good deeds, the sinner enters Jahannam (Hell). It is fundamentally a simple math question, an objective calculation, away from either cruelty or mercy; Muslim karma, if you will, except that Allah himself is both the judge and the jury since he has complete authority over the weighing process and ultimately makes the final decision, delivering his sentence upon each soul.

Despite the fact that this day of reckoning represents justice, still, one cannot help but contrast this sombre and eerie "divine courtroom" with Christ's boundless love and forgiveness. Well, there is no such thing in Islam where one's other-worldly destiny is a question of simple math, with no hope whatsoever of divine mercy or forgiveness. What? Allah might not be so merciful after all? And he also seems to hold a grudge against those who have wronged him in any way. We are far from the all-loving Christian God.

Going back to the anxiety felt by each soul as it faces the divine sentence, here again we see an unfortunate characteristic feature of Islam: the culture of fear . . . not love. Fear is the ultimate and eternal companion to the Muslims, from cradle to grave. There is always the omnipresent threat of severe punishment, and faith is driven mostly by fear of Jahannam.

- THE MUSLIM GOLGOTHA: THE PATH TO HELL

There is a very long, brutal sequence of events leading into the afterlife following the harrowing and painful experience of death and the grave. This time period involves the separation of the soul from its human sheath. For sinners, this process lasts much longer and is more painful.

The Day of Judgment starts with a trumpet blast which awakens the dead from the grave, with their *actual* bodies. Then comes what is called the "Perspiration" and "Day of the Arising" which is when all living creatures, including men, angels, Jinn (fire creatures), demons and animals gather and sweat with no shade to hide in. The non-Muslims will sweat longer on this painful day which is supposed to last for 50,000 years (!!), during which each person undergoes a veritable questioning about his life and decisions. Here, there is no room for any divine, Christ-like mercy or forgiveness. After this questioning comes the weighing process of good and bad deeds on the scale.

The final stage is the passage of the bridge of Sirat (path). This is the bridge over the fire that every individual has to try to cross. For sinners, the bridge appears as thin as a hair and as sharp as the sharpest knife or sword. Sinners will fall into the fire below and arrive at their final destination place, Jahannam. All these happenings are in no way metaphorical for Muslims, but rather literal: every Muslim absolutely believes that this is what happens after death.

- PUNISHMENTS

The Quran and Hadith offer meticulous and highly graphic descriptions of the methods of punishment in Jahannam. According to the Quran, the main punishments will be the burning of skin, only to be renewed for re-burning, again and forever; the faces, lips, back will also be burnt; the "sinners" will be forced to wear garments of fire, and boiling water will be thrown at them, scalding their skin; they shall be roasted from side to side; they shall be bound in yokes then dragged through boiling water and fire. We cannot but shudder at such sadistic torture methods, which are strangely similar to the way Daesh terrorists torture and murder those they call unbelievers. These monsters claim that they are merely following the scriptures to the letter.

As for the hadiths, they introduce other punishments. The mildest pain for the inhabitants of Jahannam will be that their brain will boil from standing on hot embers. And those who committed suicide will suffer the same death that they chose in their earthly life. As for the "hypocrites" (those who do not practice the Muslim faith as they should), they shall be thrown into the lowest depth of the fire. So, too, shall those who have spread corruption throughout their life and those who misbehave in hell—in short, all those who do not follow the path of Allah, the Right Path (al Siraat al mustaqeem).

We have described Islamic Hell in general; now we will support this description with the relevant verses from both the Quran and the hadiths, which further describe what Jahannam is like and what punishments will befall its unfortunate dwellers.

- JAHANNAM IN THE QURAN AND OTHER ISLAMIC SCRIPTURES

The Quran contains most of the description of Jahannam. Indeed, there are nearly 500 references to it in Islam's holiest book, and the rest of the elaboration came from the Hadith. Verse 15:44 of the Quran comes up with the idea of the seven gates of Jahannam, and how each level of Islamic hell would be reserved for a different class of sinner. As for verse 7:50, it describes heaven as being physically above hell, stating, *"The companions of the Fire will call to the Companions of the Garden: 'Pour down to us water or anything that God doth provide'."*

Almost every verse of the Quran in regard to Jahannam describes it as being a place of blazing fire, and verse 2:24 is very explicit when it talks about the fire "whose fuel is Men and Stones." Other verses talk about the "breath of Jahannam" (67:7) and the "voice of Jahannam" (50:30). All this definitely has a frightening effect on Muslims (and maybe also on non-Muslims), to get them to follow the right path or convert before they are doomed for all eternity.

"We have created the unbelievers out of base matters," (Quran, 70:39): this, in a nutshell, is how Islam views non-Muslims. They are inferior to Muslims and are beyond redemption. It matters not if they have led righteous, virtuous lives; their only destination in the afterworld is hell.

The following selected verses (among many others) in the Quran paint a very grim and dismal picture of what Allah's hell looks like for "unbelievers," whether they are atheists or people from other religions:

"Lo! We have prepared for disbelievers Fire. Its tent encloseth them. If they ask for showers, they will be showered with water like to molten lead which burneth

the faces. Calamitous the drink and ill the resting-place!" (Quran, 18:28–30).

"The unbelievers among the People of the Book [Christians and Jews] *and the pagans shall burn forever in the fire of Hell. They are the vilest of all creatures"* (Quran, 98:1–8).

"Garments of fire have been prepared for the unbelievers. Scalding water shall be poured upon their heads, melting their skins and that which is in their bellies. They shall be lashed rods of iron. Whenever, in their anguish, they try to escape from Hell, back they shall be dragged, and will be told: 'Taste the torment of the Conflagration!' " (Quran, 22:19–23).

"Do you not see how those who dispute the revelation of God turn away from the right path? Those who have denied the Book and the message We sent through Our apostles shall realize the truth hereafter: when, with chains and shackles round their necks, they shall be dragged through scalding water and then burnt in the fire of Hell" (Quran, 40:67–73).

"The unbelievers shall endure forever the torment of Hell. The punishment will never be lightened, and they shall be speechless with despair" (Quran, 43:74).

"That is the Hell which the unbelievers deny. They shall wander between fire and water fiercely seething. Which of your Lord's blessing would you deny?" (Quran, 55:41–52).

"For the unbelievers We have prepared chains and fetters and a blazing Fire" (Quran, 76:1–5).

"We have in store for the unbelievers heavy fetters and a blazing fire, choking food and harrowing torment: on the day when the earth shall quiver with all its mountains, and the mountains crumble into heaps of shifting sand" (Quran, 73:12).

"Woe on that day to the disbelievers! Begone to the Hell which you deny! Depart into the shadow that will rise high in three columns, giving neither shade nor shelter from the flames, and throwing up sparks as huge as towers, as bright as yellow camels . . . Eat and enjoy yourselves awhile. You are wicked men . . . " (Quran, 77:20–50).

"The unbelievers shall stare in amazement, crying: 'Woe to us! Of this we have been heedless. We have done wrong.' You and your idols shall be the fuel of Hell; therein you shall all go down" (Quran, 21:96–101).

"But for the unbelievers He has prepared a woeful punishment . . . " (Quran, 33:7–12).

"On that day they shall be sternly thrown into the fire of Hell, and a voice will say to them: 'This is the Fire which you denied . . . Burn in its flames. It is the same whether or not you show forbearance. You shall be rewarded according to your deeds" (Quran, 52:1–15).

"And burn ye him in the blazing fire. Further, make him march in a chain, whereof the length is seventy cubits.

This was he that would not believe in Allah Most high and would not encourage the feeding of the indignant. So no friend hath he here this day. Nor hath he any food except the corruption from the washing of wounds" (Quran, 31:37).

"We shall say: 'Lay hold of him and bind him. Burn him in the fire of Hell, then fasten him with a chain seventy cubits long. For he did not believe Allah the tremendous, and urged not on the feeding of the wretched. Today he shall be friendless here; filth shall be his food, the filth which sinners eat" (Quran, 69:30–37).

"Those who reject faith shall be the companions of the Fire" (Quran, 2:39).

"The curse of Allah is on the unbelievers . . . humiliating is the punishment" (Quran, 2:89-90).

"He hurls his thunderbolts at whom he pleases Yet the unbelievers wrangle about Allah" (Quran, 13:13).

"Those who resist Allah and his messenger will be humbled to dust" (Quran, 58:5).

"The fire of Hell will pluck out his being right to the skull" (Quran, 70:15–16).

"As for those who disbelieve and deny Our revelations, they are the heirs of Hell" (Quran, 5:10).

"The fruit of the Zaqqum tree shall be the unbelievers' fruit. Like dregs of oil, like scalding water, it shall simmer

in his belly. A voice will cry: 'Seize him and drag him into the depths of Hell. Then pour out scalding water over his head, saying: Taste this, illustrious and honourable man! This is the punishment which you have doubted' " (Quran, 44:40–49).

"Ye shall surely taste of the tree Zaqqum. Then will ye fill your insides therewith, and drink boiling water on top of it. Indeed ye shall drink like diseased camels raging with thirst. Such will be their entertainment on the day of Requital!" (Quran, 56:52–56).

[The infamous tree of Zaqqum, the food source of Jahannam, was also described in verses 37:62–68 and again in verse 44:43].

CHAPTER SEVEN

SHARIA OR ISLAMIC LAW: INJUSTICE IS SERVED

"When injustice becomes law, resistance becomes duty."

- THOMAS JEFFERSON

Sharia, or Islamic law, is supposed to represent Islamic justice, as it is legislation that deals with matters related to trade, inheritance, marriage, divorce, justice, and so on. However, when one reads the sharia, especially the part related to punishments, one finds it totally incompatible with modernity and human rights.

Indeed, and to a great extent, the sharia is still adopting the archaic axiom: "an eye for an eye," inflicting the most terrible punishments for crimes (and sometimes petty crimes), like beheading, stoning to death, burning, hanging, amputation; punishments that were practiced many centuries ago, and ceased to exist a long time ago in the modern civilised world, and even in many secular countries in the Third World. But unfortunately, they are still a common practice in many Islamic countries that have sharia as the origin of jurisprudence, and this is in contradiction with the UN Declaration of Human Rights (and the Geneva Conventions), rights that have become universal, applied in the majority of UN member states, except in some Muslim countries which are still applying parts of, or the whole of the sharia, whose methods amount to a barbaric and unjust practice by all accounts.

To cite but one example of a punishment that is sheer injustice: according to the sharia's arbitrary, unjust, and twisted logic, if a girl or a woman is the victim of rape, *she* gets hundreds of lashes as *punishment* (!!), in addition to a jail sentence, and sometimes even the death penalty whereby she is hanged or stoned to death. Incomprehensible, to say the least. The justification for such an inexplicable punishment of the *victim* instead of the criminal (the rapist), is that the girl or the woman was in a way responsible for rape by tempting the man (or men), and anyway, after being raped, she has violated the honour of her family and is thus unworthy of life.

Before we examine how incompatible sharia is with modernity, democracy and human rights, let us first explain what it is: its sources, categories of crimes and legal and court proceedings, penalties, fatwas, customs and contemporary practice.

WHAT IS SHARIA?
- *Meaning, sources of Sharia:*

Sharia in Arabic literally means legislation; it is the religious law and moral code or justice according to the Muslims. The sharia is the practical implementation of the Quran. Islamic law, as secular law, covers many topics, including crime, politics and economics, as well as personal matters such as sexual intercourse, hygiene, diet, prayer, and fasting. However, the difference with secular (mainly Western) law is that, according to Muslims, the sharia is considered the infallible (and hence eternal and unchangeable) law of God, as it draws its source from the Quran and Muhammad's life and example (the Sunna, which is contained in the Hadith, reports of Muhammad's sayings, his actions, and his conduct). Consequently, crime in Islam is considered sin and the offender is accused of acting against the will of God and his sins are considered an offence against Allah. His punishment will thus fit his crime.

Sharia as a "divine" law is related to but different from fiqh, which is the human interpretation of the law. The problem with sharia, therefore, is that its practices and punishments, however medieval and archaic, are as unalterable as the Quran itself since it draws its source from Allah's word. As such, this law, contrary to secular law, does not move with the times and remains stuck in the seventh century, whereas the rest of the world has largely espoused universal human rights and especially women's rights which remain conspicuously absent from Islamic scriptures and law.

In addition to the three main sources of the sharia (the Quran, the Sunna and Hadith), Islamic law also bases itself on the many, and sometimes contradictory, interpretations of the scriptures by the scholars and their religious edicts (fatwas).

Although there are many different interpretations of sharia according to the different cultures and races embracing Islam, all Muslims are in total agreement that sharia, as the Quran, faithfully reflects Allah's will for mankind. Consequently, any attempt or call to revise or modernise it is considered blasphemous and heretical, for how could Allah be wrong? It is this rigidity and refusal to revise and improve itself which makes Islamic law so impervious to change and incompatible with modernity.

- *Categories of crimes, legal and court proceedings:*

Sharia covers the following topics: purification, prayer, funeral prayer, taxes, fasting, pilgrimage, trade, inheritance, marriage, divorce, justice.

Islamic law can be divided into five main branches:

- Ibadah (ritual worship).

- Mu'amalat (transactions and contracts).

- Adab (morals and manners).

- I'tiqadat (beliefs).

- 'Uqubat (penalties or punishments).

Sharia judicial proceedings are very different from other legal traditions, including those in both common law and civil law, and this difference has crucial and dramatic consequences on whether true justice is applied, since it represents the difference between fair trials and sentences and trials and sentences based on ancient traditions and customs that don't necessarily take into account human rights or dignity.

The main reason, besides its tenets and extremely harsh punishments, that sharia may lead to *injustice* rather than justice is its legal procedure itself: according to legal experts, sharia courts customarily do *not* have lawyers; plaintiffs and defendants represent themselves. As for the trials, they are carried out exclusively by the judge, as there is no jury. There is no pre-trial process, and no cross-examination of witnesses; thus, defendants are not given a chance to prove their innocence (in case they are innocent). And, unlike civil law, sharia does not use formally codified statutes. Instead of precedents and codes, Islamic law relies on jurists' (Muslim clerics) manuals and collections of non-binding, and varying legal opinions and interpretations of the Scriptures (the Quran and hadiths); the fact which leaves a wide margin for arbitrary judgments and biased verdicts.

Sharia divides crimes into four categories: qisas, hudud, tazir, and siyastan.

A qisas (retaliation) offence involves personal injury and is treated as a common law crime, rather than a "crime against the state." If the accused party is proven guilty, the victim (or, in death, the victim's family), not the court, is the one who determines the punishment or retribution, which can range from execution, amputation of the lost limb, or literal retaliation (he would be punished with the same injury or death inflicted; the "eye for an eye" law). What makes this practice hardly legal or humane is that the next of kin of the victim would traditionally carry out the execution (or injury), rather than representatives of the legal authorities. This gives this practice a tribal, primitive aspect, as though there were no state but only tribes with flags.

The victim or his family can also alternatively choose to forgive the perpetrator, but it is hardly turning the other cheek, since in this case they would receive compensation for the loss of limb or injury. And, in case of the sentence being the death penalty, there are very few mitigating factors, which means the sentence is always carried out no matter what the circumstances surrounding it. Hence sharia sees no such thing as justifiable homicide, such as a woman killing a man who attacked her and tried to rape her.

The second category of crimes is hudud, which are crimes whose penalties were laid down by the Quran, and are considered to be "claims against God." They include:

Adultery (*zina*), which includes adultery, fornication, incest/paedophilia, rape, and pimping.

Apostasy/blasphemy.

Defamation.

Sodomy/lesbianism (or sodomy rape).

Theft.

Use of intoxicants (alcohol, drugs).

"Waging war against God and society" (hiraba, unlawful warfare; and Fasad fel Ard, mischief); armed robbery, terrorism, armed violence.

Hudud penalties for these cases are not punishments that fit the crimes, but rather they tend to be very harsh in order to set an example for the general public and sow fear in their hearts by carrying out the cruellest penalties, such as stoning or amputation or beheading. Daesh's public executions and beheadings in Raqqa province, the capital of their infamous state in Syria, are examples of these inhuman executions.

The third category of crimes is ta'zir, which refers to punishments for offences at the discretion of the judge (Qadi) or ruler of the state. While the punishments for the hudud offences are fixed by the Quran or Hadith (and therefore "defined by God"), and while qisas allows equal retaliation in cases such as murder or injury, ta'zir refers to punishments applied to the other offences for which no punishment is specified in the Quran or the Hadith. It is a "claim of the state" and it receives a discretionary sentence. The punishment can range from imprisonment to death, depending on the crime. Unlike hudud, here the punishment is meant to fit the crime.

A fourth and lesser-known category is siyastan, which is a penalty that is issued by state authorities and, unlike the other punishments, it is not derived from sharia, although it is inspired by it and cannot contradict it. A typical siyastan crime would be treason against the ruling regime. Another is drug trafficking and other crimes that are viewed as "spreading corruption on earth" (fasad fel Ard).

- PENALTIES AND PROHIBITIONS
- *Rajm (stoning to death): firmly established in Sharia*

Rajm or stoning for adultery is firmly established in Islamic law and remains a common practice in traditional Muslim societies; yes, it is inconceivable to believe that, even in this day and age, this most barbaric and demeaning practice is still and exclusively committed by many Muslims all over the world. In fact, this horrific practice is established by the Sunna (prophetic traditions). Moreover, scholars of Islam, who are considered to be the third source of Islamic law, are unanimous on the issue of stoning a married person (male or female) for adultery, as the prescribed penal punishment (hadd) of the sharia.

The *Hadith*, *Ibn Masud* reports:

"The blood of a Muslim person is not permissible except in one of three situations; the adulterer who is married, one who has killed unjustly, and the apostate" (*Bukhari* and *Muslim*).

The essence of this hadith, albeit with different wording, is also reported by such authorities as Uthmaan, Ayesha, Abu Hurairah, Jaabir and Ammaar bin Yaasir. Then there is the incident reported by Abu Hurairah and Zaid bin Khalid al-Juhani regarding a workman who committed adultery with another woman. The Messenger of Allah instructed a man from the tribe of Aslam: *"Go in the morning to this (particular) lady; so, if she confesses, then stone her"* (Bukhari, Muslim, Muatta, Musnad Ahmad, Abu Dawud, Tirmidhi, An-Nasaai). One cannot but contrast this attitude with that of Christ when faced with the same case of a woman adulterer: *"let him who is without sin among you cast the first stone,"* thus forgiving a woman adulterer by simply admonishing her thus: *"Go and sin no more."*

Based on the aforementioned narratives, as well as many others in Islamic scriptures, and even the Quran, it is proven that this command to stone adulterers was a common Muslim practice, and, alas, still remains so until this day in some traditional Muslim communities.

In accordance with the Hadith, stoning to death is the penalty for married men and women who commit adultery. As for unmarried men and women, the punishment prescribed in the Quran and Hadith is 100 lashes:

> *"The woman and the man guilty of adultery or fornication – flog each of them with hundred stripes: let no compassion move you in their case, in a matter prescribed by God, if ye believe in God and the last day"* (Quran 24:2).

However, in order to be fair, and as I mentioned earlier, there must be proof that such an act has indeed been committed. According to the Quran, there should be four witnesses to the crime. In fact, Muhammad announced in response to wrongful accusations of adultery levelled at his wife, Aisha: *"Why did they not produce four witnesses? Since they produce not witnesses, they verily are liars in the sight of Allah"* (Quran, 24:13).

Punishments are authorised by other passages in the Quran and hadiths for certain crimes (extramarital sex, adultery), and are employed by some as justification for extra-legal punitive action also known as "honour crimes" (which in fact are dishonourable crimes):

"Nor come nigh to adultery: for it is a shameful (deed) *and an evil, opening the road* (to other evils) *"* (Quran, 17:32).

- RAPE:

Rape is punishable by death in sharia law. However, many rape cases are settled out of court, with the relatives taking justice into their own hands. In some cases, rapists pay monetary compensation (jirah), and in other cases they pay diyya (compensation) for injuries inflicted.

That said, sharia makes it very hard for a woman who is the victim of rape to prove it, since she should produce four witnesses to such a crime, which is nearly impossible... consequently, rapists are seldom prosecuted and go unpunished, since there is virtual impunity for such a crime.

But the most horrible thing here for Muslim women is not impunity for their rapists, but rather a much worse injustice, which is that in most cases, the *victim* herself is punished (she gets several hundred lashes) and even sentenced to death through hanging!? So what we witness here with utter shock, horror, and disbelief is the sheer absurdity of a double injustice. First, the victim suffers the horrific act of rape; and second, instead of getting justice by seeing the rapist prosecuted, the victim *herself* is punished by being whipped then hanged. Why—we ask with horror—is the victim punished? Sharia and her relatives have an *easy answer*: because *she* has thus brought "shame" to the family which no longer recognises her and disavows her!!

- THEFT:

Traditionally, and in accordance with the Quran and several hadiths, theft is punished by imprisonment or, worse, amputation of hands. It is still a common practice today in Saudi Arabia and other Muslim countries. The Quran says:

> *"Cut off the hands of thieves, whether they are male or female, as punishment for what they have done – a deterrent from God: God is almighty and wise. But if anyone repents after his wrongdoing and makes amends, God will accept his repentance: God is most forgiving and merciful"* (Quran, 5:38)

So, repentance is acceptable only *after* mutilation. Muhammad himself says that even if his own daughter, Fatima, were to steal and then intercede that her hand should not be cut off, he would still have to cut it off (*Bukhari*, Punishments, no. 6788).

However, the sharia has several requirements for the amputation of hands, which are the following:

- There must have been criminal intent to take private (not common) property.

- The theft must not have been the product of hunger, necessity, or duress.

- The goods stolen must: be over a minimum value, not haraam (forbidden), and not owned by the thief's family.

- Goods must have been taken from custody (not from a public place).
- There must be reliable witnesses.

According to Islamic law, all of the above conditions must be met under the scrutiny of judicial authority in order to go ahead with the amputation.

Islam, to this day (as no one has dared initiate any reform), still commands that robbers be crucified or mutilated. The Quran says:

*"Those who wage war against God and His Messenger and strive to spread corruption in the land should be punished by death, **crucifixion**, the amputation of an alternate hand and foot or banishment from the land"* (Quran, 5:33).

The Hadith gives another instance for the amputation punishment:

"Narrated Anas: some people . . . came to the Prophet and embraced Islam. They turned renegades (reverted from Islam) *and killed the shepherd of the camels and took the camels away. The Prophet ordered that their hands and legs be cut off and their eyes should be branded with heated pieces of iron, and that their cut hands and legs should not be cauterised, till they died"* (*Bukhari*, Punishments, no. 6802).

In some cases, crucifixion does not even need a murder before it is imposed. This is the case of the Armenian genocide, where Turkish soldiers used to force Armenian women to line up naked, holding their babies, only to be crucified until death. History hardly recollects this horrible holocaust in its annals because politics seems to be more important than the plain truth and common decency. Armenians to this day decry the unacceptable and outrageous silence of the international community towards this unpunished genocide. Perhaps a more just world in the future will condemn such a great crime against humanity.

- LEAVING ISLAM/APOSTASY:

According to sharia, there is simply no way to opt out of the Muslim faith, whether to convert to another religion or to become non-religious (agnostic, secular, or atheist). This act is strictly forbidden to any Muslim and it is called "apostasy," a grave accusation that is equated with treason by Muslim theology and which thus entails death. Indeed, the Quran considers that "he who leaves (his religion) is killed" ("al-Murtadd yuqtal"), as his impure, treacherous blood becomes "halaal" ("permitted," even desired, we might add). Non-Muslims, however, are allowed and encouraged - when not forced - to convert to Islam.

The accusation of apostasy is also commonly, and conveniently, used against all "enemies of God" (enemies of the Islamic State), namely those brave, enlightened, moderate Muslims,- or secularists, agnostics, and atheists, who dare to make any non-conventional, progressive, reformist interpretations or criticism of the Quran. The famous author Salman Rushdie is one example of such lethal persecution made "legal" by a fatwa which called for the assassination of the author, issued in 1989 by Iran's supreme leader Ayatollah Khomeini following the publication of Rushdie's book

Satanic Verses. More recent random and arbitrary accusations of apostasy are made by Daesh, Al Nosra, Ahrar Al Sham and other extremist groups in Syria, and the punishments for such a crime are carried out in public, including crucifixion, burning, beheading, mutilation.

Those who call for the reformation of Islam also suffer the same persecution and death threats. The accusation of apostasy can also be levelled against any critic of clerical rule.

Thus, according to the Quran, the Hadith, sharia, and later legal rulings, any apostate is supposed to be killed. As typical examples (among many others), suras (verses) 9:11–12; 2:217, 9:73–74, 88:21, 5;54, 9:66 of the Quran refer to apostates and how they should be killed, or at least seem to support the death sentence for apostates. As for the hadiths, the most typical examples of death sentences for apostates are the following:

> *"The Prophet said, 'If somebody* [a Muslim] *discards his religion, kill him' "* (*Bukhari*, 52:260).

> *'*[In the words of] *Allah's Apostle, 'Whoever changed his Islamic religion, then kill him' "* (*Bukhari*, 84:57).

Other verses of the *Hadiths* calling for the execution of "apostates" are *Bukhari,* 83:37; 89:271; 84:58; 84:64–65; 11:626; *Abu Dawud,* 4346; *al-Muwatta* of Imam *Malik,* (36.18.15): *"The Messenger of Allah said, 'If someone changes his religion - then strike off his head' "* and many others.

- FOOD:

Islamic law, being comprehensive and covering every aspect of life, also has strict instructions concerning food that a Muslim should follow or risk burning in hell. Despite the fact that sharia does not provide a comprehensive list of "pure" foods, it does however prohibit: swine, blood, the meat of already dead animals and animals which are not slaughtered halal, slaughtered according to the prescribed manner of tazkiyah (cleansing), which involves cutting the throat of the animal and draining the blood.

- LIQUOR AND GAMBLING:

As for liquor and gambling, they are strictly prohibited in the Quran as well as the sharia which follows Islam's holy book. Prophet Muhammad is reported to have said: *"He who plays with dice is like the one who handles the flesh and blood of swine"* (reported by Abd-Allah ibn Amr, who claimed that Muhammad prohibited all games of chance and card playing that caused financial gain or loss).

The punishment for these two "crimes" or sins which are "haram" (religiously illegal and reprehensible) is very cruel and degrading; indeed, Islam commands that drinkers and gamblers be whipped. This is a common practice in some Islamic societies where drinkers and gamblers are flogged and caned in front of a mosque or in a public square (adding humiliation to injury). The Quran prohibits alcohol and gambling in sura 5:90–91:

> *"O you who believe! Intoxicants* [all kinds of alcoholic drinks] *and gambling... are an abomination of Shaitan's* (Satan) *handiwork. So avoid* (strictly all) *that* (abomination) *in order that you may be successful* (*Quran*, 5:90). *Shaitan* (Satan) *wants only to excite enmity and hatred between you with intoxicants* (alcoholic drinks)

and gambling, and hinder you from the remembrance of Allah and from as-Salaat (the prayer). *So, will you not then abstain?"* (Quran, 5:91).

The Quran does not expressly prescribe the punishment of flogging, but the Hadith clearly does, and so does the sharia: a "criminal" (a drinker) was brought to Muhammad who became angry: *"The Prophet felt it hard* [was angry] *and ordered all those who were present in the house, to beat him* [the drinker was dragged before Muhammad]*"* (*Bukhari,* Punishments, nos. 6774–6775).

This game prohibition has frightened most pious Muslims to this day who thus recoil from even playing Monopoly, or any other non-monetary games for fear of burning in hell.

- FATWAS: "DIVINE" DECREES OF OPPRESSION

Fatwas (or religious edicts) in the Islamic faith are juristic rulings concerning Islamic law issued by an Islamic scholar or cleric. While they are supposed to facilitate everyday life, and every aspect of life, for Muslims faced with the challenges of modernity, such as the customs of marriage, financial affairs, or moral questions. Another example is how to pray when you're on an airplane, or is one allowed to smoke or play football. Their overuse and abuse by radical or twisted clerics has led to all kinds of abominations, all in the name of the Almighty Allah.

Indeed, the scriptures have been, and are being, used and abused by Islamists to issue death sentences or justify barbaric acts against infidels or enemies of God, especially since the rise of radical Islam in the two previous decades. These edicts are issued when something is considered haraam (forbidden, blasphemous) and are tantamount to an Islamic death sentence.

Stoning, beheading, amputation, human rights violations, oppression of women, all these crimes have been given divine sanction simply by being called fatwas. Fatwas have thus become instruments of oppression at the hands of radical clerics or terrorists. But, critics of Islam say, these fatwas don't come from the void! They *are* based on Islamic scriptures, and so one cannot blame the edicts only, but also the source whence they sprang.

To go back to the nature and authority of fatwas, in Sunni Islam a fatwa is non-binding, whereas in Shia Islam it could be considered by an individual as binding, depending on his or her relation to the scholar. The person who issues a fatwa is a Muslim scholar/cleric or mufti, which means an issuer of fatwas. Also, fatwas in their greatest majority deal with issues that concern any aspect of individual life, ranging from social norms, religion, to war, peace, jihad, and politics.

To this day, thousands upon thousands of fatwas have been issued, most of them covering issues concerning ordinary Muslims, whereas the more controversial fatwas cover war, jihad, and dhimmis (and are usually issued by extremist preachers) and thus get wide media coverage because of their political nature.

However, one's conscience alone dictates that merely citing Allah does not make a law just or humane!

It must be said that a fatwa, while inspired by and based on Islamic teachings and scriptures, does not always gain universal acceptance, since its interpretation may vary according to different scholars and to the different schools of thought within the Muslim faith. Consequently, a great number of fatwas are contradictory and Muslims have to decide for themselves which cleric's edict to follow.

Some fatwas are absolutely ludicrous and even grotesque: to name but a few typical examples is the latest fatwa that allows a Muslim husband to have sex with his dead wife; the fatwa forbidding Muslim women to eat bananas or cucumbers (because of their phallic shape) unless their husbands cut them into pieces for them. Another recent fatwa issued by a Pakistani cleric as part of the violent protest among clerics against Pakistani law's banning of wife beating, allows a man to "lightly" beat his wife (not breaking her bones, in accordance with the Quran). And, last but not least, the fatwa issued by a Saudi cleric which permits a starving Muslim to *eat* his wife!! And the fatwa forbidding the Barbie doll, for it "arouses men."

One must really have a sick imagination and perverted motives to come up with such farcical fatwas. The latest ridiculous fatwa has been called a "catwa." It was issued by a Saudi cleric and it bans Muslims from taking selfies with cats.

And, of course, we have the fatwas blessing and exhorting violence and murder; as one example among many, Dr. Ali Gomaa, the Grand Mufti of Egypt (quoted in the Egyptian *Al Ahram* daily dated 4/7/2008): *"Muslims must kill non-believers wherever they are, unless they convert to Islam."* And then Muslims are surprised when people don't believe them when they say that theirs is a "religion of peace," critics rightfully say.

- PRAYER:

Muslims are obliged to pray five times a day, prayer being one of the five pillars of Islam, hence it's compulsory. But, as hard as these five prayers are difficult to perform (including a prayer in the middle of the night and one at dawn), their number was supposed to be much higher, according to Prophet Muhammad who, according to Islamic literature, had to plead with Allah to reduce the initial Almighty quota of *fifty* prayers!! :

> *"Then fifty prayers were enjoined on me. I descended till I met Moses who asked me, 'What have you done?' I said, 'Fifty prayers have been enjoined on me.' He said, 'I know the people better than you, because I had the hardest experience to bring Bani Israel [Sons of Israel] to obedience. Your followers cannot put up with such obligation. So, return to your Lord and request Him (to reduce the number of prayers.' I returned and requested Allah (for reduction) and He made it forty."*

But much more haggling had to be done with Allah to reduce the prayers to five. And so, Muhammad said:

> *"I returned and (met Moses) and had a similar discussion, and then returned again to Allah for reduction and He made it thirty, then twenty, then ten, and then I came to Moses who repeated the same advice. Ultimately Allah reduced it to five. When I came to Moses again, he said, 'What have you done?' I said, 'Allah has made it five only.' He repeated the same advice but I said that I surrendered (to Allah's Final Order)'" Allah's Apostle was addressed by Allah, "I have decreed My Obligation and have reduced the burden on My slaves, and I shall reward a single good deed as if it were ten good deeds."*

FAILED ATTEMPTS AT MODERNISING SHARIA

Muslim countries ruled (totally or partially) by sharia law have to this day remained unable *and* unwilling to reform or modernise its archaic code of harsh sanctions and punishments to make it compatible with modernity and its cherished values of human rights, diversity, democracy, and tolerance, since the first value and virtue of any civilisation worthy of that name is its ethical, humane character which respects and protects human freedom and dignity.

That being said, there *is* great variety in the interpretation and implementation of Islamic law in Muslim societies today. So-called liberal movements (inasmuch as that term could be applied) within Islam have unsuccessfully called for more leniency and flexibility in interpreting and applying sharia to make it more compatible with modernity; in other words, sharia with a human face, which is an oxymoron by all means. Some countries like Saudi Arabia have no constitution and legal code and fully apply Islamic law; others like Pakistan and Iran have constitutions which are nonetheless in total accordance with sharia. Afghanistan and Sudan also fully apply sharia.

Indonesia, Bangladesh, and Malaysia are relatively more "secular" (again, inasmuch as this term could be used) since they do have civil constitutions and laws but (and that is no minor detail) they do have Islamic provisions in family law. Finally, Turkey, which Atatürk turned into a fully secular, modern state, went back in recent years, and at an alarming rate, with Erdogan's Justice and Freedom Party, to its Islamic Ottoman roots, even though the Islamist party, Erdogan's, now in power has so far not been able to cancel its staunchly secular constitution.

As for the Middle East and North Africa, most states there maintain a dual system of secular courts and religious courts, in which the religious courts mainly regulate marriage and inheritance. Even Lebanon, which is by far the most liberal, multi-confessional and moderate country in the Arab world, also incorporates Islamic law for Muslims in family matters. Under the so-called Arab Spring, the rebels (Islamists) of Syria, Egypt, Tunisia, Libya are trying to overthrow the secular regimes in place and replace them with sharia-based theocratic states. The same goes for Africa where Nigeria, to name but one example, has reintroduced sharia courts in some of its northern states, with harsh punishments for those who break the law.

And, most alarmingly, sharia has expanded to the West and now whole areas inside cities and towns in countries such as Sweden, England, and Belgium, are considered sharia-run zones (by gangs of religious extremists) and no-go zones for the police.

The very rare and very unsuccessful attempts at trying to combine sharia law with modernity and human rights lead us to conclude that Islamic law is incompatible with modernity and its supreme values of human rights, dignity, and freedom.

Now that we've shown what *Sharia* is, let's go deeper into this unbridgeable gap between Islam and the modern world.

- Sharia is incompatible with democracy and human rights:
Serious attempts by enlightened Muslim scholars to modernise Islamic law (sharia) have so far dramatically failed, since they inevitably entail changing, or at least eclipsing, those verses upon which the sharia tenets and regulations are based, i.e. committing the most "blasphemous" act against the

sanctity of the Quran, the "revealed" word of Allah according to Muslims.

Each and every modernising attempt of the sharia was staunchly opposed by the conservative religious establishment, and aborted under the pretext of the sanctity of the Text. And it must me noted here that the sharia, as it is applied today, is used by the Islamic terrorists in their fierce fight against the secular/civil regimes in the Middle East, in a bid to replace them by *Sharia*-based governments or theocracies. And these terrorists go further to challenge the very essence of the Western model and polity. And, unfortunately, the sharia is fuelling their "sacred war" against the West with the necessary religious, intellectual, and psychological weapons; the war being for the sake of Allah, and to restore the glories of The Caliphate. Islamists have always claimed that Islam is the alternative to the Western model in both its versions: capitalism and socialism.

Being a totalitarian kind of "divine rule" allowing no room for any other beliefs than Islam in power, the sharia challenges the very essence of the Western model: Democracy and pluralism.

- Sharia is incompatible with pluralist democracy:

It doesn't take a genius to figure out that *Sharia* is undemocratic - to say the very least - seeing that, even though Islamic law does allow elections to take place and some form of plurality to appear (albeit, significantly, only *within* the Muslim spectrum), still, the socio-political rights and cultural and religious freedoms of non-Muslim minorities and those of women are not only unprotected but also unrecognised. According to the Quran, the non-Muslim believers

(Christians and Jews) are named dhimmis, and under sharia rule they are considered second-class citizens, thus negating another basic tenet of democracy, which is equal citizenship and the equality before the law. The obscurantists go further in their discrimination, they don't even consider dhimmis as human beings; thus, in some countries ruled by sharia, if a citizen runs over a Christian or a dog, the fine is the same... Those who do not espouse Muhammad's message are non-entities. As for women, we have widely shown how they are considered: lower, impure, stupid creatures, and, even worse, sex slaves. As for unbelievers, they don't even have the right to live.

So, it matters not if some Muslim scholars affirm that Islamic law is totally compatible with democracy, as *they* see it, the fact of the matter is that *it simply isn't*. And that is the main reason why Western states ban the implementation of sharia. In fact, the European Court of Human rights declared that "Sharia is incompatible with the fundamental principles of democracy." Furthermore, the archaic law of retaliation (the biblical eye for an eye), which is indeed still taken literally by Muslims after the rest of the world, including the Jews, have forsaken this savage practice, is against the rule of law, another basic principle of the modern polity.

- *Sharia is incompatible with human rights:*

Islamic law is supposed to, and claims to uphold justice, but in truth it is the epitome of injustice, sharia critics say: "Law by definition is supposed to be just, but what if the law itself were unjust and barbaric?" they wonder. The sharia, according to its Muslim and non-Muslim critics alike, is tyrannical and unjust; it infringes on men and women's freedom, dignity, privacy and their most basic human rights.

There is a tremendous difference between universal human rights on the one hand, and Islamic "human rights" on the other, that is, rights for Muslims only - and men only - , and those who strictly follow the sharia. Selective justice is no justice at all.

Several major, predominantly Muslim countries made a covenant in what came to be known as the Cairo Declaration on Human Rights in Islam, as they sought to give a semblance of justification, credibility and respectability to the practice of sharia by giving their own version (the Islamic version) of human rights and by criticising the Universal Declaration of Human Rights (UDHR) for what *they* claimed was its failure to take into account the "cultural and religious context" (i.e. Islamic) of non-Western countries. Iran in particular argued against the UDHR by saying that it was "a secular understanding of the Judeo-Christian tradition," which could not be implemented by Muslims without violating Islamic law; in other words, these Muslim countries themselves acknowledged that their law was incompatible with human rights. Consequently, in 1990, the Organisation of the Islamic Conference (OIC), which represents all Muslim majority nations, adopted the Cairo Declaration on Human Rights in Islam.

Analysts and experts pointed to some notable absences from the Cairo Declaration: provisions for democratic principles, protection of religious freedom, freedom of association and freedom of the press, as well as equality in rights and equal protection under the law. In fact, and typically in Muslim versions of democracy and human rights, article 24 of the Cairo declaration states that "All the rights and freedoms stipulated in this Declaration are subject to the Islamic Sharia." Some analysts went as far as to conclude that, according to Muslims, the concept of human rights, as applied in the European framework, is therefore unnecessary and potentially destructive to Islamic societies.

As we have seen above from the penalties imposed by the sharia, human rights and Islamic law are definitely and irremediably irreconcilable and antagonistic. From flogging to amputation to stoning to death of individuals, mostly carried out in public, these cruel, inhuman punishments are antithetical to anything that even resembles the Western model, indeed any civilised society, for the first and foremost value and virtue of Western civilisation is universal freedom and human rights. And it goes without saying that sharia tenets and principles are also incompatible with the United Nations Universal Declaration of Human Rights, especially with regard to equality of all citizens and non-citizens before the law as well as equality between men and women.

As we have seen above, the Sharia is derived from the Quran and the Hadith; there is no other kind of Islamic law. Sharia law imposes blatant and large inequalities between Muslims and non-Muslims, including Christians and Jews, and between men and women. Moreover, Islam aims to convert people, by the sword, if need be, as it was throughout history, until the whole world embraces the message of Allah's apostle. In this sense, the concept of jihad can be understood as the struggle to make the whole planet Muslim, or at least to create an international caliphate ruled by sharia law.

Sharia clerics say that all their edicts (*Fatwas*), and the sanctions that they entail, derive from the core of the Quran and Hadith; they are the source of Islamic jurisprudence, and hence their legitimacy, according to them. They advance such verses from the Scriptures, again, the word of "Allah The Great Judge," and from the Hadith, the teachings of his messenger, to defend sharia against its religious and secular critics:

"As for the thief, both male and female, cut off their hands. It is the reward of their own deeds, an exemplary punishment from Allah. Allah is mighty, wise" (Quran, 5:38).

"The punishment of those who wage war against Allah and His Messenger, and strive with might and main for mischief through the land is: execution, or crucifixion, or the cutting off of hands and feet from opposite sides, or exile from the land: that is their disgrace in this world, and a heavy punishment is theirs in the Hereafter" (Quran, 5:33).

"The fornicatress and the fornicator, flog each of them with a hundred stripes. Let not pity withhold you in their case, in a punishment prescribed by Allah, if you believe in Allah and the Last Day. And let a party of the believers witness their punishment" (Quran, *Hilali* and *Khan*, 24:2).

"And when he [Prophet Muhammad] *had given command over her and she was put in a hole up to her breast, he ordered the people to stone her. Khalid bin al-Walid came forward with a stone which he threw at her head, and when the blood spurted on his face he cursed her"* (*Muslim*, no. 4206).

(The prophet then prayed over her and buried her !?)

Of course, there are many other verses that we could cite but the above are quite typical. One might also add *Bukhari*'s verses on Punishments, nos. 6831 and 6833.

* Sharia forbids freedom of belief and expression:

In countries that are ruled by the *Sharia,* writers, thinkers, poets, artists, activists... are all deprived of their freedom of expression and oftentimes accused of heresy, apostasy or blasphemy if they dare question (or even worse, criticise) any part of the Quran or call for its reinterpretation or reform. Moreover, under Islamic law, people are forbidden to drink, play music, gamble, smoke, read literature, poetry, or philosophy, or read about art and sexuality. The Islamic State, Daesh, has imposed such a cultural nightmare (I call the Islamic State a cultural black hole) in its self-proclaimed capital *Raqqa,* which by all accounts is a living hell, even by Islamic standards and according to Muslims themselves.

* Sharia and (the lack of) women's rights:

We have already seen the place of woman in the Quran, "Allah's Book," and in the Hadith, the teachings of "Allah's Messenger," as well as her dismal status demeaned to that of a sex slave by the jihadis, "Allah's most faithful warriors." But from a legal perspective, we shall remind the reader of some of these typically misogynistic sharia regulations:

Islam allows a husband to hit his wife in case the husband merely *suspects* highhandedness in her. It is useful in this context to repeat what the Quran says:

"If you fear highhandedness from your wives, remind them [of the teaching of God], *then ignore them when you go to bed,* ***then hit them***" (Quran, 4:34).

The legal status of woman according to sharia can thus be summarised by the following, as seen earlier:

- As regards testimony in the court of law and inheritance, a woman is counted as half a man's testimony.

- As regards inheritance, a daughter's inheritance is half that of her brother's.

- As regards marriage and divorce, the woman's position in Islamic law is far less advantageous than that of the man, since polygamy is permitted (up to four wives are allowed for each man), and since a marriage can be terminated by the husband and simply by pronouncing the word "divorced" (taleq) three times. Sometimes this practice takes grotesque forms. In 2003, a Malaysian court ruled that, under sharia law, a man may divorce his wife via text messaging as long as the message is clear and unequivocal.

- Another discriminatory rule is that a Muslim woman is not allowed to marry a non-Muslim whereas Muslim men are allowed to marry non-Muslims. Worse, a woman, in some backward and tribal Muslim communities, does not have the right to choose her husband (her family usually does that *for* her). And, the worst thing is that the despicable crime of paedophilia is *in principle* permitted since the legal age for a "woman" to marry is as low as *six* years!

- As regards clothing and appearance under sharia, a woman is obliged to cover herself from head to toe, including the face, by wearing the burqa or the niqab, according to the various "customs" in Islamic countries. In more "liberal" Islamic countries like Iran (everything is relative), a woman can show a part of her face by wearing the tchador or simply the hijab and a dress covering her pants.

Once again, in order to protect so-called morality, sharia dictates that women cannot be in contact with men to whom they are not related without the presence of some male relative. The segregation of sexes makes it impossible for women to leave their houses. Islamic law in this way totally prevents women from taking part in society and keeps them locked up, isolated and unable to take part in society and to reach their potential as free and productive citizens.

- As regards violence against women (whether domestic or social), and as already mentioned above, a husband has the right to hit his wife and oblige her to have sex with him, as part of her marital duties.

- As regards rape (as explained earlier), a woman must secure the testimony from four direct witnesses, the fact which makes it virtually impossible to prosecute rapists. And, to make matters worse, testimony from women is given only half the weight of men, and testimony from non-Muslims may be dismissed altogether...

To sum up, the sharia commits a blatant inequality between the sons and daughters of Allah: a Muslim woman has barely any rights and is considered her husband's "property" (hurrma) with which he can do as he pleases.

* Sharia and (the lack of) rights of non-Muslims:

Based on Quranic verses and other Islamic scriptures and traditions, *Sharia* distinguishes between Muslims, followers of other monotheistic religions, and Pagans or people belonging to other polytheistic religions. As monotheists, Jews and Christians have traditionally been considered by Muslims as "People of The Book" and allowed as dhimmis to practice their faith, provided they pay a tax. Atheists, pagans and people of other faiths like Buddhists and Hindus do not have that special status; they are considered non-entities and consequently they are not afforded the rights and protections of monotheists, according to sharia. In fact, they have no rights whatsoever and should either be eliminated or convert to Islam.

As a result of their being considered non-beings by *Sharia,* millions of Hindus and Buddhists were persecuted and murdered by zealots throughout Islamic history (and continue to be so until today) in majority Muslim countries.

In any case, and in practice, even Christians and Jews were not spared and still aren't today in many parts of the Islamic world: indeed, ISIL (Daesh), when forcing Christians and Yazidis in Iraq and Syria to choose between forcibly converting to Islam or being murdered, is not even practising the rules of the sharia which allows them to survive provided they pay the tax...

The undeniable fact is that sharia practices unabashed and blatant discrimination against non-Muslims. Thus, in addition to the imposition of Islamic morality on non-Muslims, Islamic law dictates that there should *not* be equality between Muslims and non-Muslims (in flagrant violation of the Human Rights Charter). Under sharia, only Muslims can be full citizens of a Muslim state. Thus, non-Muslims in majority Muslim states have limited rights and cannot participate in public life or hold positions of authority over Muslims. Crimes against Muslims are often punished more severely than crimes against others. In many countries, the testimony of a non-Muslim in court is not equal to that of a Muslim. dhimmis are second-class citizens at best...

Freedom of religion does not just mean the freedom to hold a faith but also the freedom to change one's religion or belief or the freedom to hold *no* faith, the freedom to be an Atheist. No such freedom exists under sharia: the ultimate crime of apostasy is when a Muslim abandons his or her faith, and thus is left to face the most ruthless violence, often being sentenced to death. Again, this discrimination is clearly contrary to freedom of belief and religion and the principle that religion should be a private affair of the individual.

* *Homosexuality:*

Under sharia, homosexuality is prohibited and often punishable by death. Many Islamic verses are clear in their denunciation of homosexual activity; thus, the Hadith shows Muhammad's punishment of homosexuals:

> *"If you find anyone doing as Lot's people* [homosexuals] *did, kill the one who does it, and the one to whom it is done"* (*Dawud*, no. 4447).

> *"Ali had two people* [homosexuals] *burned and Abu Bakr had **a wall thrown down on them**"* (*Mishkat*, vol. 1, p. 765, Prescribed Punishments).

This again contradicts gay rights, and LGBT rights in general, which are protected nowadays in the West under the banner of human rights and freedoms, including freedom of sexual orientation.

Sharia: Islamic (in)justice

As we can clearly see from what we have shown above, the concept of justice embodied in sharia is different from that of secular Western law and universal standards and values of human rights. In fact, according to many, sharia law is totally incompatible with modernity, indeed it represents its very antithesis, as it violates all basic and universal human rights: women's civil rights and individual freedom, freedom of expression, freedom of religion and belief, and freedom *from* religion for those who choose not to believe.

Moreover, sharia and pluralism belong in two different, indeed antagonistic, worlds. A true democracy is pluralistic in nature, i.e. it allows all communities to live their beliefs and express them in society, and in politics as well. Furthermore, democracy is based on the principles of equality of citizenship and gender equality. All this renders sharia and pluralist democracy irreconcilable.

Sharia could only fit majoritarian democracy where Muslims are the majority, as is the case with today's Turkey and Iran. But sharia and pluralistic, true, representative democracy remain alien to each other.

In addition to this, sharia and parliamentary democracy as conceived in the West are also incompatible. Islamic law adopts the shura concept, which is mainly of advisory nature; it is a kind of representative council (mainly tribal), as it were, advising the Muslim ruler on the state affairs. And there is no parliament to legislate and hold the ruler, or the government, accountable.

PART TWO

ISLAM: RELIGION OF MERCY?
THE OTHER SIDE OF ISLAM

"Let there be no compulsion in religion...
If anyone slew a person unjustly, it would be as if he slew
the whole of mankind"

- Quran, 2:256, 5:32

CHAPTER EIGHT

"POSITIVE" ISLAM:
THE FORGOTTEN VERSES

"Neglected, the sacred verses rust."

- LORD BUDDHA

After having read everything that has been said about Islam above, one wonders (or doesn't even want to) whether it makes any sense seeing any "other side" to Islam—that is, if there is such a side, and if so, why has it been hidden for all these centuries? With such negative aspects that characterise the religion of Muhammad, critics say, one does not need or want to know more.

Indeed, anyone who reads the numerous verses that have been cited throughout this book, verses filled with wrath, hatred, resentment, violence, lust, misogyny, will most certainly have a very negative impression of Islam as being a religion of sex and merciless violence. Islamists in particular have made sure we only remember these verses that they use and abuse in order to kill, maim, and exploit in the name of Allah. However, and yes, it is hard to believe based on the aforementioned verses, this is but one side of the coin, the dark side of Islam. And yes, there is a bright side, or at least a brighter side to this religion that has been almost totally ignored, neglected, willingly or unwillingly, consciously or unconsciously, by Muslims, moderates and extremists alike, whose majority probably isn't even aware of the existence of such verses, or, in the case of Islamic terrorists, couldn't care less about them.

This positive Islam, yes, there is such a thing, if we want to be fair and objective and give credit and justice where credit and justice are due, is the "religion of peace" that moderate followers of that religion refer to when they defend their faith from charges of being a religion of war and intolerance, arguing that Islam has been "hijacked" by extremists who abuse and misuse its verses to justify their evil deeds. The peace-loving Muslims base their affirmation on the few but existing verses in the Quran relating to mercy, compassion, peace, and tolerance.

Yes, the verses that are about to be mentioned in this chapter may now seem totally irrelevant to the reader, shocked and appalled by the verses of hate and violence so characteristic of the Islam of the Islamists, but the following verses are indeed what I have called the forgotten verses of positive Islam, the other side of Islam, the light at the end of the long and dark tunnel. The relief that comes as a result of reading the verses below will come too late to change one's view of Islam, but it is there, and gives hope to those Muslims who still care to save their religion from its mad extremists.

So, after having read the Quran's verses of war, violence, and punishment, critics of Islam wonder how could the same book which preaches the most barbaric practices (as they rightfully say), be it against people of other faiths, or against women, apostates, and so forth, how could this book also contain verses of mercy, compassion and forgiveness? And yet it does, and herein lie both its mystery and its biggest flaw, but perhaps also its last and only hope. In view of how the Quran is nowadays being used by the Islamists to justify the most horrible crimes and barbaric atrocities humanity has ever witnessed in history, could Islam be saved from the clutches of fanatic terrorists by highlighting its brighter side? And could the other negative side be simply discarded or eclipsed? This will be our challenge in the coming chapter, but for now let us thus cross to the other side of Islam and let us simply shed light on the lighter side of Muhammad's religion.

To counterbalance the hundreds of verses of violence and intolerance in the Quran, there are dozens of peaceful verses in Islam's holy book which, although they take up a relatively lesser space in Allah's book, and remain overshadowed and discarded by Muslim fanatics and terrorists for the sake of other verses, they nonetheless cannot be ignored or eclipsed. They remain the very essence of Islam as a religion of peace and tolerance, as the moderate Muslims continue to affirm and confirm. Indeed, these peaceful verses, which have been all but forgotten or neglected by Muslims themselves, are quite unknown to non-Muslims who would probably scoff at the very idea of the existence of such verses, given what the fanatic extremists have done in the name of their religion.

These forgotten verses, as I call them, are rarely cited, let alone heeded by the most loyal and fiercest followers of Islam, the Islamist fanatics. Why? In a weird and twisted sense, they are less appealing to them instead of being more appealing, as with other religions which focus on love and compassion. Perhaps words like jihad seem to draw more attention and admiration among the zealots who need a cause to fight for.

The Islamist jihadis use the book, not to pray, but to rally for war. The Quran is their religious manifesto: "Muslims of the world unite to combat the enemies of God, and to establish his government on earth, the Caliphate, and to make his law fulfilled, the sharia."

In any case, as the great Buddha said, *"Neglected, the sacred verses rust."* What good are these verses if they are not cited, heeded, and practiced? Still, cited or not, heeded or not, practised or not, these verses of peace, tolerance, mercy, and compassion do exist right there in the Quran, making strange bedfellows with the verses of violence, hatred, and intolerance.

Let us take the reader on an exclusive journey into the other side of Islam, alas nowadays silenced. Some Muslim scholars, though certainly and unfortunately not the majority, do cite and appreciate these peaceful verses. Thus, the full picture of Islam and the Quran, say Khouj and Nyang, is captured by chapter 5, verse 32 of Islam's holy book:

"If anyone slew a person - unless it be for murder or spreading mischief in the land - it would be as if he slew the whole of mankind. And if anyone saved a life, it would be as if he saved the life of the whole mankind."

How could the same book preach the beautiful verse above and at the same time the most horrific verses of violence, death, destruction, beheading, stoning to death that we have cited throughout this book? The first question which comes to the mind of any thinking being, and which, alas, ultimately leads to his death, if uttered out loud, is the following: was the Quran perverted? And the answer is very swift: if so, it is *not* (or no longer) the word of God. If not, this *cannot* be the word of God! Both ways, Islam loses its divine justification and legitimacy.

The second question that is allowed by some moderate Muslim clerics is: are the Quran's verses misinterpreted or misused? But a quick answer eliminates this question, for most verses, indeed, almost all, are very clear with instructions to chop off the heads and limbs of unbelievers and "sleep with as many women as you want" etc.

Here, as objective readers and academic scholars, we are faced with two hypotheses: either the Quran was perverted, and many verses have been manipulatively inserted into the original text to serve power and dominion, rather than religiosity and human redemption, and the Quran that we now hold in our hands is not the true one; or the original text carries a duality that touches the frontier of contradiction, as several verses contradict each other, and are mutually exclusive, as if we have *two books* merged in one, for reasons beyond understanding, unless one admits the historical context of the message, in such a way that we have a Quran, or verses, for a certain time and not for every time.

Before issuing our verdict or judgment on which of the two hypotheses is more plausible, let us invite the reader to wander into uncharted territory, mainly the largely unknown, gentler, merciful side of Islam.

- *Mercy, compassion and forgiveness in Islam*

In the Muslim tradition, foremost among God's qualities are his mercy and compassion or, in the Arabic language, rahman ("compassionate") and rahim ("merciful"). Each of the 114 chapters of the Quran, with one exception, begins with the verse, *Bism-i-llah a-Rahman-i-Rahim* (*"In the name of God the Merciful, the Compassionate"*).

The Arabic word for mercy is rahmah. This word is scattered throughout the Quran as one of God's main attributes. Practising Muslims begin each prayer and each significant action by invoking Allah "the Merciful and Compassionate" through reciting the familiar Islamic mantra Bism-i-llah a-Rahman-i-Rahim.

According to the Quran, mercy is supposed to be a Muslim characteristic which encompasses all aspects of life, including warfare. This may seem very strange to the reader, after becoming acquainted with the very brutal verses of violence and intolerance in the biggest part of this book, but this is nonetheless true: mercy is *also* a characteristic of Islam's holy book, making very strange bedfellows with other words like "slaughter," "whip," "behead," "stone." Yes, Islamic scriptures *also* urge compassion towards captives as well as towards widows, orphans and the poor. Indeed, zakat, a toll tax to help the poor and needy, is obligatory upon all Muslims (Quran, 9:60).

One of the practical purposes of fasting or sawm during the month of Ramadan is to help one empathise with the hunger pangs of those less fortunate, to enhance sensitivity to the suffering of others and develop compassion for the poor and destitute, which is hardly the case in the way that this holy month is lived by most Muslims with their succulent and opulent festivities, without taking real care of the needy.

Be that as it may - and however strange it might seem after reading all the verses of violence throughout this book - Prophet Muhammad is supposed to be the *"Mercy of the World"* (Quran, 21:107); and one of his sayings informs the faithful that, *"God is more loving and kinder than a mother to her dear child."* Yes, the Quran said that; the same book that exhorted Muslims to chop off the heads of infidels. Incredible but true.

The purpose of this book is to analyse the religion which is used and abused by the terrorists to justify the most horrific crimes; but we should show the total picture of Islam, in order to be fair and objective, and in order to analyse how and why this discrepancy between verses is so characteristic of the Quran, which is holy to over 1.5 billion people around the globe. By showing the totality of Islam, we strive to highlight both sides of this religion and let the reader decide for himself what he thinks of it and whether the murderers are justified in quoting their holy book or whether they are abusing its verses and only focusing on the bad ones.

To go back to the question of mercy in the Quran, we quote the following verses:

"We sent thee not but as a mercy for all creatures" (Quran, 21:107).

"Say,' O My servants who have transgressed against your own souls: do not despair of God's mercy, for God forgives all sins. It is He who is the Forgiving, the Merciful' " (Quran, 39:53).

"He is God, other than whom there is no deity, Knower of the unseen and the witnessed. He is the Most-Merciful, the Dispenser of Mercy" (Quran, 59:22).

Allah is thus the *"Dispenser of Mercy,"* and his prophet also described himself as *"Ar Rahmatu al mozjah"* and *"Al Neemat al Mohadat,"* the mercy presented by Allah to mankind.

In the Islamic lexicon, ar-rahman and al-raheem are the characteristics of Allah. both are derived from the noun rahmah, which, as said above, means "mercy," "compassion," and "loving tenderness." *Ar-Rahman* describes *Allah's* nature of being All-Merciful, while *ar-Raheem* describes His acts of mercy dispensed to His creation, a subtle difference, but one which shows His all-encompassing mercy:

"Say, 'Call upon God or call upon the Most-Merciful (ar-Rahman), whichever name you call – to Him belong the most Beautiful Names....' " (Quran, 17:110).

In fact, these two names are some of the most frequently used names of God in the Quran: *ar-Rahman* is used 57 times, while *al-Raheem* is used twice as much (114 times).

By now the reader is flabbergasted upon reading these verses of mercy and kindness. Gone is all the wrath, violence, intolerance, incitement to slaughter and maim. This is the other side of the religion of Muhammad; the side which speaks of loving kindness. The Prophet said:

"Indeed, God is Kind, and loves kindness. He grants with kindness what He does not grant with harshness" (*Saheeh Muslim*).

Both mercy and compassion are also divine attributes signifying *Allah's* relationship with creation; in a prayer which Muslims recite at least 17 times a day, they start by saying:

"In the Name of God, the Most Merciful, the Dispenser of Mercy. Praise be to God, the Lord of All the Worlds; the Most Merciful, the Dispenser of Mercy." (Quran, 1:1–3).

And *Allah* the All-merciful responds to such powerful words by saying:

"When the servant says: 'Praise be to God, the Lord of All the Worlds,' I (God) say: 'My servant has praised Me.' When he says: 'the Most Merciful, the Dispenser of Mercy,' I (God) say: 'My servant has extolled Me' " (Saheeh Muslim).

As incredible as it may seem, this is *also* the Quran, the lesser known, forgotten verses of the holy book of Islam.

Allah's mercy is infinite and includes all existence:

"Say: 'Limitless is your Lord in His mercy... ' " (Quran, 6:147).

" . . . but My mercy encompasses all things . . . " (Quran, 7:156).

Creation itself is an expression of God's mercy:

"Behold, then, (O man,) these signs of God's mercy - how He gives life to the earth after it had been lifeless! " (Quran, 30:50).

Mercy is Allah's gift to mankind:

"And (thus, O Prophet) We have sent you as [an evidence of Our] mercy towards all the worlds" (Quran, 21:107).

Just as Jesus was God's mercy to people:

"And that We may make him a symbol unto mankind and an act of mercy from Us" (Quran, 19:21).

The Prophet said with tears in his eyes upon hearing the news of his son's death:

"This is compassion God has placed in the hearts of His servants. Of all His slaves, God only has mercy on the compassionate" (Saheeh Al-Bukhari).

According to the Messenger of God, the merciful will be shown mercy:

"God will not have mercy on one who is not compassionate towards people" (Saheeh Al-Bukhari).

"The Merciful shows mercy to those merciful. Have mercy to those on earth, and the One above the heavens will have mercy upon you" (At-Tirmidhi).

One cannot but contrast these verses of mercy and compassion with the verses promoting the most brutal violence. The reader is left with more questions than answers upon reading these virtually unknown verses of the religion of Muhammad.

God's mercy, the Quran says, displayed itself in the *Torah* of Moses:

". . . In the writing whereof there was guidance and mercy for all who stood in awe of their Lord" (Quran, 7:154).

And the faithful must revere and obey the revelation of the Quran bestowed on mankind to benefit from *Allah's* boundless mercy and compassion:

"This [revelation] *is a means of insight from your Lord, and to provide guidance and, mercy unto people who will believe"* (Quran, 7:203).

"And this [Quran] *is a Book which We have bestowed from on high, a blessed one: follow it, then, and be conscious*

of God, so that you might be graced with His mercy" (Quran, 6:155).

"Hence, when the Quran is recited, listen to it, and listen in silence, so that you might be graced with [God's] *mercy"* (Quran, 7:204).

"Hence, (O believers!) *be constant in prayer, and render the purifying dues, and obey the Messenger, so that you might be graced with God's mercy"* (Quran, 24:56).

"Affliction has befallen me: but You are the most merciful of the merciful! " (Quran, 21:83).

"O our Lord!, let not our hearts swerve from the truth after You have guided us; and bestow on us the gift of Your mercy: verily, You are the [true] *Giver of Gifts"* (Quran, 3:8).

"O my Lord!, Bestow Your mercy upon them [the parents], *even as they brought me when I was a child! "* (Quran, 17:24)

However, and that is a significant difference with (and departure from) Christianity, Allah's mercy is exclusively reserved for the faithful alone (the Muslims) in this life and on Judgment Day:

"Muhammad is the messenger of Allah. And those with him are hard against the disbelievers and merciful among themselves (Quran, 48:29).

"With My chastisement do I afflict whom I will - but My Mercy overspreads everything: and so I shall confer

it on those who fear Me and spend in charity, and who
believe in Our messages - those who shall follow the [last]
Messenger, the unlettered Prophet whom they find described
in the Torah that is with them, and in the Gospel."
(Quran, 7:156–157).

And here, one may legitimately ask: how could God's
mercy be "without limits," whilst being exclusive for
Muslims?

Be that as it may, the Prophet thus describes *Allah's*
bestowal of mercy on his "slaves" (not sons!):

"God created a hundred portions of mercy. He placed
one portion between His creation due to which they have
compassion on each other. God has stored the remaining
ninety-nine portions for Judgment Day to grace His slaves"
(*Saheeh Al-Bukhari, Saheeh Muslim, Al-Tirmidhi,* and
others).

Another sign of God's mercy is, *"If a believer were to know*
what punishment God has stored, he will despair and not a single
one will anticipate making it to Paradise. If an unbeliever were to
know the abounding mercy of God, not a single one will despair
to make it to Paradise. " (*Saheeh Al-Bukhari, Saheeh Muslim,*
Al-Tirmidhi).

However, the consolation is that divine mercy supersedes
divine anger:

"Indeed, My mercy supersedes my punishment." (Saheeh
Al-Bukhari, Saheeh Muslim).

Since God has created man weak with a propensity to
sin, divine mercy and forgiveness encompasses those who sin

- provided they repent (and enter Islam) - for *Allah* accepts repentance, even if sins are repeated (as the following verses show:

> *"All the children of Adam constantly err..."* (*Al-Tirmidhi, Ibn Majah, Ahmad, Hakim*).

> *"... but the best of those who constantly err are those who constantly repent"* (*Al-Tirmidhi, Ibn Majah, Ahmad, Hakim*).

> *"Say: if you love God, then follow me, God will love you and forgive you your faults, and God is forgiving, merciful"* (*Quran*, 3:31).

> *"Say, 'O My servants, who have transgressed against their souls! Despair not of the Mercy of God: for God forgives all sins, for He is Oft-Forgiving, Most-Merciful'"* (*Quran*, 39:53).

> *"Tell My servants that I am indeed the Oft-Forgiving, Most Merciful"* (*Quran*, 15:49).

> *"...Why do you not, rather, ask God to forgive you your sins, so that you might be graced with His mercy?"* (Quran, 27:46).

> *"... God's mercy is ever near unto the doers of good!"* (Quran, 7:56).

> *"And so, when Our judgment came to pass, by Our mercy We saved Hud and those who shared his faith . . . "* (Quran, 11:58).

"And so, when Our judgment came to pass, by Our mercy We saved Shu'ayb and those who shared his faith . . . " (Quran, 11:94).

"God does wish to turn to you, but the wish of those who follow their lusts is that you should turn away (from Him), - far, far away" (Quran, 4:27).

"Know they not that God accepts repentance from His votaries, and receives their gifts of charity, and that God is indeed He, the Oft-Forgiving, Most-Merciful" (Quran, 9:104).

"For God loves those who turn to Him constantly . . . " (Quran, 2:22).

"Say: Unto whom belongeth whatsoever is in the heavens and the earth? Unto Allah. He hath prescribed for Himself mercy, that He may bring you all together to the Day of Resurrection whereof there is no doubt. Those who ruin their souls will not believe" (Quran, 6:12).

"And when those who believe in Our revelations come unto thee, say: Peace be unto you! Your Lord hath prescribed for Himself mercy, that whoso of you doeth evil through ignorance and repenteth afterward thereof and doeth right (for him) lo! He is Forgiving, Merciful" (Quran, 6: 54).

"If mankind were not to commit sins, God would create other creatures who would commit sins, then He would forgive them, for He is Oft-Forgiving, Most-Merciful" (Al-Tirmidhi, Ibn Majah, Musnad Ahmed).

"God is more delighted with the repentance of His slave when he repents, than any of you would be if (he found his) camel, which he had been riding in a barren desert, after it had escaped from him carrying his food and drink. After he despaired of it, he came to a tree and laid down in its shade. Then while he was despairing of it, the camel came and stood by his side, and he seized its reins and cried out in joy, 'O God, You are my servant and I am your Lord!' – making this mistake (in wording) out of his excessive joy" (Saheeh Muslim).

"God extends His Hand at night to accept the repentance of one who has sinned during the day, and He extends His Hand during the day to accept the repentance of one who has sinned during the night – until [the day comes when] the sun rises from the West [one of the major signs of the Day of Judgment]" *(Saheeh Muslim).*

" . . . and when We appointed for Moses forty nights [on Mount Sinai], *and in his absence you took to worshipping the* [golden] *calf, and thus became evildoers: yet, even after that, We blotted out this your sin, so that you might have cause to be grateful"* (Quran, 2:51–52).

"A man committed a sin, and then said, 'O my Lord, forgive my sin,' so God said, 'My slave has sinned, then he realized that he has a Lord who can forgive sins and can punish him for it.' Then the man repeated the sin, then said, 'O my Lord, forgive my sin.' God said, 'My slave has sinned, then he realized that he has a Lord who can forgive

*sins and can punish him for it.' The man repeated the sin
(the third time), then he said, 'O my Lord, forgive my
sin,' and God said, 'My slave has sinned, then he realized
that he has a Lord who can forgive sins and can punish
him for it. Do what you wish, for I have forgiven you' "
(Saheeh Muslim).*

- "Love" in the Quran

The reader might wonder why the word love above is used
between quotes; that is simply because that word in Islam greatly
differs from love in the Christian sense. It should be understood
as compassion and not love in the unconditional, boundless
sense as is the case with Christianity. Still, it is significant to find
that word uttered in the same book which contains dozens of
verses of violence, wrath and harsh punishments.

The word *love* appears about 45 times in the whole of the
Quran, mostly in expressions such as "in love; love of wealth;
love of life; love of Allah; love of woman; love of self; love of
other believers"; or love in the abstract, in verses such as 2:177;
3:31; 103; 119; 5:54; 9:23; 19:96; 38:32. The following are
some verses of love in Islamic scriptures:

*"And among His signs is this, that He created for you mates
from among yourselves, that you may dwell in peace and
tranquillity with them, and He has put love and mercy
between your* (hearts): *Verily in that are signs for those
who reflect"* (Quran, 30:21).

*"O Humans revere your Guardian Lord, Who created you
from a single person created of like nature its mate, and
from this scattered (like seeds) countless men and women.*

Reverence Allah through Whom you claim your mutual rights" (Quran, 4:1).

"And if a bounty from Allah befell you, he would surely cry, as if there had been no love between you and him: oh, would that I had been with them, then should I have achieved a great success!" (Quran, 4:73).

"Lo! Those who believe and do good works, the Beneficent will appoint for them love" (Quran, 19:96).

"And I endued thee with love from Me that thou mightiest be trained according to My will" (Quran, 20:39).

"The most perfect in faith and amongst believers is he who is best in manners and kindest to his wife" (*Sunnan* of *Abu Dawud*).

"This is which Allah announceth unto His bondmen who believe and do good works. Say (O Muhammad, unto mankind): *'I ask of you no fee therefore, save loving kindness among kinsfolk. And whoso scoreth a good deed We add unto its good for him. Lo! Allah is forgiving, responsive"* (Quran, 42:23).

"It may be that Allah will ordain love between you and those of them with whom ye are at enmity. Allah is mighty, and Allah is forgiving, merciful" (Quran, 90:7; 76:7; 60:7; 49:7).

We notice from the "positive" verses above that, even in its verses of mercy and compassion, Islam teaches that God shows love exclusively towards his own, i.e. Muslims, for "Islam is

Allah's religion," says the Book, whilst promising punishment and showing spite towards the "infidels" and more or less towards the dhimmis (Jews and Christians, who are Ahl al-Kitāb, People of the Book). This love/hate combination (critics would say contradiction) has been repeated in at least forty verses of the Quran, with a clear definition for two distinct groups, the "good" people (Muslims) and the "bad" people (all other religions). As previously said, this makes the Muslim concept of "love" radically different from Christianity and Buddhism's unconditional, infinite love for and mercy towards all of mankind.

Notwithstanding this exclusive, partial concept of "conditional" love in Islamic theology, still, these verses represent a radical departure from the verses of war, wrath and violence mentioned in earlier chapters.

Allah loves those who follow *"Al Sirat Al Mustaqim"* (the "Right Path") and do good deeds, and this is clearly shown in five verses of the Quran (2:195; 3:134; 3:148; 5:13 and 5:93), which focus on doing good to others, like helping poor people, supporting orphans or even respecting one's parents, and other good deeds which have also been mentioned in various verses of Islam's holy book.

Other "good people," according to the Quran, are those who:

- Guard themselves against sin (3:76; 9:4; 9:7).

- Judge fairly (5:42; 49:9; 60:8).

- Fight in God's way (61:4).

- Purify themselves (2:222; 9:108).

- Turn much to God (2:222).

- Trust in God (3:159).

- And are patient (3:146).

On the other hand, God does not love the person who is:

- An unbeliever (3:32; 30:45).

- Arrogant (16:23; 4:36; 31:18; 57:23).

- Cruel (3:57; 3:140; 42:40).

- Unfaithful and ungrateful (2:276; 22:38).

- Exceeding the limits (2:190; 5:87; 7:55).

- Extravagant (6:141; 7:31).

- Mischief-maker (2:205; 5:64; 28:77).

- Treacherous (8:58; 4:107).

- And exulting in riches (28:76).

- *Verses of peace and tolerance in the Quran*

Islam showing tolerance towards other religions? Islam, a religion of peace? Yes, it is so - despite the many verses that could be taken as absolutely intolerant towards other faiths - or rather it is *also* so... this "also" is the reason Islam is such a "contradictory" religion, as many view it... We shall see in the verses below another side to Islam, the side which lets moderate Muslims say that theirs is a "religion of peace." Let us delve into this other dimension of Muhammad's religion.

- *Peace in the Quran*

Wishing peace is the way of greeting in Islam: when meeting and parting with each other, Muslims say *"As-Salâmun 'Alaikum"* ("peace be upon you"). This greeting finds its source in the *Quran*:

"Salâmun 'Alaikum [peace be upon you] *for that you persevered in patience! Excellent indeed is the final home!"* (Quran, 13:24).

"But if the enemy incline towards peace, do thou (also) *incline towards peace"* (Quran, 8:61).

Accordingly, Prophet Muhammad ordered his fellow Muslims to salute each other and non-Muslims alike with peace when he said: *"Peace before Speech."*

As for the word *Islam,* it does mean submission and not peace, but the root of that word is *salama,* which is the origin of both words peace and/or submission; peace to the world and submission to God.

Peace is the ultimate reward in the hereafter:

"(It will be said to them): *'Enter therein* (Paradise), *in peace and security' "* (Quran, 15:46).

Allah calls paradise "a home of peace":

"Allah calls to the Home of peace and guides whom He wills to a Straight Path" (Quran, 10:25).

The Quran also relates how Abraham prayed for peace:

"And (remember) *when Ibrahim* (Abraham) *said: 'O my Lord! Make this city* [Mecca] *one of peace and security, and keep me and my sons away from worshipping idols"* (Quran, 14:35).

As well as Noah:

"It was said: 'O Nûh (Noah)! *Come down* (from the ship) *with peace from Us and blessings on you and on the people who are with you* (and on some of their off spring), *but*

(there will be other) *people to whom We shall grant their pleasures* (for a time), *but in the end a painful torment will reach them from Us' "* (Quran, 11:48).

When one thoroughly reads the *Quran,* one would be pleasantly surprised by the following three verses of peace in that same book, where *Allah* shows His appreciation towards him who strives for peace:

"But he who fears from a testator some unjust act or wrongdoing, and thereupon he makes peace between the parties concerned, there shall be no sin on him. Certainly, Allah is Oft Forgiving, Most Merciful" (Quran, 2:182).

"Say: 'If there were on the earth, angels walking about in peace and security, We should certainly have sent down for them from the heaven an angel as a Messenger' " (Quran, 17:95).

"But if they incline to peace, you also incline to it, and (put your) *trust in Allah. Verily, He is the All-Hearer, the All-Knower"* (Quran, 8:61).

- *Tolerance in the Quran:*

At the same time that Islam urges its followers to *"slay the idolaters wherever you find them,"* it also issues antithetical commandments of complete mercy and tolerance. The "other," positive side of Islam preaches the absence of coercion and tolerance towards non-Muslims, who should be treated with fairness and respect, as the many following verses will show:

"Let there be no compulsion in religion. Truth stands out clear from Error. Whoever rejects false worship and believes

in Allah has grasped the most trustworthy handhold that never breaks. And Allah hears and knows all things" (Quran, 2:256).

"If it had been thy Lord's Will, they would all have believed, all who are on earth! Wilt thou then compel mankind, against their will, to believe!" (Quran, 10:99).

"And so, (O Prophet!) *exhort them your task is only to exhort; you cannot compel them to believe"* (Quran, 88:21, 22).

"But if they turn away from you, (O Prophet remember that) *your only duty is a clear delivery of the Message* (entrusted to you)" (Quran, 16:82).

"Yet if God had so willed, they would not have ascribed Divinity to aught besides him; hence, We have not made you their keeper, nor are you (of your own choice) *a guardian over them"* (Quran, 6:107).

"And whoso takes for patrons others besides God, over them does God keep a watch. Mark, you are not a keeper over them. But if they turn aside from you (do not get disheartened), *for We have not sent you to be a keeper over them; your task is but to preach . . . "* (Quran, 42:6, 48). *"Obey God then and obey the Messenger, but if you turn away* (no blame shall attach to our Messenger), *for the duty of Our Messenger is just to deliver the message"* (Quran, 64:12).

"(Three Messengers to their people) *Said* (the Messengers), *'Our Sustainer knows that we have indeed been sent unto you, but we are not bound to more than clearly deliver the Message entrusted to us'* " (Quran, 36:16, 17).

"Assuredly, We have sent down the Book to you in right form for the good of man. Whoso guided himself by it does so to his own advantage, and whoso turns away from it does so at his own loss. You certainly are not their keeper" (Quran, 39:41).

"And tell my servants that they should speak in a most kindly manner (unto those who do not share their beliefs). *Verily, Satan is always ready to stir up discord between men; for verily; Satan is man's foe . . . Hence, We have not sent you* (Unto men O Prophet) *with power to determine their Faith"* (Quran, 17:53, 54).

"(O Prophet) *We have not sent you except to be a mercy to all mankind: Declare, 'Verily, what is revealed to me is this, your God is the only One God, so is it not up to you to bow down to Him?' But if they turn away then say, 'I have delivered the Truth in a manner clear to one and all, and I know not whether the promised hour* (of Judgment) *is near or far'* " (Quran, 21:107–109).

"And they ask, 'When shall the promise be fulfilled if you speak the Truth?' Say, 'The knowledge of it is verily

with God alone, and verily I am but a plain warner' "
(*Quran, 67:25, 26*).

"Allah forbids you not, with regard to those who fight you not for (your) *Faith nor drive you out of your homes, from dealing kindly and justly with them: for Allah loveth those who are just"* (*Quran, 60:8*).

"Allah only forbids you, with regard to those who fight you for (your) *Faith, and drive you out of your homes, and support* (others) *in driving you out, from turning to them* (for friendship and protection). *It is such as turn to them* (in these circumstances), *that do wrong"* (Quran, 60:9).

What needs to be pointed out—a thing which is both funny and pathetic—is the fact, that in the days of the Prophet, some non-Muslim communities were given protective status (provided they paid the tax), but the Islamic State in Syria and Iraq (Daesh) today beheads, crucifies and burns non-Muslims who are unfortunate enough to live in its self-declared Caliphate. Daesh's warmongers are killing Muslims too, their fellow Sunnis who reject their fanatic rule, as well as Muslims from other sects (such as Shias, Alawites), as Daesh does not consider them as true Muslims.

The Prophet did call for the protection of non-Muslims who had made peace with his followers:

"Whoever kills a person who has a truce with the Muslims will never smell the fragrance of Paradise" (*Saheeh Muslim*).

"Anyone who kills a non-Muslim who had become our ally will not smell the fragrance of paradise" (*Bukhari*).

The above verses would be a great card in the hands of those who defend Islam as being a religion of peace and tolerance if it were not for the fact that this same religion contradicts itself when it calls for exterminating all non-Muslims. This alone would explain the fact that Islam today is in deep crisis and faces a big dilemma: which Islam to follow, Daesh's, which has all the verses it needs for religious legitimacy, or the positive Islam of the moderates, which also has all the verses it needs to support it?! Verily, a question upon which will depend the future of Islam.

Be that as it may, so long as the upper hand was with the Muslims, the Prophet forbade any maltreatment of people of other faiths. Confirming that tolerance towards non-Muslims living in the Islamic Caliphate, Muhammad said:

"Beware! Whoever is cruel and hard on a non-Muslim minority, or curtails their rights, or burdens them with more than they can bear, or takes anything from them against their free will; I (Prophet Muhammad) *will complain against the person on the Day of Judgment"* (*Abu Dawud*).

"He who believes in God and the Last Day should honour his guest, should not harm his neighbour, should speak good or keep quiet" (*Bukhari, Muslim*).

"Whoever hurts a Non-Muslim citizen of a Muslim state hurts me, and he who hurts me annoys God" (*Bukhari*).

"He who hurts a Non-Muslim citizen of a Muslim state, I am his adversary, and I shall be his adversary on the Day of Judgment" (*Bukhari*).

"Beware on the Day of Judgment; I shall myself be complainant against him who wrongs a non-Muslim citizen of a Muslim state or lays on him a responsibility greater than he can bear or deprives him of anything that belongs to him"(Al-Mawardi).

Moreover, monasteries, churches and synagogues must be respected, since they are mentioned in the Quran as places of worship of God:

"If God had not driven some people back by means of others, monasteries, churches, synagogues and mosques, where God's name is mentioned much, would have been pulled down and destroyed. God will certainly help those who help Him - God is All-Strong, Almighty (Quran, 22:40).

Of course, this protection came at a price: these non-Muslims had to pay the tax (jizya). But wasn't that better than nowadays in IS-occupied parts of Syria and Iraq, where Islamic State terrorists slay all those who don't believe in their twisted, Satanic version of religion? Finally, as said above, Islam recognises Christians and Jews as Ahl al-Kitāb (People of the Book), and confirms the Torah and the Gospel as books revealed by God:

"And We (God) sent after them in their footsteps Jesus, son of Mary, verifying that which was before him of the Torah; and We gave him the Gospel containing guidance and light, and verifying that which was before it of the Torah, and a guidance and an admonition for the dutiful. (Quran, 5:46)

PART THREE

THE TRUTH SHALL SET YOU FREE: ENDING THE CONTROVERSY

"And ye shall know the truth,
and the truth shall set you free."

- John 8:32

CHAPTER NINE

PERVERSION, MISREPRESENTATION OF THE QURAN . . . OR THE PLAIN TRUTH?

"Beware of false knowledge: it is more dangerous than ignorance."

- GEORGE BERNARD SHAW

There is no doubt that Islamic terrorists are selecting the verses from the Quran that serve to justify their horrific crimes, thus using and abusing the Quran, whilst there are other verses that preach mercy and tolerance in that same holy book, verses which these terrorists simply and conveniently choose to ignore. *Yet the very fact* that there are verses of extreme violence in a religious book is in itself disturbing, as religions are supposed to preach love, compassion, and peace. And that is precisely what makes them religions.

Be that as it may, we should accept the very odd reality which is: Islam is *both* a religion of war, violence, intolerance, *and* a religion of peace, mercy and compassion. That is in principle. In practice, unfortunately, the world has only witnessed - with very few exceptions - the violent side of this religion, especially that the Islamists, throughout the ages, as is the case today with the terrorist fundamentalists, have managed to obscure the peaceful version of Islam in favour of the violent one, and have also succeeded in mediatising their version and exploiting it to a very large extent, whilst silencing - through force and terror - the majority of Muslims who are eager to practice what they call "the Islam of the middle (i.e. moderation)," *Islam al-Wasat*, which is praised and embraced by mainstream Islamic authorities like al-Azhar of Egypt, al-Najaf of Iraq, as well as by the Sufis, the Muslim mystics.

Nevertheless, after reading the verses of peace, mercy, compassion and tolerance in the previous chapter, one finds oneself totally confused and filled with suspicion, and the following question immediately pops in his mind: what is real Islam? *Which* is real Islam? Daesh's, the bloodthirsty, hateful, wrathful, violent, intolerant, repressive and oppressive Islam, or the peaceful, merciful, tolerant, compassionate Islam of al-Azhar, al-Najaf, and the Sufis?

But the discerning reader, after reading the positive verses, would never simply dismiss the violent side as not being true Islam, for these verses are right there in black and white on the pages of the Quran, and they have just as much weight and importance as the positive verses. Yet, the one explanation for these blatant contradictions could be the very likely possibility of the perversion of the text, for a book cannot preach one thing and its very opposite only verses away from each other.

Were these contrasts intended, or was the Quran edited? If the contradictions were part of the integral text, how divine is the Quran, critics of Islam, or even the average reader, ask. Can God's word mix cruelty with mercy, and wrath with compassion, and war and violence with peace? What kind of a "God" contradicts himself, or speaks two languages at the same time? And, if the Quran was edited, as many, seeing two contradictory versions coexisting side by side, tend to believe, then it is no longer the Word of God and loses its legitimacy, its divine legitimacy and justification. These are very legitimate questions that even many Muslims are critically, albeit discreetly, asking nowadays, when they see a Daesh criminal reciting a verse from the very sacred text of the Quran before beheading his innocent victim in the name of God!

Herein lies the real problem, the deep crisis of Islam. And here again we ask the question: is Islamism the same as Islam?

The problem (and the obstacle in the way of reforming Islam) is that the very possibility of the perversion of the Quran is a taboo subject among Muslim clerics, moderates and extremists alike, since that book is supposed to be the untainted, unchanging word of God for all ages until the Day of Judgment. If the Quran was perverted, as many tend to believe, their logic goes that it is not perfect, nor is it supreme truth, which means the whole edifice of moral and religious self-proclaimed supremacy and holiness collapses like a deck of cards. And suddenly Allah is not great.

In any case, the verses of peace and tolerance of the previous chapter leave the reader baffled, after having read the verses of violence throughout the book. Thus the reader asks himself, over and again, with no clear answer in sight: were these contradictions intended, or was the Quran edited? We do not know; what we do know for sure is that Islamic terrorists are using and abusing *ad nauseum* the verses that justify their heinous acts of barbarism and sheer ignorance.

As for those Muslim clerics who warn critics of Islam of the "pitfalls" of "misinterpreting" and "misconstruing" their holy book (thus clinging to their authority as sole interpreters of Allah's book), arguing that one should read this book "very carefully" (conveniently adding that only clerics can and should interpret the Quran), one can rightfully ask them with total confidence: how is it possible to misinterpret, misconstrue crystal-clear and absolutely non-allegorical and literal verses like *"slay the idolaters wherever you find them,"* *"I will instil terror into the hearts of the unbelievers, smite ye above their necks and smite all their fingertips,"* *"they should be murdered or crucified or their hands and their feet should be cut off on opposite sides,"* and countless similar verses of extreme violence and brutality?

The ludicrous theory of the "Western conspiracy against Islam"—namely, the bizarre, far-fetched theory by some Muslims that the West is conspiring against Islam by spreading a distorted version of it through Islamic terrorists, and that the latter are mere puppets of this conspiracy—goes up in flames, since the Quran itself contains those very verses that Islamic terrorists are using to justify their horrific crimes against humanity. And, because of the countless very clear and literal verses of violence which are sadly overwhelming the peaceful ones (which gives Islam its characteristic image of a religion of war), the accusation of "misrepresentation" does not stand. Indeed, how can one possibly misrepresent verses which are flagrant exhortations to slaughter "infidels"?

Muslims would argue that one should study the context of the verses of violence and intolerance, because they were written in a context of war where Muslims often found themselves on the defensive and even being persecuted for their beliefs (at the onset of Muhammad's time, before the Muslim conquests and the establishment of the caliphate). These Muslim scholars argue that the Quran is "a book of peace," saying that many of the Quranic verses are being quoted out of context in a deceitful misrepresentation to wrongly justify terrorist actions. This explanation is very plausible. Yet, their argument goes, most of those verses are only referring to a particular situation, such as the Battle of Badr or the battle of Uhud. And, as said above, these verses were in self-defence against the enemies of Islam and only held true when Muslims were attacked. Here are the verses in question:

"Fight in the cause of Allah those who fight you, but do not transgress limits; for Allah loveth not transgressors."

"And slay them wherever ye catch them, and turn them out from where they have turned you out; for tumult and oppression are worse than slaughter; but fight them not at the Sacred Mosque, unless they (first) *fight you there; but if they fight you, slay them. Such is the reward of those who suppress faith."*

"But if they cease, Allah is Oft-Forgiving, Most Merciful."

"And fight them on until there is no more tumult or oppression, and there prevail justice and faith in Allah; but if they cease, let there be no hostility except to those who practice oppression" (Quran, 2:190–193).

To be fair, the preceding verses were clearly written in a context of war and self-defence. But what about the hundreds of other verses of war, violence, and intolerance that were not written in the context of war and self-defence? The argument of "misrepresentation" simply does not stand against such countless exhortations to kill, maim, oppress and torture all "unbelievers." And, anyway, one might ask, aren't the verses of the Quran supposed to be open-ended, universal and eternal?

If they are subject to their historical context, where is their eternal and divine nature? Isn't Allah's word supposed to be applied for all eternity, and not limited to a certain historical context which is human, all-too human? Is the Quran human, all too human?

This brings out a third, more plausible hypothesis, which is neither the Quran's perversion (as some Western scholars argue) nor its misrepresentation (as Muslim moderates argue, accusing extremists of doing just that in order to justify terrorism), but rather - and we already touched on that subject earlier in the present work - the fact that Prophet Muhammad's mission passed by two historical stages in spreading his religion, an earlier peaceful period when his message was attracting very few converts, and a more violent one which coincided with his religion's expansion through conquests and rule by the sword, and the fact that the increasing numbers of enemies against the new faith were *necessarily* faced with more coercive verses (!).

It is worth mentioning in this context that, according to the Islamic historical narrative, the verses were not revealed to Mohammad all at once, but rather gradually and according to each situation he had to deal with, whether ethical, social, or political. In other words, the Quran was given to accompany the prophet throughout his life or mandate, and, for each problem encountered, an *ad hoc* sura (chapter) or aya (verse) was given, which gives numerous verses of the Quran, namely the warlike ones, a very historical conditioning or make up, and hence necessitates reading it in its historical, and socio-political, context.

Although this explanation does not satisfy the Muslim clerics, moderates, and fundamentalists alike, as it is touching what they call "the eternity" of the Quran, meaning that it applies to every time and space, nevertheless, this "historical" approach to the Quran is the most plausible one, and it saves it from its enemies within, the Islamists who are ruining the ethical legitimacy of their religion with their barbaric, inhuman, unethical, and evil deeds.

Thus the "historical" approach classifies the Quranic verses according to two main phases of Muhammad's religious life or ministry: the earlier, peaceful phase in Mecca, with its positive verses, better known as the Meccan verses, which were unfortunately, and accordingly, superseded by violent Medina verses which came during the more tumultuous phase in Medina when Muhammad had to face his enemies, the Quraishis (a prominent tribe in the Arab peninsula), as well as people from other faiths. That second phase was the phase of conquests and forced conversion of non-Muslims.

So here, some Western historians of Islam, feel compelled to say that when Muslims were subdued, they kept a low profile and preached peace and tolerance, but when they gained the upper hand, they unleashed the most brutal violence to spread their religion throughout the whole world. And they nearly did, reaching the shores of Europe and China.

But the dangerous deduction, if we adopt and accept this two-stage hypothesis, the Mecca and Medina phases, with their differing verses in spirit, rationale, context, and purpose, is that the Quran was *not* revealed and dictated by Allah to Muhammad, as Muslims confirm, as they staunchly defend the divine source of the Quran as the word of Allah, who transcends time and space, and the earth and the universe alike and whose word must consequently not change or falter, as it does, according to the *earthly* historical and geographical context. Indeed, Muslims embrace this absolute transcendence of God - Allah Ta'alah. So how could the "transcendent" God be wholly immersed, totally involved, in His spirit and word, somewhere in Mecca and Medina, these insignificant places compared to the infinite universe!

The word of God, the Eternal and Universal, must be in his image: eternal and universal. And not differing from one place to another on earth, or from one planet to another, or not even from one galaxy to another. Eternal and universal mean the same essence, everywhere and forever.

With these philosophical and theological insights, one is compelled to utter, say the harsh critics of Islam, that, in view of its inherent contradiction, in explicit wording and in spirit, the Quran was not God's work and word, but rather that it was simply man-made. Indeed, this would mean in their opinion and logical reasoning that Islam is not divine but human.

But here the Muslims would surely reply: so, the Quran, written by Muhammad himself? It simply couldn't be; the prophet was illiterate since boyhood until receiving the revelation. What, then? Written by someone else, wonder the critics, using the same reasoning? It couldn't be, Muslims fiercely reply, since they consider the Quran as a linguistic masterpiece, a literary miracle that no human hand or mind could create or even come close to producing.

We can see that Muslims refuse all these legitimate questions or scepticism when it comes to the divine source of the Quran, even when they don't have any reasonable or convincing answer to questions regarding the blatant contradictions we spoke about. They answer: God knows. So they reject any doubt regarding the revelation of the Quran by

God himself, *and in Arabic*, otherwise the whole edifice of this religion, the revelation, falls like a deck of cards. Indeed, this, the harsh critics of Islam contend, would mean that Islam is not divine but human. And that would be the plain truth. Full stop: the Quran is *not* Allah's word, these critics would say. It was neither edited nor perverted, neither misrepresented nor misconstrued. It is just a human book written by a human. And here we find yet another layer, not to say the mother of all layers, of the crisis of Islam: the supposed divinity of the Book!

Let's be straight about it: it is extremely hard to defend Islam strictly as a religion of peace, as the moderates claim, because there are so many verses of war and violence that contradict and eclipse their peaceful sister-verses. This raises the question of the incoherence of the text, due to many contradictions it contains, whether intentionally or unintentionally, God knows! But what we *do* know is that the verses of violence are *right there* in the scriptures. They might be misused and abused by Islamic terrorists, but still, they are neither misrepresented nor distorted, since terrorists are using the exact same verses that are preached by their holy book. You don't see the Christians and the Buddhists making an effort to defend the New Testament or the Buddha's Dhammapada! Simply because they don't need to be defended, since these holy books only contain verses of love and compassion.

Does Islam carry the seeds of Islamism, the seeds of its own destruction, since Islamists, with their bloody barbarism, are destroying the very ethical and "divine" legitimacy of their own religion? This question has to be answered by Muslims themselves.

So, perversion or misrepresentation of the Quran? Or just the plain truth, which is the double nature, the Dr Jekyll and Mr Hyde, of Islam? And hence its human nature? Is there a controversy regarding the nature of Islam, warlike or peaceful, as the objective and rational scholars say, or is it *simply* a misuse and abuse of the text, as the moderate Muslims subjectively affirm and confirm, in a bid to defend their religion against the obvious: Muhammad's cult of war? Muslim scholars themselves must answer these questions and decide to reform and redefine their religion in order to save it from itself.

A ray of hope was cast upon the Muslim World when secular Egyptian president Sisi called for a "religious revolution." Sadly, this call received no echo at all from Muslim clerics and scholars, and remained a cry in the wilderness. This conspiracy of silence among mainstream Muslim authorities regarding the barbarous Islamist crimes in Syria, Iraq, and elsewhere in the Muslim world and their terrorist acts against the West, is what makes Islam stand today in the culprit's seat, having no advocate in the non-Muslim world to seriously defend it.

This book is not about reforming or redefining Islam; this is the task of moderate Muslims themselves. The present work only shows that Islamists are selectively misusing and abusing the verses of violence which are there, in their holy book, to further their murderous ends. They are not hiding that fact; on the contrary, they are claiming full legitimacy and responsibility for their *crimes*, which they don't see as crimes but rather as honourable and brave deeds by soldiers of Allah to fulfil his will, which is explicitly expressed in his book. So, the present book shows how Islam's deep crisis lies not only in the fact that it has been hijacked by extremists, but also, and more importantly, in the (disturbing and dangerous) fact that this holy book itself contains verses that preach and justify terrorism. Doesn't this make the task of saving Islam from Islamism a mission impossible?! Again, the answer lies in the hands of moderate Muslims.

Islam or Islamism? This is an existential question for Islam: *to be or not to be*. Hence, the moderate Muslim scholars should rise to this historical and existential task: saving Islam from the *inside enemy*.

A TYPICAL EXAMPLE OF THE CONTROVERSY SURROUNDING ISLAM: The concepts of Greater and Lesser Jihad

- Greater (vs. lesser) Jihad: the other nature of Jihad

The word jihad makes us think of the events of 9/11, Osama bin Laden, the Madrid and London bombings, the Paris and Brussels terrorist attacks, ISIL's and al-Nusra's savage beheadings and other horrific crimes in Syria and Iraq, and so on. Indeed, throughout Islamic history, this term has almost always been used in a military sense, in most cases to justify the most horrific crimes.

However, there exists another, loftier, allegorical dimension to that most dreaded word in the lexicon of humanity, and that is known as "greater jihad" - the soul's jihad - (jihad al-nafs). Unfortunately, this spiritual jihad has been ignored, neglected, or misunderstood by Muslims. And it is a real shame, since that word is of a spiritual nature and bears a meaning that is totally antithetical to the bloody meaning which has stained the image of Islam and continues to stain it until today.

- WHAT IS JIHAD?

The word *jihad* stems from the Arabic root word *jahada*, which means "strive," "struggle." Other words derived from this root include "labour," "effort" (juhd or ijtihad). In the context of the Quran, jihad is a struggle or effort to strive *"in the path of God"* (22:78). That seems very noble and commendable, but *how?* Peacefully, by doing good deeds and spreading peace and love, or by waging war against, and slaughtering "unbelievers"? The difference is great, and up till now Muslims, namely the Islamic zealots, have chosen the latter version of jihad, thereby doing the greatest damage to both their religion and the world.

If, as some moderate and enlightened Muslim scholars define that word, jihad is the effort to purify oneself from within, to purify oneself of selfish appetites and desires, if this is the root meaning of jihad, as these moderates affirm, then when and how, one wonders with dismay, did it come to mean "holy war" or a "war to kill the infidels"? To answer that, we need to look at jihad in the Quran and its historical development.

However, before we examine the verses themselves, we should distinguish between what is known as "greater" and "lesser" jihad. Muslim clerics define these two forms of jihad as follows:

-1- **Lesser (outer) jihad, "jihad by the sword"** (al-jihad al-asghar, jihad bil saif); a military struggle, a holy war. Lesser jihad is the physical holy war, the struggle to establish the Muslim Caliphate or Islamic State (and that is the Caliphate that ISIL self-declared in parts of Iraq and Syria, totally in line with the *Quran*'s injunction). This jihad is done either by waging war to expand the empire or by defending it against its enemies. Indeed, the Quran itself refers to "lower jihad, " a struggle sanctioned by Allah:

> *"To those against whom war is made, permission is given* [to fight] *because they are wronged; and verily, God is most powerful for their aid"* (Quran, 22:39).

The Quran also states in chapter 2, verse 190: *"Fight in the cause of Allah those who fight you, but do not transgress limits; for Allah loves not transgressors. "* The two above-mentioned verses clearly exhort Muslims to fight only in self-defence and not indiscriminately, which means sparing innocent civilians (a rule that ISIL terrorists are certainly not applying, thus violating the Quran).

However, it would be great if all of the Quran's verses preaching Jihad limited this struggle to self-defence. But that is obviously and unfortunately *not* the case, as Islam's holiest book is jam-packed with verses of Jihad which are not in self-defence but rather clear exhortations to forcibly convert "infidels" or exterminate them if they refuse to submit to *Allah's* religion. Muslim moderates keep conspicuously silent when these verses are mentioned, and their silence speaks a thousand words.

-2- Greater (inner) jihad, "jihad of the soul" (al-jihad al-akbar, jihad al nafs); the personal inner and spiritual struggle on the part of every Muslim to follow the teachings of Allah in word and deed throughout his or her life, overcoming base desires such as anger, greed, pride, and hatred. This higher struggle also entails forgiving those who have wronged us, and working to achieve social justice. The following verse gives us an idea about this internal struggle each Muslim must pursue:

"Of those who answered the call of Allah and the messenger, even after being wounded, those who do right and refrain from wrong have a great reward." (Quran, 3:172).

The Greater jihad is thus mainly about being good.

During Muhammad's lifetime, and until this day, the word *jihad* was, and still is, almost always used in a military sense, and abused *ad nauseum* by Islamic terrorists to justify their horrendous crimes. The idea of a greater and lesser *Jihad* was a later development which originated from the eleventh-century book, *The History of Baghdad,* by the Islamic scholar al-Khatib al-Baghdadiis, by way of Yahya ibn al 'Ala', who said:

"We were told by Layth, on the authority of 'Ata', on the authority of Abu Rabah, on the authority of Jabir, who said, 'The Prophet returned from one of his battles, and thereupon told us (his followers), *'You have arrived with an excellent arrival, you have come from the Lesser Jihad to the Greater Jihad. They asked: what is the greater Jihad?'* He said: - the striving of a servant [of Allah] *against his idle desires' "* (*Mujahadat al-'abdi Hawah*).

This saying, while lofty and commendable, is dismissed by the proponents of the lesser Jihad as being "weak," since it derives from a hadith whose authenticity is not proven. However, Ibn Hajar Al-'Asqalani said in *Tasdid al-Qaws:* "this saying is widespread and it is a saying by Ibrahim ibn Ablah according to Nisa'i in al-Kuna. Ghazali mentions it in the *Ihya'* and *al-'Iraqi* said that Bayhaqi related it on the authority of Jabir and said: 'there is weakness in its chain of transmission' " (*'Ali al-Qari, al-Asrar al-marfu'a,* Beirut 1985, p. 127).

Although this saying attributed to Prophet Muhammad cannot be confirmed as hadith because of its weak chain of one or two of its transmitters, nonetheless Ibn Taymiyya, who is otherwise often used for more rigid interpretations, said of it:

> "[it] *leaves no doubt as to the fact that Jihad al-nafs* [struggling to overcome one's base desires] *comes first and is the precondition sine qua non of military Jihad."*

So even greater jihad is tainted with war? It seems Islam cannot but be a religion of war.

- WHICH JIHAD?

Jihad, according to Muslim scholars, is divided into five types of struggle:

- Jihad of the soul/heart (jihad bin nafs/qalb): the struggle for moral reformation and faith.

- Jihad of the tongue (jihad bil lisan): the struggle to proclaim God's word; right speech.

- Jihad by the pen/knowledge (jihad bil qalam/'ilm): this form of jihad involves scholarly research of Islam in aiding the spread and defence of Islam.

- Jihad by the hand (jihad bil yad): doing good deeds.

- Jihad by the sword (jihad bis saif): the lesser jihad or holy war.

When Prophet Muhammad was asked which people fought in the name of Allah, he said:

> *"The person who struggles so that Allah's word is supreme is the one serving Allah's cause"* (*Hadith*).

"Allah said': 'Those who have striven for Our sake, We guide them to Our ways" (Quran, 29:96).

Thus, the Muslim who spends his life pursuing jihad is the one who will go to heaven, according to the Messenger of Allah. But here one asks oneself: *how* does one best serve Allah? By the soul or the sword? Through greater or lesser jihad? Although the Quran clearly quoted Allah as saying, *"Fight in the cause of Allah those who fight you, but do not transgress limits; for Allah loves not transgressors,"* and although the prophet told his followers, his warriors, that they had arrived *'from the lesser jihad to the greater jihad, the striving of a servant* [of Allah] *against his idle desires',* the absence of a clear and permanent answer to the above questions makes the concept of jihad a controversial one. While few Muslim scholars believe that the greater jihad is the internal spiritual struggle, based on the Prophet's statement, other scholars (a majority, it must alas be said) believe that this inauthentic saying is unreliable and that jihad meaning holy war is the more important meaning. And that precisely is the reason why Islam is called a religion of war by most of the world, since that latter definition largely prevails, and since jihad is Islam's holiest and most important concept.

Now that we have explained what greater jihad means, thus distinguishing it from Lesser jihad, we can move to examine more closely the concept of jihad in the Quran and the Hadiths.

- JIHAD IN THE QURAN

The word *jihad* - and its derivatives meaning struggle in the path of God - appears in 164 verses in the Quran, which makes it by far Islam's most important, indeed, main concept.

The word *qital*, a synonym which more directly means "fighting," appears no less than 36 times in the Quran, and most prominently in verses 2:190, 9:13, and 4:91–93.

- *Greater Jihad in the Quran:*

There are many more verses on striving (jahada) in the Quran. The following are some typical ones:

"And whosoever strives (jahada), strives (yujahidu) only for himself, for lo! Allah is altogether independent of the universe" (Quran, 29–69).

"And those who strive (Jahadu) for Us - We will surely guide them to Our ways. And lo! Allah is with the doers of good" (Quran, 29–69).

"By the Nafs and the proportion and order given to it, and its inspiration as to its wrong and its right; truly he succeeds who purifies it, and he fails that corrupts it" (Quran, 91:7–10).

"But as for him who feared to stand before his Lord and restrained his soul from lust, Lo! The garden will be his home" (Quran, 79:40–41).

As one can notice, these are Meccan, peaceful verses that mainly seem to focus on spiritual purification. Other verses are less clear and could be construed as either relating to lesser or greater jihad, such as the following ones:

"So obey not the rejecters of faith, but strive (Jahidu) against them by it [the Quran] with a great endeavour" (Quran, 25–52).

"And strive (Jahidu) for Allah with the endeavour (Jihadihi) which is His right. He has chosen you and has not laid upon you in the religion any hardship" (Quran, 22–78).

- Lesser Jihad in the Quran:

The following are typical verses of holy war or lesser jihad:

"Fight [qatilu] in the way of God against those who fight you, but do not attack them first. God does not love the aggressors. Slay them wherever you find them. Drive them out of the places from which they drove you. Idolatry is worse than carnage . . . Fight against them until idolatry is no more and God's religion reigns supreme. But if they desist, fight none except the evil-doers" (Quran, 2:190).

"Will ye not fight a folk who broke their solemn pledges, and proposed to drive out the Messenger and did attack you first?" (Quran, 9:13).

"If they withdraw not from you, and offer you not peace, and refrain not their hand, take them, and slay them wherever you come to them; against them We have given you a clear authority" (Quran, 4:91–93).

It is important to note that in each of these examples, qital is referred to in a defensive manner. Therefore, it is fair to say that even the lesser jihad is *sometimes* not aggressive but defensive. That would be fine if it were the case with *all* verses exhorting Muslims to jihad, which is far from being the case, hence the crisis in which Islam finds itself today, as it often rhymes with terrorism.

Indeed, the following are verses that justify offensive fighting:

"Make war on them until idolatry shall cease and God's religion shall reign supreme. If they desist, God is cognizant of all their actions; but if they give no heed, know then that God will protect you" (Quran, 8:39–40).

"Fight those who do not believe in God or the last day, and do not hold forbidden that which was forbidden by God and His Apostle, or acknowledge the religion of truth (even if they are) *of the people of the book, until they pay jizya* [tax] *with willing submission, and feel themselves subdued"* (Quran, 9:29).

So, greater or lesser jihad? This dual nature of the Quran is what makes Islam contentious. While greater jihad is essentially an inner struggle of spiritual purification that has nothing to do with killing, lesser jihad is clearly and obviously a cult of war and violence, whether in self-defence or in a blatant war against "idolatry" and "apostasy," as well as forced conversion. And it has nowadays become barbaric terror and mass murders with the jihadis of the twenty-first century: the al-Qaeda-inspired terrorist organisations such as the Islamic State (Daesh), al-Nusra, Taliban, Boko Haram, and the like.

It is the controversy over the Quran's verses on jihad, as with many other issues, and the ambiguity of these verses which could take the reader simultaneously in the two directions of "lesser" (religious cleansing) and "greater" (spiritual purification and cleanliness) jihad. It is this controversy or ambiguity that leaves a large manoeuvring room for terrorists to commit their horrific crimes against humanity in the name of Allah, whilst having a "heavy religious weaponry," the verses themselves, to use against their critics and enemies alike. It is not an exaggeration to say that the verses have become "weapons of mass destruction" in the hands of the terrorists; *WMD verses*, one might say, to annihilate, not only their enemies, but humanity as a whole.

The ambiguity of the Scriptures, or rather its dualistic nature, makes the Islamic terrorists quote the very verses that justify their horrific crimes and serve their interests of power and dominion, and disregard those other verses of religious purification and elevation. It goes without saying that this selectivity, this arbitrary reading of the Book, lies at the heart of the crisis of Islam since it stems from antithetical, or at best dual, verses which make nearly every issue controversial since it has simultaneously a metaphorical as well as a literal meaning. The Quran itself admits that "the verses bear many faces" (Hammalatt Awjoh), and that only the "knowers," those "well-versed in knowledge" (al-rassikhoun bil Elm) know how to interpret them: *"Wala yaalam ta'wilouha ella Al rassikhoun bil Elm"* ("only those well-versed in knowledge know how to interpret the verses"), the Quran itself says.

- Jihad outside the Quran

The word *jihad* - with its derivatives, including the verb *jahada* ("strive") - appears hundreds of times in the standard collection of *Hadith, Bukhari.*

- Greater Jihad in the Hadith:

We have already cited above the hadith in which the Prophet tells his followers that they have come from the lesser jihad and must embark on the greater jihad. Unfortunately, this hadith, - as shown above, - has been deemed "weak" and discredited, especially by the radical clerics and Islamists in their warlike and violent version of Islam, and in their literature on jihad. So the controversy remains as to whether or not Muhammad actually said these lofty words.

Be that as it may, other verses from the hadiths - some authentic, others less authentic (less authentic, according to Islamist radicals and warmongers), also show that the notion of Greater jihad was not alien to Islam. The Prophet said in another hadith:

"On another occasion a man asked: 'should I join the Jihad?' The prophet pbuh [peace be upon him] *asked him, 'do you have parents?' The man said yes. The prophet said: 'then do Jihad by serving them!' "* (*Sahih Bukhari*, 5972). This hadith is very authentic and shows the great value Islam put on honouring one's parents.

In another "weak" hadith (some proponents of lesser jihad would even say fake hadith) Muhammad said in what was known as the Farewell Pilgrimage:

"*The Mujahid is he who makes Jihad against his Nafs* (ego) *for the sake of obeying Allah*" (*Ibn Hibban* no. 1624, 2519; *Al-Hakim: Sahih*. Also in *Tirmidhi, Ahmad*, and *Tabarani*).

Muhammad also said in a similar hadith:

"*The strong one is not the one who overcomes people, the strong one is he who overcomes his Nafs* (ego)" (*al-Haythami* declared this *Hadith* authentic in *Majma' al-Zawa'id*).

Other hadiths of the Prophet whose authenticity is not questioned show that he espoused some aspects of greater jihad:

> *"Aisha, Allah be well-pleased with her, asked: 'Messenger of Allah, we see Jihad as the best of deeds, so shouldn't we join it?' He replied: 'But the best Jihad is a perfect Hajj* (pilgrimage to Mecca)' " (*Sahih Al-Bukhari* no. 2784).

> *"Another man asked: 'what kind of Jihad is better?' The Prophet pbuh replied: 'a word of truth spoken in front of an oppressive ruler' "* (*Sunan al-Nasa'i* no. 4209)

> *"The Prophet pbuh said to Abu Sa'id al-Khudri: 'Even if one strikes unbelievers and idolaters with his sword until it breaks, and he is completely dyed with their blood, the Rememberers of Allah are above him one degree"* (related on the authority of *Abu Sa'id al-Khudri* by *Ahmad,* 3:75, *Tirmidhi* no. 3376, *Baghawi* in *Sharh al-Supnna,* 5:195, *Ibn Khatir* in his *Tafsir,* 6:416, and others).

> *"The prophet said: 'shall I tell you something that is the best of all deeds, constitutes the best act of piety in the eyes of our Lord, elevates your rank in the hereafter, and carries more virtue than the spending of gold and silver in the service of Allah, or taking part in Jihad and slaying or being slain in the path of Allah?'They said: "yes!' He said: 'Remembrance of Allah"* (related on the authority of *Abu al-Darda'* by *Ahmad, Tirmidhi, Ibn Majah, Ibn Abi al-Dunya, al-Hakim* who declared it sound, and *Dhahabi* who confirmed him; *Bayhaqi, Suyuti* in *al-*

Jami' al-saghir, and *Ahmad* also related it from *Mu'adh ibn Jabal*).

Muhammad said: *"The example of the Mujahid* [he who performs *Jihad*] *in the Cause of Allah, and only Allah knows who is truly performing Jihad in His Cause, is the example of he who is both a Saa'im* [fasting] *and a Qaa'im* [standing up in voluntary prayers] *" (Al-Bukhari).*

- Lesser jihad in the Hadith:

Totally in line with Islam's dual nature, the *Hadiths* also contain verses which exhort followers to pursue the lesser jihad or holy war. There is no room for controversy or misinterpretation, the verses are crystal-clear:

"The Messenger of Allah was asked about the best Jihad. He said: 'The best Jihad is the one in which your horse is slain and your blood is spilled' " (also cited by Ibn *Nuhaas* and narrated by *Ibn Habbaan*).

Ibn *Nuhaas* also cited a hadith from *Musnad Ahmad Ibn Hanba,* where Muhammad states that the highest kind of jihad is that of *"the person who is killed whilst spilling the last of his blood"* (*Ahmed,* 4:144).

"Standing for an hour in the ranks of battle is better than standing in prayer for sixty years" (*Saheeh* related by *Ibn Ade* and *Ibn Asakir* from *Abu Hurayrah* 4:6165, *Sahih al Jaami* as *Sagheer* no. 4305).

"Allah's Apostle was asked, 'What is the best deed?' He replied, 'To believe in Allah and His Apostle (Muhammad).' The questioner then asked, 'What is the

next (in goodness)?' *He replied, 'To participate in Jihad* [religious fighting] *in Allah's Cause' "* (*Sahih Bukhari*, 1:2:26).

It was narrated that *Amr bin Abasah* said: *"I came to the Prophet and said: 'O Messenger of Allah, which Jihad is best?' He said: ' (That of a man) whose blood is shed and his horse is wounded' "* (*Sunan Ibn Majah*, 2794).

> *"A morning or evening spent in the path of Allah is better than the world and all it contains"* (*Saheeh al Bukhari*, 4:50).

> *"Shall I tell you who has the best degree among people? A man who takes the rein of his horse to do Jihad in the way of Allah"* (*Al-Muwatta*, 21 21.1.4b).

> *"On the authority of Rashid, on the authority of Sa'd (radiallaahu 'anhu), on the authority of one of the Companions, that a man said, 'Oh Messenger of Allah! Why is it that the believers are all put to trial in their graves, except for the martyrs?' He (salallaahu 'alayhee wa sallam) said, 'The clashing of swords above his head was sufficient trial for him' "* (*Sahih al-Jam'i*).

The importance placed on physical jihad in Islam is most conspicuous in *Sahih Hadith* which relates Muhammad referring to Muslims who refuse to fight or consider going to *Jihad* as "hypocrites":

> *"It has been narrated on the authority of Abu Huraira that the Messenger of Allah (may peace be upon him) said: One who died but did not fight in the way of Allah nor did he*

express any desire (or determination) *for Jihad died the death of a hypocrite"* (*Sahih Muslim,* 2:4696).

"Whoever dies but neither fought (i.e., in Allah's cause), *nor sincerely considered fighting, will die a death of Jahiliyyah* [pre-Islamic era of "ignorance"] *"* (*Sahih Hadith, Tafsir Ibn Khatir*).

- Lesser Jihad is much more widespread in Islamic scriptures and among Muslim scholars and laymen

As we have shown, the concept of jihad as "Holy War" - Jihad of the sword - is much more authentic in Islamic scriptures and much more widespread among Muslims, both scholars and laymen, than its loftier, spiritual counterpart of *Jihad* of the soul. That is the main reason why it is much more typical of Islam and more popular among Muslims - including Islamic terrorists, who use and abuse it to carry out their conquest of the land of "infidels"...

As for the "weak, the very weak" (according to radical clerics and Islamist warmongers) argument of moderate Muslims who accuse critics of their religion of "misusing" the term jihad by using it "out of context," the answer is simple, critics of Islam say: What context? Islam has *always* been in the context of war! Whether in the days of the Prophet or today. And, if there is a context, then what happens to the eternal word of God that is supposed to be above time? If this word is the hostage of time, then it is not timeless and should therefore be reformed. And this also means it is not God's word.

In fact, all four schools of Sunni jurisprudence (fiqh) as well as the Shiite tradition hardly make any reference to the greater jihad. Only the Sufis, the Muslim mystics wholeheartedly embrace the greater jihad, the jihad of the soul against the earthly desires of the flesh, as well as the desires of the nafs for power and dominion, and they are condemned for heresy by orthodox Muslims. So, unfortunately, the concept of the greater jihad is unorthodox and heretical to the majority of the world's Muslims. The Quran is much more crystal-clear about the lesser jihad than it is about the greater jihad, as the following verses show (which some scholars cite as contradicting the hadith about the greater jihad):

"Not equal are those believers who sit (at home) *and receive no hurt, and those who strive and fight in the cause of Allah with their goods and their persons. Allah hath granted a grade higher to those who strive and fight with their goods and persons than to those who sit* (at home). *Unto all* (in Faith) *Hath Allah promised good: But those who strive and fight Hath He distinguished above those who sit* (at home) *by a special reward"* (Quran, 4:95).

"Think not of those who are killed in the Way of Allah as dead. Nay, they are alive, with their Lord, and they have provision" (Quran, 3:169).

In all six major *Hadith* collections (*Sahih Bukhari, Sahih Muslim, Dawud, al-Sughra, Tirmidhi and Ibn Majah*), jihad almost always refers to the lesser, outward physical struggle and not the greater, inward spiritual struggle. As an example, there are nearly 200 references to jihad in the most trusted collection of Hadith, *Sahih Bukhari,* and *every single one* assumes that jihad means literal warfare.

Ibn Taymiyyah, the famous Islamic scholar and theologian also known as Shaykh ul-Islam, said the following of the famous but "weak" hadith where the Prophet supposedly praises greater jihad:

"There is a Hadith related by a group of people which states that the Prophet [peace be upon him] said after the battle of Tabuk: 'We have returned from Jihad Asghar [lesser jihad] to Jihad Akbar [greater jihad].' This Hadith has no source, nobody whomsoever in the field of Islamic Knowledge has narrated it. Jihad against the disbelievers is the most noble of actions, and moreover it is the most important action for the sake of mankind."

That was many centuries ago, but even today Muslim scholars deride the above-mentioned "fabricated" hadith which gives preference to the method of Da'wah ("the call," "preaching") over jihad for spreading Islam. These scholars and clerics argue that the best method for spreading Islam is through the sword. *"The Book in one hand, the sword in the other,"* Muhammad (reportedly) said, as Islamic history clearly shows. Indeed, the Prophet spent thirteen years in Mecca preaching his message, but he was only able to convert a few dozen people to Islam; whereas, when he entered Mecca with his armies years later, thousands converted to Islam. This achievement, these so-called learned Islamic teachers say, shows that it is only by conquering land that Islam can be, and was indeed, spread to the world.

Moreover, these clerics go as far as to postulate that this "fabricated" hadith actually contradicts the Quran, citing the following verse which they claim certainly does not refer to an inner struggle:

"When the Prophet (sallallahu 'alayhe wassallam) said: Narrated by Abu Huraira: Allah's Messenger said:

'Whosoever dies without participating in Jihad nor having the intention to do so, dies on a branch of hypocrisy' " (*Sahih Muslim*).

According to these same Islamic scholars, the whole concept of a lesser and greater jihad has no validity within Islam, and they believe that the highest stage of jihad is fighting the enemies of Muslims and Islam. In that same vein, the highly influential Muslim Brotherhood leader, Sayyid Qutb, preached in his book *Milestones* that jihad *"is not a temporary phase but a permanent war."* And after that, Muslims still wonder why Islam is called a "religion of war," when the crushing majority of Muslims, scholars and laymen alike, still consider that the lesser jihad is the only real jihad.

CONCLUSION

WHAT IS REAL ISLAM?
THE JURY IS STILL OUT

"If the God for whom you kill so blindly made us in His image, each bullet in my wife's body would have been a wound in His heart."

- ANTOINE LEIRIS, HUSBAND OF ONE OF THE VICTIMS OF THE
PARIS MASSACRE PERPETRATED BY ISLAMIC STATE TERRORISTS ON
NOVEMBER 13TH, 2015

Where do we go from here? We have reached the end of the book and still we lack clear answers as to what real Islam is: religion of war or religion of peace? Or both? If so, then how could the Almighty *contradict* Himself? Or could He use a double - alas, explicitly double - language; and if so, why? Or maybe, just maybe, this is *not* Allah's word? Is the Quran the unadulterated word of God, or was the text perverted?

To those who might, and surely will, accuse the author of blasphemy for raising these "sacrilegious" questions, we respond: Islam itself says that it is a "religion of reason" (Deen al-aql). So it's only legitimate, and very *rational*, to ask these questions when we are faced with the inherent, or rather explicit, duality of the text. And our aim is to find the truth, and nothing but the truth.

Islam also says that it is a "religion of nature," human nature, (Deen al-fitra): "We *naturally* know God," says Islam, i.e. our innermost nature discerns right from wrong, good from evil. Furthermore, fitra means conscience; that inborn "divine" voice that makes us human, that guides us to God, that leads us to live an ethical life. And when we are faced with those *evil, inhuman* atrocities that the Islamic fundamentalists are committing in the name of God, and justifying their barbaric, horrendous crimes with verses from *God's Book* itself, we *naturally* say, we are *humanely* compelled to say, our conscience (fitra) pushes us to say, that these verses are *not* God's words; our innermost human nature tells us that God would never condone or advocate killing, while, at the same time, saying: *Thou shalt not kill!*

What we do know for certain is that Islam's holy book has been and continues to be misused and abused by Islamic terrorists. Islamism is the plague that is corrupting the whole religion, and sowing death and destruction on the four corners of the planet, but let us not hide the fact that it draws its strength and justification from the fact that it is using *actual* verses of the Quran which glorify war, jihad, violence, intolerance, and preach the oppression of women, and the implementation of the barbaric and backward sharia. But we have also seen the "other," lesser known side of Islam, "Islam with a human face," one might say, which preaches peace, tolerance, mercy, and compassion.

How could good *and* evil coexist in the same book? How could peace and violence, mercy and cruelty, compassion and hatred, religious freedom and oppression, accepting others and denying their rights to exist, mix and clash in the mind of Muslims? Very few other religions contain such contradictions.

Hence the crisis of Islam, and the dilemma of Muslims. Islam, to the objective observer and to the keen seeker of truth, is not one religion but two. What is being preached is not one but *two*, and, what's more, contradictory, messages. And, although the verses of violence and intolerance largely predominate, still, one should not neglect the other positive verses.

In any case, after reading this book, moderate Muslims and their friends can no longer say *"those who commit acts of terror have not read the Quran,"* because the Quran *does* condone violence in its crystal-clear verses praising and exhorting jihad.

Islamism, and Islamic terrorism, its unholy offspring, is the scourge. It is waging a total war of annihilation against the whole world; against mankind at large; against non-Muslims and Muslims alike, against believers and atheists, against thinkers, writers, artists, poets, journalists, men of science, women . . . in the name of Allah. And no city or town on this earth has been left unscarred by its bloody killing spree. One need only turn on the TV and watch news from all over the world, and one will find with shock and dismay that almost all the violence on this planet nowadays is committed by Muslim extremists; Muslims, but extremists; extremists, but Muslims nonetheless. Therefore, if the religion does not dissociate itself from its extremists, it will fall with the death of the last terrorist. Islamism has already lost the moral battle, and it is jeopardising the very moral ground of Islam itself.

We have *dissected*, we have critically (but objectively) read, rationally analysed, and morally studied, the Quran and shown its many aspects and its dual nature, yin and yang, war and peace, violence and tolerance. We have shown that orthodox Islam is incompatible with modernity, especially when it comes to human rights, and more specifically women's rights. Moreover, Islam, being an all-encompassing religion that controls and regulates (and interferes in) everything, the public and the private spheres, is a totalitarian ideology in the era of universal and individual freedom. Man, according to Islam, is not the son but the servant of God who is asked to blindly fulfil his will and word. The Islamists are proving to be *his faithful, blind servants!*). There is compulsion everywhere and freedom nowhere.

This book's aim is to end the eternal, and very false, cliché that we hear, each time there is a crime committed by Islamic terrorists: this is not Islam, and those who commit terrorist acts have never read the Quran. Now that we have shown the countless verses of violence, this very weak defence no longer stands. The terrorists might have not read the *whole* book, but they have surely read *enough!* For, on the contrary, it is those who have actually *read* the Quran who will know and realise that it does, to a great extent, condone and even encourage violence. Whereas it is mostly those who say that Islam is a religion of peace that have not read the *whole* Quran, or read so little of it! How is that for irony? Those who defend Islam as a peaceful religion and the terrorists alike, both haven't read the whole book, but part of it, each according to his own choosing. The terrorists have read the Quran, and they perfectly understood *their* part, and they are applying it to the letter!

Asserting that Islam, in its totality and completeness, is a peaceful religion would mean one of two hypotheses: One has either not read the Quran *at all*, or has read it *all* and has chosen to disregard the violent part! So enough of this *this is not real Islam,* because it *is*, at least partly, to be fair! If

Muslims are eager to save their religion, they must face facts, which are that the Quran does preach violence, and of the most brutal sort. The truth shall set you free.

So, Islam or Islamism? Are they different, or the same? Is it merely a difference of degrees, but they are essentially the same thing, as critics of Islam insist? Or is Islamism a distortion of true Islam, as moderate Muslims equally insist? Who is the true Muslim, the moderate or the fundamentalist? The Islamic terrorist simply chooses to focus on the "negative" side of his religion, while the moderate Muslim chooses to stick solely to the positive side. Both are Muslims, but with a difference of perspective, depending on which end of the spectrum one chooses to look into.

The Paris massacre, perpetrated by Islamic State terrorists on November 13th, 2015, left 129 dead, 359 injured with 99 in critical condition. Antoine Leiris, the husband of one of the victims shot dead on that fateful day, posted a heart-wrenching message on social media, a message that is an act of defiance, the resistance of the spirit of freedom, enlightenment and civilisation against the backward, dark forces of ignorance and barbaric medievalism.

The message was so moving and significant that it deserves to be quoted in full:

"On Friday night, you stole away the life of an exceptional being, the love of my life, the mother of my son, but you will not have my hatred. I do not know who you are and I don't want to know, you are dead souls. If the God for whom you kill so blindly made us in His image, each bullet in my wife's body would have been a wound in His heart.

Therefore I will not give you the gift of hating you. You have obviously sought it but responding to hatred with anger would be to give in to the same ignorance that that has made you what you are. You want me to be afraid, to cast a mistrustful eye on my fellow citizens, to sacrifice my freedom for security. Lost. Same player, same game.

I saw her this morning. Finally, after nights and days of waiting. She was just as beautiful as she was when she left on Friday evening, as beautiful as when I fell madly in love with her more than 12 years ago. Of course I'm devastated with grief, I will give you that tiny victory, but this will be a short-term grief. I know that she will join us every day and that we will find each other again in a paradise of free souls which you will never have access to.

We are only two, my son and I, but we are more powerful than all the world's armies. In any case, I have no more time to waste on you, I need to get back to Melvil who is waking up from his afternoon nap. He's just 17 months old; he'll eat his snack like every day, and then we're going to play like we do every day; and every day of his life this little boy will insult you with his happiness and freedom. Because you don't have his hatred either."

Two visions clash in the aforementioned message: civilisation and enlightenment versus ignorant barbarism; the enlightened sons of life versus the sons of darkness, fanaticism and ignorance.

Therefore, even if the jury is still out on what real Islam is, the main thing moderate Muslims should do is to acknowledge the hard fact that Islam has been hijacked by *its* extremists, the most loyal servants of Allah, who have waged war on the whole world... consequently, all moderate Muslims should speak loudly against such extremists and condemn their crimes and join the international war against terrorism (World War III), making a clean break between Islam and Islamism represented by the black plague Daesh and its sisters al-Nusra and al-Qaeda. This war on terror takes place both with weapons and with the mind, to make sure this ideology does not resurface one day in the minds of deluded Muslims after it is obliterated on the battleground.

What is sure is that after reading this book, moderate Muslims will no longer be able to merely shrug their shoulders when atrocities are committed by Islamic terrorists in the name of Islam by simply saying that these horrific acts "are alien to the teachings of our religion," for were they truly acquainted with their religion, they would know better than to just deny some of its teachings and deal with the reality of Islam's dual nature.

POSTFACE

IS ISLAM BEYOND REDEMPTION?

"Ignorance is always afraid of change."

- JAWAHARLAL NEHRU

- *The need for a Muslim Luther . . . or another Nietzsche?*

Can Islam overcome its crisis and save itself through a reformation akin to the one undertaken by Martin Luther, or is this the end? Will Islamism destroy Islam? Reform, or fall; that is the equation which saved Christianity from its Inquisition and its horrors. Will it save Islam from *its* inquisition and its horrors? Indeed, Islam is passing through *its* Dark Ages; the same Dark Ages that Christianity endured, and overcame, in medieval times. The Muslim world is in dire need of an Age of Enlightenment. Where are the Muslim Voltaires, Rousseaus, Hugos? Reform will need its martyrs; there is no question about that: brave, enlightened, moderate Muslims who refuse to see their religion hijacked by a fringe group of mad and fanatic murderers.

Islam is in deep crisis, but the way out of this crisis is fraught with dangers, indeed, dangers that threaten its very survival, as the religion of Muhammad also faces an existential dilemma; the Muslim dilemma could be summed up thus: if there is resistance to reform, as is sadly the case now, because of the sacredness and untouchability of Allah's unadulterated and eternal word and supreme truth, then more and more moderate Muslims will turn away from their religion and it will continue to be reviled worldwide as a religion of war and violence which does not "move with the times" and is therefore incompatible with modernity.

However, if Islam *is* reformed - as unlikely as this seems presently, in the absence of any sign or movement pointing in that direction, it will never be the same again, since the Quran will be edited, which means it will no longer be considered "divinely inspired," thus losing its heavenly legitimacy and sacredness, its revelatory character which makes it so hallowed among Muslims, who believe that Muhammad, an illiterate, received Allah's revelation and wrote a literary masterpiece, the Quran, which is precisely the "miracle" of Islam; a miracle akin to Christ's resurrection for Christians.

Does this mean that either way Islam is doomed? There is no doubt about the need to reform Islam; but reform will entail amending the scriptures by eliminating the incriminating verses of violence, which means shattering the celestial nature of the religion of Muhammad. So the question is not so much: reform or die? But rather reform *and* die? If no reform is made, Islam can no longer endure as a religion, for it is totally incompatible with modernity and its universal values of human rights, and it has been totally smeared with the stain of violence and terrorism. But if reform is made, Islam will also eventually die as a divinely-inspired religion, for revelation is its very essence. Is Islam beyond redemption? It certainly seems to be a lose/lose situation.

Can Islam be saved? Or is it intrinsically flawed and doomed for destruction? Do we need a Muslim Luther who will reform Islam, or another Nietzsche who will destroy it, as the original one destroyed Christianity? What is certain is that if no serious, or even drastic, reform is undertaken, there will be more and more Salman Rushdies who will expose and condemn the verses of violence. A Muslim reformation, if it is to see the light of day, should be the battle of Muslim scholars and secular thinkers alike.

A historical approach must be adopted, meaning to agree that the warlike, violent, misogynistic verses *have served their time*, and must be re-shelved, and only the very universal and peaceful verses should be kept. That is Islam's sole guarantee for survival, and ticket for the future.

It must be said in this regard that Christian reform was an easier task. First, because, unlike the Quran, the New Testament is not a revealed book; it was written by ordinary people who related the life of Jesus Christ. Second, Christ's teachings are crystal-clear and cannot be distorted or manipulated.

The battle to reform Islam *from within* is one of legitimacy. The Islamists will advocate, as they did throughout history, the "eternity" of the Quran, Allah's message and words, its validity for all times and circumstances. Nevertheless, legitimacy stems from the ability to evolve according to reason, human progress, and civilisation; what might have been valid centuries ago, cannot be valid anymore.

The battle to reform Islam, like any other reform, is a battle of minds: a battle between dinosaur-like minds stuck in the past, and hence doomed to extinction, and progressive minds open to the future against all odds.

Adapt or perish! This is the rule of the game of survival.

In an article he published in *National Interest* in the spring of 2000 entitled "Islam and Islamism – Faith and Ideology," Daniel Pipes wrote:

> Searching for explanations for their predicament, Muslims have devised three political responses to modernity - secularism, reformism and Islamism. The first of these holds that Muslims can only advance by emulating the West. Yes, the secularists concede, Islam is a valuable and esteemed legacy, but its public dimensions must be put aside. In particular, the sacred law of Islam (called the Shari'a) - which governs such matters as the judicial system, the manner in which Muslim states go to war, and the nature of social interactions between men and women - should be discarded in its entirety. The leading secular country is Turkey, where Kemal Atatürk in the period 1923–38 reshaped and modernized an overwhelmingly Muslim society. Overall, though, secularism is a minority position among Muslims, and even in Turkey it is under siege.
>
> Reformism, occupying a murky middle ground, offers a more popular response to modernity. Whereas secularism forthrightly calls for learning from the West, reformism selectively appropriates from it. The reformist says, 'Look, Islam is basically compatible with Western ways. It's just that we lost track of our own achievements, which the West exploited. We must now go back to our own ways by adopting those of the

West.' To reach this conclusion, reformers reread the Islamic scriptures in a Western light. For example, the Quran permits a man to take up to four wives - on the condition that he treat them equitably. Traditionally, and quite logically, Muslims understood this verse as permission for a man to take four wives. But because a man is allowed only one in the West, the reformists performed a sleight of hand and interpreted the verse in a new way: the Quran, they claim, requires that a man must treat his wives equitably, which is clearly something no man can do if there is more than one of them. So, they conclude, Islam prohibits more than a single wife.

Reformists have applied this sort of reasoning across the board. To science, for example, they contend Muslims should have no objections, for science is in fact Muslim. They recall that the word algebra comes from the Arabic, al-Jabr. Algebra being the essence of mathematics and mathematics being the essence of science, all of modern science and technology thereby stems from work done by Muslims. So there is no reason to resist Western science; it is rather a matter of reclaiming what the West took (or stole) in the first place. In case after case, and with varying degrees of credibility, reformists appropriate Western ways under the guise of drawing on their own heritage. The aim of the reformists, then, is to imitate the West without acknowledging as much.

Though intellectually bankrupt, reformism functions well as a political strategy.

Secularists believe that the law of the state should be based on secular principles, not on Islamic legal doctrines. Traditionalists believe that the law of the state should be based on the traditional legal schools. However, traditional legal views are considered unacceptable by some modern Muslims, especially in areas like women's rights or slavery. Reformers believe that new Islamic legal theories can produce modernised Islamic law and lead to acceptable opinions in areas such as women's rights. However, traditionalists believe that any departure from the legal teachings of the Quran as explained by the Prophet Muhammad and put into practice by him is an alien concept that cannot properly be attributed to "Islam".

Pipes wrote his article sixteen years ago, and it is safe to say by now that all three solutions he mentioned which Muslims have come up with to overcome the crisis of Islam are essentially doomed to failure, and have actually already failed. In a nutshell: if you reform Islam, it is no longer Islam. If you don't reform it, it is heading for oblivion. Either way, it is doomed, say its harsh critics. Pipes had a critical and pessimistic outlook for Islam sixteen years ago, before Daesh. Can you imagine what he would write today, if he were asked to reassess the crisis of Islam?

That being said, reformation, whatever its consequences, is a moral duty for each moderate Muslim who rejects his religion's proclivity to violence and terrorism. The following are recommendations for moderate Muslims which I have come up with for an Islam "with a human face":

- Acknowledge that Islam is (partly) intolerant and warlike, and stop saying it is *only* a religion of peace. That is not how you can reform and save it. The verses of violence and intolerance are *right there* in the Quran. Stop denying what is a fact.

- Focus on preaching and applying the forgotten, disregarded "positive" verses of mercy, compassion, forgiveness, peace and tolerance, and even love (in the Sufi sense) in the Quran. Muslims can *make* Islam a religion of peace, the same way the Islamists have made it a religion of war; the ethical, religious battle is between Muslims and Islamists.

- Distinguish between Islam and Islamism. Even if, as we have seen throughout this book, this distinction is sometimes blurred because the Islamists are using actual verses from the Quran, still, there is a great amount of misuse of these verses by extremists.

- Forgo the brutal, outdated, archaic sharia and its cruel and unjust practices of stoning, beheading, mutilating, amputating, which are totally incompatible with humanity and civilisation.

- Acknowledge women as daughters of God and Life who have just as much the right to live and thrive as their male counterparts. In the era of universal human rights, it is absolutely inconceivable and forbidden to still treat women as inferior non-entities with no rights whatsoever, no better than goats or camels, as the backward Islamists are doing and want to do to women all over the earth.

- Adopt the moral, higher meaning of jihad, the greater jihad, as self-conquest and purification, and abandon its definition as holy war and thence the Muslim obsession with this lower jihad or holy war, which is nothing but a war for dominion and material gains in disguise, conveniently cloaked in religious garb.

- Adopt an allegorical and spiritual, instead of physical and material, interpretation of *Jannah* (heaven) and *Jahannam* (hell) as respectively the soul's elevation and fall.

- Only Ibn Rushd-like rationalism, or Sufi-like spirituality, in great doses, could or might just save Islam. Sufism is the only solution for the crisis of Islam. These could be the only solutions for the crisis of Islam, as for any other religion, to cure it from the scourge of dogmatic Islamism its true and lethal enemy. If "this is not real Islam," then *this* is how it *should* be! Show what "true Islam" is, instead of being stuck in denial. Even if Allah himself is wrong, correct him! Choose conscience over scripture. I wrote in one of my books: "I only believe in one God: he is called my conscience." Make Islam truly Deen al-futra.

- Regarding the misrepresentation of the scriptures: moderate and enlightened Muslim clerics should issue fatwas against the misuse of the Quran and Hadith. Morality should be heavily injected into Muslim teachings and practice: it is high time to practice ijtihad (interpretation) not just for day–to-day matters, but to reinterpret the scriptures in a mystical, ethical, rational way. Ijtihad must go all the way, beyond mere rituals and religious practices. Make Islam truly *Deen al-akl.*

- The inconsistencies in the Quran should be addressed head-on, thus lifting the taboo of "touching" the Quran. The verses of violence should cease being applied. This is both possible and desirable; the Old Testament is also full of violence and cruelty, but the significant difference with Islam is that the former's bad side is no longer practiced in our day and age.

Only love can save Islam. Muslims should understand that "convert or die" doesn't win the hearts and minds of people, and that is the only way a true religion worthy of that name spreads and endures. If you don't bow to the winds of change, you will be broken like an old branch.

But to even consider the above recommendations, Muslims must be willing to take a good hard look at the mirror of reality: the dual nature of the Quran. Another reading of the Quran needs to be undertaken, a reformation of Islam.

However, there is strong resistance from Muslim scholars to reassess or reinterpret the scriptures because they know the high and risky cost of such a crucial endeavour: many passages in the Quran and Hadith will have to be rejected, which means the Word of Allah is not infallible, it is contradictory and even (sometimes) cruel and inhuman; the whole edifice will fall. That is why so much resistance faces the reformists, if any, because the whole religion rests on the revelation.

Enlightenment means steering away from the original Quran and Hadith, as it's a lose/lose situation. If the scriptures remain the same, with resistance to change or reform, Islam will continue to be demonized and associated with terrorism; if Islam is reformed, it is no longer Islam. A reformed Islam is no longer . . . Islam!

But we are not there yet. Reform seems like a faint light at the end of an interminable tunnel. We'll cross that bridge when we come to it; the more pressing concern is the following: how can Islam be saved when Muslims themselves aren't even conscious that their religion in crisis? Or rather, more plausibly, they don't want to believe it. Who other than the Muslims themselves can reform Islam?

Westerners, facing the Inquisition (with the significant difference that the tyrannical priests were *not* applying Jesus' teachings, so their twisted version of Christianity was easier to discard), turned away from theocratic Christendom, political Christianity, if you will, and secularism, which is the rule of positive law, took over and ruled the public sphere, relegating religion to the private sphere. Religion no longer became a relation between the *community* and God, but rather a strict relation between the individual and the Lord.

In stark contrast, Muslims, despite the Inquisition-like Islamic State's atrocities, have not yet shown - in their overwhelming majority - any sign of turning *away* from their religion, or at least its violent side, and relegating it from the public to the private sphere (and heaven knows it is high time they did!); but rather, and shockingly, they are turning *back* to religion and more specifically to the sharia and the Caliphate (the counterpart of Christendom, or Kingdom of God). Alas, they are becoming *more* religious! And Islam for them has become, in the East and more dangerously in the West, a political-communitarian expression of their existence and way of life. And the few enlightened and secular Muslims live in hiding or are slaughtered. And that is mainly the difference between Western and Muslim culture and ethics.

After the Paris massacre of 2015, horrified and outraged, I published the following post on Facebook:

"Where are the millions of 'moderate' Muslims (supposedly the majority) demonstrating around the world against the Islamic State and saying 'not in my name? ' Until and unless the civilised world sees that, don't blame it for blaming ALL Muslims for terrorism. There is a very pertinent French saying: *'qui ne dit mot consent'* (' silence is consent')."

Is Islam beyond redemption? That is a question that Muslims themselves must address, and decide, since the fate of their religion lies in their own hands.

Enlightened Aristotelian philosophers like Ibn Rushd, Ibn Sina, Farabi, and the great Sufi poet Rumi tried to introduce mind into the Quran in order to save it from ignorance. This is still possible today:

> *"The strong light of the mind in but a flash will burn the veil of ignorance"* (The Song of Mahamudra).

Therefore, instead of telling non-Muslims to *"convert or die,"* Muslims must tell *themselves "reform or die."*

But the problem is that the mere act of questioning the scriptures is considered blasphemous and heretical by *all* Muslims, moderates and extremists alike. So when evolution is impossible, revolution becomes necessary. Resistance to change brings collapse. And that is the fate that awaits everything that does not evolve, since evolution is the law, essence, and purpose of life.

In the absence of a serious will to reform Islam - "the *Quran* is divine, so it cannot be changed," Muslims insist - and rid it of its extremist, distorted version, Islamism, the future of the religion of Muhammad looks bleak, and Muslims themselves are to blame for not reforming their religion. Will Islam rid itself of Islamism, or will Islamism kill Islam by distorting it beyond redemption? We do not see any Muslim Luther anywhere today. Will a new Nietzsche sound the death knell for Islam? After all, wasn't it Nietzsche himself who wrote *"That which is falling, deserves to be pushed!"*?

REFERENCES

BOOKS, ARTICLES, AND INTERNET LINKS

- http://www.thereligionofpeace.com/Quran/023-violence. htm.

- Hilali and Khan, *The Noble Quran* (Riyadh: Darussalam, 1996).

- http://www.faithfreedom.org/ Islam and forced conversion.htm, *6/6/2011.*

- *Weekly Synopsis 4th June 2011, "Convert or die."*

- http://www.bibleprobe.com/muhammad.htm.

- http://www.thereligionofpeace.com/Quran/023-violence. htm, August 13, 2005.

- *Top ten reasons why Sharia is bad for all societies* by James Arlandson and Soliman al-Buthe: http://www.americanthinker.com/2005/08/top_ten_ reasons_why_sharia_is.html.

- *Islam and Islamism - Faith and Ideology* by Daniel Pipes, National Interest, Spring 2000: http://www.danielpipes.org/366/islam-and-islamism-faith-and-ideology.htm.

- *Distinguishing between Islam and Islamism*, Centre for Strategic and International Studies, June 30, 1998: http://www.danielpipes.org/954/distinguishing-between-islam-and-islamism.

- http://en.wikipedia.org/wiki/Islamism.

- http://hnn.us/articles/1671.html, George Mason University's History News Network. What Is the Difference Between Islam and Islamism? by Melvin E. Matthews, Jr.

- *Is It Islamic or Islamist? The West's confusion spells trouble.* Murad Sezer / Rueters-Landov: http://www.newsweek.com/2010/10/22/is-it-islamic-or-islamist.html.

- http://www.civitas.org.uk/pdf/cs29.pdf, The 'West', *Islam and Islamism.*

- Is ideological Islam compatible with liberal democracy? Caroline Cox and John Marks, Civitas: Institute for the Study of Civil Society, London.

- *The roots of terror: Islam or Islamism?* Meghnad Desai, 6th February 2007: http://www.opendemocracy.net/democracy-terrorism/

islamism_4326.jsp.

- *No distinction between Islam and Islamism.* Jonathan Kay
  May 8th, 2011:
  http://www.theblogmocracy.com/2011/05/10/geert-wilders-no-distinction- between-islam-and-islamism/
  Geert Wilders.

- *Islamism Is Not Islam* by Maajid Nawaz: http://online.wsj.
  com/article/SB100014240527487039597045754532119
  43767790.html.

- *No pressure, then: religious freedom in Islam:*
  http://www.opendemocracy.net/patricia-crone/no-compulsion-in-religion.

- *Islamic Hell - Torture Chamber for Unbelievers. Abdullah
  Yusuf Ali* and N.J. *Dawood*:
  http://www.flex.com/~jai/satyamevajayate/hell.html.

- *Terrorism in the Quran:*
  http://muhammadanism.org/Muhammad/Muhammad_
  Terrorism.htm.

- *Killing by Beheading is Islamic!* by *Syed Kamran Mirza*:
  http://www.faithfreedom.org/oped/SKM40715.htm.

- *The Holy Quran,* translated by A. Yousuf Ali, published by
  Amana corporation, Brentwood, Maryland, 1983.

- *Al-Sira al-nabawiyya,* 4:296ff.

- *The Sacred Muslim Practice of Beheading,* By Andrew G.
  Boston: FrontPageMagazine.com, May 13th, 2004:

http://www.frontpagemag.com/Articles/ReadArticle.
asp?ID=13371.

- *The Laws of Islamic Governance*, translated by Dr.
  Asadullah Yate, (London), Ta-Ha Publishers Ltd., 1996,
  p. 192.

- The Baburnama -Memoirs of Babur, Prince and Emperor,
  translated and edited by Wheeler M. Thacktson, Oxford
  University Press, 1996, p. 188.

- *Where's the Arab Media's Sense of Outrage?* By Mamoun
  Fandy, Washington post, Sunday, July 4, 2004.

- *Question Authority: The Quran mentions beheading. Why
  does the U.S. press claim otherwise?* July 1, 2004, by Lee
  Smith.

- *164 Jihad Verses in the Quran.* Compiled by Yoel Natan:

  http://www.answering-islam.org/Quran/Themes/jihad_
  passages.html.

- http://conservativecolloquium.wordpress.
  com/2008/03/11/violent-and-intolerant-quran-verses/

- http://www.prophetofdoom.net/

- ' *Ali al-Qari, al-Asrar al-marfu'a*, Beirut 1985.

- *What the Quran says about Polygamy*:
  http://skepticsannotatedbible.com/quran/says_about/
  polygamy.html.

- *Polygamy and the Quran:*
  http://www.suite101.com/content/polygamy-and-the-quran-a121193.

- http://infidelsarecool.com/2008/01/top-10-quran-quotes-every-woman-must-see/

- *Wondrous Treatment of Women In Islam:*
  http://www.flex.com/~jai/satyamevajayate/women.html.

- *Rajm* (stoning) *firmly established in Shariah:*
  http://www.answering-islam.org/Shamoun/stoning.htm

- *The (lack of) Rights of a Muslim woman.* Weekly Synopsis
  30th May 2011:
  http://www.faithfreedom.org/

- *Allah wants to see women illiterate*, by *FFI Contributing Editor* Dr Radhasyam Brahmachari:
  http://www.faithfreedom.org/

- *Joys of Muslim Women*, by Nonie Darwish:
  http://www.flex.com/~jai/satyamevajayate/heaven.html

- David B. Barrett, Todd M. Johnson, *World Christian Trends, AD 30–AD 2200,* William Carey Library, 2001.

- *Mercy in Islam,* by Dr. Hassan Hathout:
  http://members.cox.net/arshad/mercy.html.

- *Love And Mercy In Al Qur'an*:
  http://www.scribd.com/doc/11520747/Love-and-Mercy-in-Al-Quran.

- *The Divine Mercy of God* (3 parts): http://www.islamreligion.com/articles/419/ by IslamReligion.com Published on 09 Oct 2006.

- The Quran on God's Love: http://www.parsquran.com/eng/articles/love.htm.

- http://www.sunniforum.com/forum/showthread. php?36693-Verses-of-Peace-in-the-Holy-Quran.

- *Quran a Book of Peace, Not War, Scholars Say,* Peter Standring, National Geographic Today, September 25th, 2001.

- *Concept of Peace in Islam*: http://saif_w.tripod.com/questions/violence/concept_of_ peace_in_islam.htm.

- *Verses of the Holy Quran About Peace,* by Aena Joseph: http://ezinearticles.com/?Verses-of-the-Holy-Quran- About-Peace&id=5627208

- http://en.wikipedia.org/wiki/Compassion, from WikiIslam, the online resource on Islam.

- www.wikiislam.net

- http://www.scu.edu/ethics/publications/submitted/heit/ whatisjihad.html

- http://wikiislam.net/wiki/Lesser_vs_Greater_Jihad

- Donner, Fred M. *The Sources of Islamic Conceptions*

of War. Chapter in *Just War and Jihad: Historical and Theoretical Perspectives on War and Peace in Western and Islamic Traditions.* John Kelsay and James Turner Johnson Eds. Greenwood Press: New York, 1991.

- *Feldman, Noah. After Jihad: American and the Struggle for Islamic Democracy.* Farrar, Straus, and Giroux: New York, 2003.

- Johnson, James Turner. *The Holy War Idea in Western and Islamic Traditions.* Pennsylvania University Press: Pennsylvania, 2002.

- http://www.peacewithrealism.org/jihad/jihad03.htm

- http://www.livingislam.org/d/jih_e.html

- http://en.m.wikipedia.org/wiki/Jihad

- http://www.justislam.co.uk/product.php?products_id=2

- 'Ali al-Qari, al-Asrar al-marfu'a (Beirut 1985 ed), p. 127.

- www.sunnah.org

- *Jihad Al Akbar* from Shaykh Hisham Kabbani's *Islamic Beliefs and Doctrine According to Ahl al-Sunna: A Repudiation of "Salafi" Innovations.*

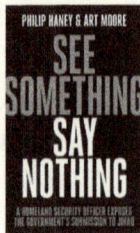

www.ingramcontent.com/pod-product-compliance
Lightning Source LLC
Chambersburg PA
CBHW031944080426
42735CB00007B/260